Take Another Look

The Quran, The Sunnah And The Islam of The Honorable Elijah Muhammad

By

Wesley Muhammad, PhD

A TEAM PUBLISHING .COM

Take Another Look

Second Edition
First Printing
August 2011

A-Team Publishing
PO Box 551036
Atlanta GA, 30355

To order additional copies or to reach Dr. Muhammad for speaking engagements, please contact the Publisher.

ISBN: 978-0-9833797-1-3

Table of Contents

Chapter I: ***Assessing Elijah Muhammad's Islamicity*** 1-24

1. *Did The Honorable Elijah Muhammad Teach True Islam?*
2. *Al-Ghazzālī: Proof of (What) Islam?*
3. *Whose Orthodoxy? The Black Sheep and the White Sheep*
4. *A**ḥ**mad b. **Ḥ**anbal: Champion Among the Black Sheep*
5. *Ibn al-Jawzī as Criterion of Faith?*
6. *The Affair of al-Q**āḍī** Abū Ya'l**ā***

Chapter II: ***Formless and Invisible?*** 25-42

1. *Formless and Immaterial?*
2. ***Sūrat al**-Ikhl**āṣ** and Islam's Corporeal God*
3. *Deus Invisibilis in the Qur'**ā**n?*
4. *The Qur'**ā**n's Morphic God*

Chapter III: ***The Man-God of the Sunnah*** 43-79

1. *The Sunnah's Morphic Deity*
2. *The Prophet's Vision of God*
3. *A Real Vision?*
4. *'**Ā'isha**'s Denial and Sunnism's Affirmation*
5. *The Hon. Elijah Muhammad on the Prophet's Vision*
6. *Is Allah a Man?*
7. *The Coming of Allah*
8. *Literal or Metaphorical?*

Conclusion: ***The Hon. Elijah Muhammad and the Islam of the Black Sheep*** 80-81

Appendix: ***The Long Overdue Scholarly Dialogue Between Students of Imam W.D. Mohammed and the Honorable Minister Farrakhan*** 82-226

Chapter I
Assessing Elijah Muhammad's Islamicity

1. *Did The Honorable Elijah Muhammad Teach True Islam?*

The late, renowned historian of Black Religion, C. Eric Lincoln, appropriately observed in 1983:

> But controversy aside, in terms of the impress he made on the world (Elijah Muhammad) must be reckoned one of the most remarkable men of the 20th century. Among his more commonly recognized achievements were his enormous contributions to the dignity and self-esteem of the Black undercaste in America. Beyond that, and with infinitely more far-reaching implications, Elijah Muhammad must be credited with the serious re-introduction of Islam to the United States in modern times, giving it the peculiar mystique, the appeal, and the respect without which it could not have penetrated the American bastion of Judeo-Christian democracy. If now, as it appears, the religion of Islam has a solid foothold and an indeterminate future in North America, it is Elijah Muhammad and Elijah Muhammad alone to whom initial credit must be given.[1]

Lincoln's observation regarding the decisive role played by the Honorable Elijah Muhammad (THEM) in Islam's successful "penetration of the American bastion of Judeo-Christian democracy" is still worth quoting, even while Robert Dannin's ethnographic study suggests that some African Americans encountered and embraced Sunni Islam long prior to the late Imām Wārrithuddīn Muhammad's transformation and

[1] C. Eric Lincoln, "The American Muslim Mission in the Context of American Social History," in Earle H. Waugh, Baha Abu-Laban, and Regula B. Qureshi (edd.), ***The Muslim Community in North America*** (Canada: The University of Alberta Press, 1983) 221 [art.=215-233].

incorporation of the Nation of Islam (NOI) into the larger Sunni Muslim world.[2] Though there is today general consensus regarding THEM's catalytic role in this process of 'Islamizing' Black America, there are many scholars – Muslim and non-Muslim alike – as well as many in the lay African American Muslim community who refuse to apply the terms 'Islam' and 'Muslim' to him and his message; the NOI rather was a 'proto-Islamic' nationalist movement, whose doctrine was "Islamic only in name," we are told.[3] The central and allegedly most disqualifying tenet of NOI doctrine was/is THEM's bold claim that "God is a man, and we just cannot make Him other than man."[4] This point is given some specificity in the creedal statement called "Point Number Twelve", which is the twelfth item in a 12-item list of "What the Muslims Believe," written by THEM:

> 12. WE BELIEVE that Allah (God) appeared in the Person of Master W. Fard Muhammad, July, 1930; the long-awaited "Messiah" of the Christians and the "Mahdi" of the Muslims.

This anthropomorphist doctrine, "Despite its Islamic trappings," Zafar Ishaq informs us, "is far too foreign for ordinary Muslims

---

[2] Robert Dannin, ***Black Pilgrimage to Islam*** (New York: Oxford University Press, 2005). Cf. Edward E. Curtis IV, ***Black Muslim Religion in the Nation of Islam 1960-1975*** (Chapel Hill: The University of North Carolina Press, 2006) 176.

[3] Ernst Allen, Jr, "Religious Heterodoxy and Nationalist Tradition: The Continuing Evolution of the Nation of Islam," ***The Black Scholar*** 26 (Fall 1996/Winter 1997) 8 [art.=2-34]; Lincoln, "American Muslim Mission," 227; Sherman Jackson, ***Islam and the Blackamerican: Looking Toward the Third Resurrection*** (Oxford: University Press, 2005).

[4] Elijah Muhammad, ***Message to the Black Man in America*** (Chicago: Muhammad's Temple No. 2, 1965) 6. Basic sources on Black Muslim theology include, but are not limited to, the following: idem, ***Our Saviour Has Arrived*** (Chicago: Muhammad's Temple of Islam No. 2, n.d.); idem, ***The Theology Of Time*** Lecture Series printed transcript by Abass Rassoul. U.B.U.S., Hampton. 1992.

even to understand, let alone accept."[5] M. Amir Ali, founder of the Institute of Islamic Information and Education (III&E), in a brochure entitled "Islam and Farrakhanism Compared," contrasted Point Number Twelve with the central creedal tenet of "true Islam": that God (Allah) is "One (who is) Unique, never appeared in any physical form, hence, no physical representation is possible, He is recognized through his 99 names."[6] Indeed Islam is often viewed as the religion *par excellence* of divine transcendence of the Hellenistic type, i.e. characterized by incorporeality.[7] God is *khilāf al-ʿālam*, "the absolute divergence from the world" and this characteristically Islamic doctrine of *mukhālafa* "(divine) otherness" is said to preclude divine corporeality and anthropomorphism.[8] That Point Number Twelve is "sufficiently distant from…the teachings of the Qur'an and the Hadith or Sunna" and thus completely irreconcilable with Muslim orthodoxy is stated frequently in the literature.[9]

---

[5] Zafar I. Ansari, "Aspects of Black Muslim Theology," ***Studia Islamica*** 53 (1981): 142 [art.=137-176].

[6] M. Amir Ali, PhD, *Islam and Farrakhanism Compared*, III&E Brochure Series No. 19 (Chicago: The Institute of Islamic Information and Education, n.d.).

[7] See e.g. William A. Graham, "Transcendence in Islam," in Edwin Dowdy (ed.), *Ways of Transcendence; Insights From Major Religions and Modern Thought* (Bedford Park, South Australia: Australian Association 1982) 7-23; Abdoldjavad Falatâri, "How can a Muslim Experience God, Given Islam's Radical Monotheism" in Annemarie Schimmel and Abdoldjavad Falatâri (edd.), ***We Believe in One God: The Experience of God in Christianity and Islam*** (New York: The Seabury Press, 1979) 77ff. On the Hellenistic model of divine transcendence vs. the Semitic model, see Wesley Williams, "'A Body Unlike Bodies ': Transcendent Anthropomorphism in Ancient Semitic Tradition and Early Islam," ***Journal of the American Oriental Society*** 129 [2009]: 19-44.

[8] Muhammad Ibrahim H.I. Surty, "The Concept of God in Muslim Tradition," ***Islamic Quarterly*** 37 (1993): 127f; Faruq Sherif, ***A Guide to the Contents of the Qur'an*** (Reding, 1995), 24.

[9] Allen, Jr, "Religious Heterodoxy ," 8; Mattias Gardell, "The Sun of Islam Will Rise in the West: Minister Louis Farrakhan and the Nation of Islam in the Latter Days," in Yvonne Yazbeck Haddad and Jane Idleman Smith (edd.), ***Muslim Communities in North America*** (Albany, NY: State University of New York Press, 1994) 32. See further Lawrence H. Mamiya, "Minister Louis Farrakhan and the Final Call: Schism in the Muslim Movement," in

This popular presumption of THEM's irredeemable heterodoxy is the elephant in the room whenever followers of his (e.g. modern day followers of the Honorable Minister Farrakhan) and African American Sunni Muslims come together; it thus has strained relationships within the African American Muslim community. In July 2010 I had the distinct honor to be among those fortunate enough to join Brother Minister Farrakhan for dinner at the National House in Chicago. Among the many jewels of wisdom he shared with his guests, he revealed his desire to see his followers and the followers of Imām Wārrithuddīn to come together as a unified community descendant from the spiritual loins of THEM. He acknowledged that Point Number Twelve is the obstacle to this unity. Because

---

Waugh, Abu-Laban, and Qureshi, ***The Muslim Community***, 240 [art.=234-255] who claims that Point Number 12 is "doubly heretical in orthodox Islam (to identify a human being as God, and to say that one saw God)." Similarly Denis Walker, ***Islam and the Search for African-American Nationhood: Elijah Muhammad, Louis Farakhan and the Nation of Islam*** (Atlanta: Clarity Press, Inc., 2005) 273, 274, 282, who claims that "The central doctrine of Sunni Islam...is that there is no God but a non-corporeal Allah". He points out THEM's "anthropomorphist blurring of the Qur'an-affirmed transcendent God," for "the Islamic concept of God reiterated throughout the Qur'an is that the Omnipotent Creator is beyond human sense-perception and unbounded by both time and space." See further Ernest Allen, Jr. "Minister Louis Farrakhan and the Continuing Evolution of the Nation of Islam," in Amy Alexander (ed.), ***The Farrakhan Factor: African-American Writers on Leadership, Nationhood, and Minister Louis Farrakhan*** (New York: Grove Press, 1998) 58. Amina Wadud charges the seminal "proto-Islamic groups," i.e. the Moorish Science Temple of America (MSTA) and the NOI, with failing to "sustain the integrity of Islamic dogma involving belief in on supreme transcendent God, Allah, and in the prophecy an living example of the Prophet Muhammad." "American Muslim Identity: Race and Ethnicity in Progressive Islam," in Omid Safi [ed.], ***Progressive Muslims: On Justice, Gender, and Pluralism*** (Oxford: One World) 276. Jackson, ***Islam and the Blackamerican***, 45, 59 speaks of THEM's "irredeemable heterodoxy," "theological and doctrinal excesses, omissions, and downright blasphemes," among which Jackson includes the claim that "God is a man" which is "certainly condemnable from the standpoint of Muslim orthodoxy". See also Dannin, ***Black Pilgrimage to Islam***, 4; Mustafa El-Amin, ***The Religion of Islam and the Nation of Islam: What is the Difference?*** (Newark: El-Amin Productions, 1991) 3-4.

members of the Imām's community tend to be more learned in the Arabic Islamic tradition and frequently engaged the Qur'**ā**n and the Sunna of the Prophet Muhammad (s) in the Arabic, they are convinced of the theological error of this pillar of THEM's "Islam" and that it is nothing less than *shirk* (associating in worship others with Allah), the gravest of sins according to the Qur'ān. But what if this conclusion by many in the Islamic world was based on a rather shallow engagement of the Classical Arabic sources and tradition? What if the theological interpretation of the Qur'ān and Sunna that is held up as the criterion by which THEM's islamicity is judged and found lacking is in fact grounded less in the Arabic Qur'ān and Sunna themselves but rather in non-Arabic ideas that have accreted within Islam over the last several centuries and which today, ironically, merely *pass* as 'true Islam'?

It is often pointed out that THEM's 'Islam', in particular his doctrine of God, is radically at odds with the view of the Orthodox Muslim world.[10] But it is precisely this god of today's orthodoxy that THEM expressly condemned:

> The ignorant belief of the Orthodox Muslims that Allah (God) is some formless something and yet He has an Interest in our affairs, can be condemned in no limit of time. I would not give two cents for that kind of God in which they believe.[11]

While rejecting the god of the Orthodox Muslim world, THEM seems to distinguish that view from the view of the Qur'ān itself,

---

[10] Thus Mustafa El-Amin, ***Religion of Islam***, 5-6: "As the reader can clearly see, the concept of God in the Religion of Al-Islam is extremely different than that of the Nation of Islam. Over one billion Muslims and others believe and accept the concept of Allah (God) as it is presented in the Religion of Al-Islam and the Holy Qur'an. Only a few thousand believe and accept the concept of God as it is presented by the Nation of Islam." See also Ansari, "Aspects," 147: "When all these various characteristics are pieced together in order to obtain an integrated view of the 'Nation of Islam's' concept of God, the concept that emerges does not even remotely resemble the one to which the Muslims all over the world subscribe."

[11] Cited by Ansari, "Aspets," 147.

which, he affirms, "has all Truth in it if you understand."[12] And with a proper understanding of the Qur'ān, THEM indicates, his Teaching about God is not at odds with Islam's scripture.[13] In other words, according to THEM, there is a difference between the God of the Qur'ān and the god of the Orthodox Muslim world. Thus, while he would certainly object to the interpretations of the latter (i.e. the Orthodox Muslim world) being advanced as the criterion by which his islamicity is judged, THEM recognized the authority of the Qur'ān and regularly anchored his 'New Islam' in it. By doing so he also tacitly recognizes the Orthodox Muslim world's departure from the 'truths' of Islam's holy book.

2. *Al-Ghazzālī: Proof of (What) Islam?*

THEM's claim that God is a man is certainly at odds with the normative or orthodox Islamic view, a view well articulated by the Persian scholar Muḥammad Abū Ḥāmid al-Ghazzālī (d. 1128), called *Ḥujjat al-Islām* or the 'Proof of Islam,' in his ***Kitāb al-qawā'id al-ʿaqā'id***, 1.3:

> He [God Most High] is not a body with a form, or a limited, quantitative substance…He does not resemble anything that exists, nor does anything that exists resemble Him. There is nothing whatsoever like unto Him, nor is He like unto anything. He is not delimited by magnitude, contained by places, encompassed by directions, or bounded by heavens or earth.
>
> He sees without a pupil or eyelids. He hears without ear canals or ears. Likewise, He knows without a heart, He seizes without an extremity, and He creates without an implement-because His attributes do not resemble the attributes of the creation.

[12] Muhammad, ***Theology of Time***, 379.
[13] See discussion by Herbert Berge, ***Elijah Muhammad and Islam*** (New York: New York University Press, 2009) Chapter 3.

Likewise, His essence does not resemble the essences of the creation.

Al-Ghazzālī's influence on later (and current) orthodox theology is unparalleled. He is called 'The Proof of Islam,' ***Ḥujjat al-Islām*** in part because his articulation and rationalization of a formless, bodiless, immaterial God is *the* articulation and rationalization of Islamic orthodoxy today. Thus, the theological interpretation of the scriptures of Islam against which THEM is often judged and found guilty of *shirk* and *kufr* (unbelief), and the interpretation which he himself rejected, is an interpretation substantively influenced and informed by al-Ghazzālī. And while THEM has been accused of reading his anthropomorphist doctrine *into* the Qur'ān where it (presumably) does not naturally exists, it is demonstrable that al-Ghazzālī read his anti-anthropomorphist doctrine of incorporeality into the Qur'ān and Sunna where, by his own admission, this doctrine is completely absent. In his important treatise, ***Iljām al-awām an ilm il-kalām*** ("Bridling the Common Folk Away From the Science of Theological Speculation") the Persian Proof of Islam confesses that, even though the Prophet Muḥammad was in no way lax in terms of his desire to propagate the full truth as he knew it; though he had no intellectual deficiency that would have limited the truth as far as he possessed it; though he lacked nothing in terms of linguistic and semantic facility that would have precluded his clear articulation of the truth as he knew it; yet the Prophet never affirmed this incorporeal god to whom he (al-Ghazzālī) and the

Alleged portrait of Al-Ghazzālī

speculative theologians were calling the people. Why didn't the Prophet, fully capable of affirming the truth of this incorporeal deity, actually do so? Because, al-Ghazzālī claims, the Prophet was commanded by God to speak "only at the level of the people's intellects." Because the people to whom the Prophet was sent were not intellectually capable of grasping this 'truth' and therefore would have rejected this god as an impossibility and rejected Islam, the Prophet withheld the truth of the incorporeal god (see below)! It is not necessary here to deconstruct al-Ghazzālī's elitist and condescending presumptions regarding the masses of the Muslim followers of the Prophet. It is enough to emphasize that al-Ghazzālī here clearly admits that the 'Islam' of which he is said to be the 'Proof' is NOT the Islam that the Holy Prophet articulated!

فإن قيل: فلم لم يكشف الغطاء عن المراد بإطلاق لفظ الإله ولم يقل إنه موجود ليس بجسم ولا جوهر ولا عرض ولا هو داخل العالم ولا خارجه ولا متصل ولا منفصل ولا هو في مكان ولا هو في جهة، بل الجهات كلها خالية عنه، فهذا هو الحق عند قوم، والإفصاح عنه كذلك، كما أفصح عنه المتكلمون ممكن ولم يكن في عبارته ﷺ قصور، ولا في رغبته في كشفه الحق فتور، ولا في معرفته نقصان؟

قلنا: من رأى هذا حقيقة الحق اعتذر بأن هذا لو ذكره لنفر الناس عن قبوله، ولبادروا بالإنكار وقالوا: هذا عين المحال ووقعوا في التعطيل ولا خير في المبالغة في تنزيه ينتج التعطيل في حق الكافة إلا الأقلين، وقد بعث رسول الله ﷺ داعياً للخلق إلى سعادة الآخرة رحمة للعالمين. كيف ينطق بما فيه هلاك الأكثرين، بل امر أن لا يكلم الناس إلا على قدر عقولهم، وقال ﷺ: «مَنْ حدَّثَ الناس بحديثٍ لا يفهمونه كان فتنة على بعضهم». أو لفظ هذا معناه.

فإن قيل: إن كان في المبالغة في التنزيه خوف التعطيل بالإضافة إلى البعض ففي استعماله الألفاظ الموهمة خوف التشبيه بالإضافة إلى البعض.

قلنا: بينهما فرق من وجهين.

أحدهما: أن ذلك يدعو إلى التعطيل في حق الأكثرين، وهذا يعود إلى التشبيه في حق الأقلين، وأهون الضررين أولى بالاحتمال، وأعلم الضررين أولى بالاجتناب.

والثاني: أن علاج وهم التشبيه أسهل من علاج التعطيل. إذ يكفي أن يقال مع هذه الظواهر: ﴿لَيْسَ كمثله شيءٌ﴾[1]. وأنه ليس بجسم ولا مثل الأجسام. وأما اثبات موجود في الاعتقاد على ما ذكرناه من المبالغة في التنزيه شديد جداً، بل لا يقبله واحد من الألف لا سيما الأمة العربية.

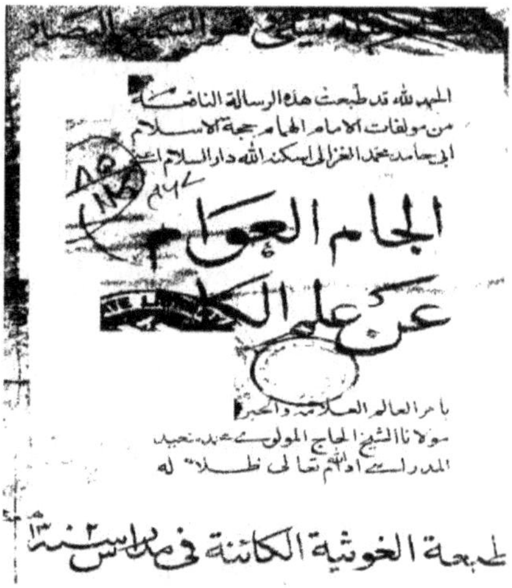

Relevant page from al- Ghazzālī's ***Iljām al-awām an ilm il-kalām***

Al-Ghazzālī thus had to read his incorporeal god into the Qur'ān and Sunna by applying allegorical exegesis (*ta'wīl*) to the passages that would otherwise seem to affirm or support an anthropomorphist reading. His *ta'wīl* was informed by Hellenistic logic, in particular Aristotelian Logical Analogies (*al-*

qiyās al-manṭiqī al-arasṭī). It is therefore no surprise that his incorporeal god is but the god of the Greek philosophers in a turban.

3. *Whose Orthodoxy? The Black Sheep and the White Sheep*

To understand the full significance of this 'Persian Proof of Islam' and his *revision* of the Prophetic legacy, one must see him in the light of a *prophetic* report of Muḥammad.

> Zayd b. Aslam related that the Prophet (s) saw a vision and told his companions about it. He said: "I saw a group of black sheep and a group of white sheep then mixed with them [until the white sheep became so numerous that the black sheep could no longer be seen in the herd of sheep.] I[14] interpreted it to mean that [the black sheep are the Arabs. They will accept Islam and become many. As for the white sheep, they are the non-Arabs (i.e. Persians, Turks, Byzantines, ect.)] They will enter Islam and then share with you your wealth and your genealogy [and become so numerous that the Arabs will not be noticed amongst them.]" The Companions became surprised by what he (s) said. Then one said, "The non-Arab Persians will enter our land, O' Messenger of Allah?!" The Prophet (s) then said, "Yes. By He Who Has my soul in His Hand, if the religion was hanging on the distant star, men from the non-Arab Persians would reach it and the luckiest of them would be the people of Faris."[15]

The original recipients of the Prophet's message, the Arabs or 'black sheep,' are here said to have been (or in the future to be) engulfed by later non-Arab converts to Islam or 'white sheep'

---

[14] Or Abu Bakr with the approval of the angel.

[15] There are several versions of this report here conflated. Al-Suyūṭī, ***Tārikh al-khulafā***, ed. **Jamāl Maḥmūd Muṣṭafā** (Cairo: Dār al-Fajr lil-Turāth, 1999) 86; **Rāghib al-Iṣfahānī, *Muḥāḍarat al Udabā'*, I,** 219; 'Alā al-Dīn b. Husām al-Dīn al-Muttaqī, ***Kanz al-'ummāl*** (Haydarabad, 1312/1894-98) VI: 215 # 3755; al-Tha'ālibī, ***Mukhtaṣarāt***, ed. Gustav Flügel, ***Der vertraute Gefährte des Einsamen in schlagfertigen Gegenreden*** (Wien, 1829) 270 # 313.

who will not only 'share' their wealth (e.g. the riches generated from Middle Eastern oil), but also share or, rather, 'appropriate' Arab genealogy. In other words, non-Arab converts to Islam will assume Arab identity to such an extent that the actual ethnicity of the original Arabs will be forgotten. The fact that the original Arabs and Arab followers of Muḥammad were black is well-documented.[16] So too is the fact that these original Muslims have been lost within an influx of non-Arab converts to Islam.[17] The face of Islam went from black to white.

It is not to be doubted that the 'black sheep' metaphor in this report alludes to the black ethnicity of the original Arabs. This is confirmed by numerous reports. See especially the example of Muḥammad b. **'Abd Allāh** (d. 762), known also as al-Nafs al-Zakiyya ("The Pure Soul"). He was a pure descendent of the Prophet himself through the latter's daughter Fāṭimah, wife of 'Alī b. Abī Ṭālib, and in fact "prided himself on being a Qurayshi [Arab] of pure lineage…[with] a pure descent from the Prophet."[18] This point is clearly evident in a letter he sent to the 'Abbāsid caliph Abū Ja'far al-Manṣūr (r. 754 – 775), against whom he rebelled in 762. Al-Nafs al-Zakiyya felt Abū Ja'far al-Manṣūr's mixed lineage (his mother was a Berber) disqualified him for leadership over the community. He wrote to the caliph:

> You well know that no one has laid claim to this office (the caliphate) who has a lineage, nobility, and status like ours. By the nobility of our fathers, we are not the sons of the accursed, the outcasts, or freedmen…I am at the very center of the Banū

[16] See Wesley Muhammad, ***Black Arabia and the African Origin of Islam*** (Atlanta: A-Team Publishing, 2009) Chapters Six and Seven.

[17] Robert Goldston, ***The Sword of the Prophet: A History of the Arab World From the Time of Mohammed to the Present Day*** (New York: Dial Press, 1979) 87: "the original Arabs, those lords of the desert who had formed the vanguard of Islam and presided over its golden age…(almost) all had long since become so submerged into the cosmopolitan empire that they were indistinguishable from their neighbors."

[18] Muhammad Qasim Zaman, "The Nature of Muḥammad al-Nafs al-Zakiyya's Mahdiship: A Study of Some Reports in Iṣbahānī's *Maqātil*," ***Hamdard Islamicus*** 13 (1990): 60-61.

> Hāshim's lines. My paternity is purest among them, undiluted with non-Arab blood, and no concubines dispute over me.[19]

What did this pure Arab descendent of the Prophet look like? "Muḥammad (Al-Nafs al-Zakiyya) is described as tall and strong with very dark skin".[20] Indeed, al-Dhahabī describes him as "black-skinned and huge."[21] But it is al-**Ṭabarī**'s description that is most informative:

> Muḥammad (Al-Nafs al-Zakiyya) was black, exceedingly black, jet black (*ādam shadīd al-udma adlam*) and huge. He was nicknamed "Tar Face" (*al-qārī*) because of his black complexion (*udmatihi*), such that Abū Ja'far used to call him "Charcoal Face" (*al-muḥammam*).[22]

Muḥammad al-Nafs al-Zakiyya, a Qurayshī Arab whose pure lineage on both his father's and his mother's side put him "at the center" of the genealogical lines of the Banū Hāshim, the Prophet's kinsfolk, was so black he was called 'Tar face' and 'Charcoal face'. He best represents those 'black sheep' to whom the message of Islam first came and who disappeared from view once non-Arab groups converted in large numbers.

It is not incidental that the Qur'ān emphasizes that it is an Arabic, not a non-Arabic (*a'jamiyya*) revelation (41:2-3, 44). This suggests that the proper context in which to understand the revelation is a 7th century Arab linguistic and, thus, cultural context. It is the case that the Bedouin Arabs (*a'rābī*) were seen as the purest representatives of the Arabic Islamic way. Fine points of Islamic law were frequently decided by appeal to Bedouin

---

[19] Quoted from al-**Ṭabarī**, ***The History of al-Ṭabarī*, Vol. XXVIII: *'Abbāsid Authority Affirmed***, trans. annot. Jane Dammen McAuliffe (Albany: State University of New York Press, 1985) 167-68.

[20] ***The Encyclopedia of Islam*** (New Edition; hereafter ***EI²***) 7:389 s.v. Muḥammad b. **'Abd Allāh** by F. Buhl.

[21] ***Al-'Ibar fī khabar man ghabar*** (Kuwait: Turāth al-Arabī) 4:198.

[22] Al-**Ṭabarī, *Ta'rīkh al-rusul wa'l-mulūk***, edd. Michael Jan de Goeje and Lawrence Conrad, ***Annals of the Apostles and Kings. A Critical Edition Including 'Arib's* Supplement** (Gorgias Press, 2005) 10:203.

tradition, and Arabic philologists privileged 'pure' desert Bedouin usage over the more cosmopolitan Arabic of the town when ruling on matters of correct Arabic grammar. The pure Arab was the Black Arab, the black sheep of the Prophet's vision. This was the original recipient community of the message of Islam, and their linguistic-cultural way provided the context in which to properly understand the revelation.

The Persian al-Ghazzālī best represents the 'white sheep' – those non-Arabs who converted to Islam and appropriated the wealth and even identity of the original Muslims, the black sheep or Black Arabs. It is quite telling that al-Ghazzālī would dismiss the original Muslim followers of the Prophet, the black sheep, as too dim-witted to have received the 'truth' of the incorporeal god from the Prophet – thus the conspicuous absence of this god from the Prophet's message. This sentiment no doubt reflects not only a condescending elitism on al-Ghazzālī's part, but also racism: the latter characterized much Iranian (Persian) Muslim literature in his day.[23] These 'white sheep' introduced non-Arab, even non-Islamic elements into Islam, such as an anti-black racism. They also, however, introduced the 'God of the Philosophers' and the Hellenized interpretation (*ta'wīl*) of scripture so as to locate that god within Islamic revelation.[24]

4. *Aḥmad b. Ḥanbal: Champion Among the Black Sheep*

If Muḥammad al-Nafs al-Zakiyya is the best representative of the ethnicity of the black sheep, the best representative of their theological orthodoxy is no doubt the famous Imām Aḥmad b. Ḥanbal (d. 855), eponym of the Ḥanbali school, one of the four legal schools recognized as orthodox by all Sunni Muslims. Imām Aḥmad was a pure Arab, and thus a black sheep. Al-

---

23 Mino Southgate, "The Negative Images of Blacks in Some Medieval Iranian Writings," ***Iranian Studies*** 17 (1984): 3-35

24 See Wesley Williams, "A Body Unlike Bodies: Transcendent Anthropomorphism in Ancient Semitic Tradition and Early Islam," ***Journal of the American Oriental Society*** 129 (2009) 19-44.

Dhahabī (d. 1348) reports in his ***Siyar a'lām al-nubalā'***: "Ibn Durayy al-'Akbarī said: 'I searched for Aḥmad b. Ḥanbal (and then) found him and gave him the salaams and he was a tall, black-skinned man with a dyed beard." When Sunni orthodoxy first consolidated in Baghdad in the ninth century, it did so around the theological creed of Imām Aḥmad.[25] As Christopher Melchert, the primary biographer of Ibn Ḥanbal today points out, during the ninth and tenth centuries "Men would assert as a badge of orthodoxy that their creed was **Aḥmad**'s."[26] Examples include al-Muzanī (d. 878),[27] al-**Ṭabarī** (d. 923),[28] and al-**Ash'arī** (d. 936).[29] Al-Khāṭib al-**Baghdādī** (d. 1071) introduced Ibn **Ḥanbal** as "the champion of the Sunna, the senior figure of his community, and the exemplar of his class (*ta'ifa*)."[30] His school, the Ḥanbali school, was the leading *theological* school (vs.

---

[25]As noted by Christopher Melchert, the primary biographer of Ibn Ḥanbal today: "A**ḥmad ibn** Ḥanbal…was the central, defining figure of Sunnism in the earlier ninth century CE": Christopher Melchert, "**Aḥmad Ibn Ḥanbal and the Qur'an**," *JQS* 6 (2004): 22 [art.=22-34].

[26] Melchert, "**Aḥmad Ibn Ḥanbal and the Qur**'an," 22.

[27] Fuat Sezgīn, *Geschichte des arabischen Schrifttums* 9 vols. (Leiden, E.J. Brill, 1967-)1:493 # 2 and 508 #22.

[28] Dominique Sourdel, "Une profession de foi de l'historien al-**Ṭabarī**," ***REI*** 36 (1968): 177-99; Claude Gilliot, *Exégèse, lanque et théologie en islam: l'exégèse coranique de Tabari* (Paris: J. Vrin, 1990) 258-9.

[29] "The belief we hold and the religion we follow are holding fast to the Book of our Lord, to the Sunna of our Prophet, and to the traditions related on the authority of the Companions and the Successors and the imams of hadith. To that we hold firmly, professing what Abū 'Abd Allāh **Aḥmad Ibn Ḥanbal** professed, and avoiding him who dissents from his belief, because he is *the* excellent imam and the perfect leader, through whom God declared the truth, removed error, manifested the modes of action, and overcame the innovations of the innovators, the deviation of the deviators, and the skepticism of the skeptics."Al-Ash'**arī, *al-Ibāna 'an uṣūl al-diyāna,*** translated into English by Walter Conrad Klein (New Haven, 1940) 49; Daniel Gimaret, "Bibliographie d'Ash'**arī**: un réexamen," *JA* 273 (1985): 278.

[30] Al-Khāṭib al-**Baghdādī, *Ta'rikh Baghdād***, 14 vols. (**Cairo: al-Maktabat al-'Arabiya bi-**Baghdad, 1931) 3:336.

legal school) for the next three centuries.[31] Traditionalist Sunnism among the other *madhhab*s or schools was distinctly **Ḥ**anbalite. This is clearly seen by examining the creeds of such non-**Ḥanbalī** Traditionalist Sunnis as Ibn Khuzayma (d. 924)[32] and Ab**ū** Bakr al-**Ā**jurr**ī** (d. 971),[33] both Sh**āfi'īs, and al-**Qayraw**ānī (d.** 996), a M**ālikī.**[34] As early as 908 the **Ḥanbalī** leader al-Barbah**ārī (d.** 941) was recognized as leader of the majority Sunn**ī** population of Baghd**ā**d, the cultural and intellectual center of the Muslim world long after it ceased being the political and economic center.[35] In 1040, the caliph al-Q**ā**'im (r. 1031-1075) publically proclaimed the **Ḥanbalī** theological creed, *I'tiq**ā**d Q**ā**dirī*, making **Ḥ**anbalism "the 'official credo' of the state."[36]

It has been conclusively demonstrated that A**ḥ**mad Ibn **Ḥ**anbal's creed and that of his school were characterized by an unambiguously anthropomorphist doctrine: Allah (God) has a human-like form (***ṣū**ra*), after which Adam's physique was patterned, but one that was in some fundamental way unlike that

---

[31] See esp. Wesley Williams, ' *Tajallī wa-Ru'ya*: A Study of Anthropomorphic Theophany and *Visio Dei* in the Hebrew Bible, the Qur'ān and Early Sunnī Islam,' unpublished Ph.D. dissertation (University of Michigan, 2008) 223-

[32] **Ibn Khuzayma, *Kitāb al-tawhīd wa-ithbāt ṣifāt al-*Rabb.** Edited by Mu**ḥ**ammad Khal**īl Harrās** (Cairo: 1968)

[33] Ab**ū Bakr al-'Ajurī, *Al-Sharī'a*. Edited by Muhamma Hāmid al-Fiqī (Cairo:** 1950).

[34] See William Montgomery Watt, *Islamic Creeds: A Selection* (Edinburgh: Edinburgh University Press, 1994) 69-72.

[35] Ibn **al-Athīr, *Kāmil fī al-ta'rīkh*** 7 **vols. (Cairo:** Idārat al-**Ṭ**ibā'**ah** al-Munīrīyah, 1929/30), 6: 121f; Al-Muqaddas**ī, *Aḥsan al-taqāsīm* (ed. M.J. de Goeje; Leiden,** 1906) 126; Ibn al-Jawz**ī, *al-Muntaẓam fī tārikh al-*** *mul**ūk** **wa** 'l-umam* 6 vols. [=vols. V-X, yrs. 257-574/870-1197], Hyderbad, 1358/1940) 8: 312.

[36] George Makdisi, "**Ḥ**anbalite Islam." In Merlin Swartz (ed.) ***Studies on Islam***. New York: Oxford University Press, 1981; Kh**ā**lid Ya**ḥyā** Blankinshp, « Introduction », in '**Abd al-**Ra**ḥman Ibn al-**Jawz**ī, *The Attributes of God*,** Translated by 'Abdull**ā**h bin **Ḥ**am**ī**d '**A**l**ī** (Bristol, England : Amal Press, 2006) xiv.

of Adam's.[37] The orthodoxy of this black sheep, then, is radically different from the orthodoxy of al-Ghazzālī, a white sheep. Whose 'orthodoxy,' if any, is to be used to assess the 'islamicity' of THEM? Or rather, whose understanding of the sources of Islam – the Qur'ān and Sunna – should we privilege in our attempt to assess the viability of THEM's interpretation? It is time to take another look at the Islam of THEM in the light of the Qur'ān and Sunna, but these sources looked at through an exegetical lens other than the one normally employed. We will see that, while judged by the standards of the orthodoxy of the white sheep – e.g. al-Ghazzālī – THEM's Islam seems strange and 'un-islamic'; but when judged by the standards of the orthodoxy of the black sheep – e.g. Imām Aḥmad – THEM's Islam appears as a very legitimate understanding of the Islamic sources.

5. *Ibn al-Jawzī as Criterion of Faith?*

It is frequently claimed by Muslims influenced by al-Ghazzālī's anti-anthropomorphist ideas that Imām Aḥmad and his school are actually 'free' of the 'charge' of anthropomorphism. While this claim as far as Imām Aḥmad is concerned has been sufficiently refuted on the basis of the available sources attesting to his creed, this false claim that Imām Aḥmad has been 'exonerated' is based on the misrepresentation and misuse of the text, ***Daf' shubah al-tasbīh bi-Akaff al-tanzīh*** ("Dispelling the Doubt of Anthropomorphism with the

[37] Wesley Williams, 'Aspects of the Creed of Ahmad Ibn Hanbal: A Study of Anthropomorphism in Early Islamic Discourse,' *International Journal of Middle East Studies* 34 (2002): 441-463; idem, ' *Tajallī wa-Ru'ya*: A Study of Anthropomorphic Theophany and *Visio Dei* in the Hebrew Bible, the Qur'ān and Early Sunnī Islam,' unpublished Ph.D. dissertation, (University of Michigan, 2008), 208-243; idem, "Black Muslim Theology and the Classical Islamic Tradition: Possibilities of a Rapprochement," ***American Journal of Islamic Social Sciences*** 25 (2008): 61-89; idem, "A Body Unlike Bodies: Transcendent Anthropomorphism in Ancient Semitic Tradition and Early Islam," ***Journal of the American Oriental Society*** 129 (2009) 30-32.

Most Repelling Exoneration") by the **Ḥ**anbal**ī**, 'Abd al-Ra**ḥ**m**ā**n b. al-Jawz**ī** (d. 1201).[38] The claim is made that Ibn al-Jawz**ī** was a 'strict **Ḥ**anbal**ī**' (i.e. strict follower of Im**ā**m A**ḥ**mad) and that the anti-anthropomorphist views he expressed in this book represent the views of strict **Ḥ**anbalism. Nothing could be further from the truth. The attempt to pass Ibn al-Jawz**ī**'s ***Daf' shubah al-tasbīh*** off as representative of the Sunnism of his day is highly misleading. To clarify issues, one must understanding the Sunnism of the period.

During the period 945-1055 an Iranian Shi'ite dynasty, the Buyids, dominated Baghdad and completely controlled the Sunni 'Abb**ā**sid caliphs based there. In order to gain strength in the face of this Shi'ite encroachment, the caliphs clung to the **Ḥ**anbal**ī** school of Im**ā**m A**ḥ**mad b. **Ḥ**anbal because it was a popular movement: it commanded the allegiance of the masses in Baghdad. This alliance between the 'Abb**ā**sid caliphs and Baghdadi **Ḥ**anbal**ī**s culminated in 1018 when the Caliph al-Q**ā**dir issued *al-Ris**ā**la al-Q**ā**diriyya*, a **Ḥ**anbal**ī** theological creed condemning as heretics the Ashariyya and Mu'tazila, the two leading Sunni anti-anthropomorphist theological schools at the time and making Hanbalism the official state and popular orthodoxy. This creed was reiterated in 1041 by the following Caliph al-Q**ā**'im with a public proclamation of *al-Risala*. As Professor Khalid Yahya Blankinship of Temple University puts it:

> thus affirming the Hanbali creed in its literalist form as worked out in the previous century…the favor of the 'Abbasid caliphs for the anthropomorphist Hanbali creed may go back as early as the 3rd/9th century.[39]

---

[38] See e.g. 'Abdull**ā**h bin **Ḥ**am**ī**d 'Al**ī**'s comments in his translation to this work: **'Abd al-**Ra**ḥman Ibn al-**Jawz**ī,** ***The Attributes of God,*** Translate by 'Abdull**ā**h bin **Ḥamīd 'Alī** (Bristol, England: Amal Press, 2006) 3.

[39] Blankinship, "Introduction," xiv, xvi.

As Professor Blankinship correctly notes, the **Ḥ**anbal**ī** creed that was there declared official Sunni orthodoxy was anthropomorphist, i.e. it affirmed for God an anthropoid form. This creed was largely the creed of the major **Ḥ**anbal**ī** imam al-**Qāḍī Abū Ya'lā** (d. 1066).[40] When Caliph al-Q**ā**'im publicly proclaimed *al-Risala* in 1041 he did so in specific support of al-**Qāḍī Abū Ya'lā**, whose Sunnism was indeed anthropomorphist (see below).

This is the Sunnism that was orthodox in Ibn al-Jawz**ī**'s Baghdad and it was the Sunnism that Ibn al-Jawz**ī** himself originally championed! He rose to fame in Baghdad as a champion of this Sunnism, consequently being granted the privilege of preaching from the pulpit of the staunchly orthodox Jami' al- Man**ṣūr**, the main Sunni mosque in West Baghdad. In fact, Ibn al-Jawz**ī** was such a staunch defender of this Sunnism that the pro-Hanbalī government selected him to lead the charge against the heretical Asharites and Mu'tazilites, both of whom denied the literal reality of God's Attributes because of their anti-anthropomorphist theologies. In 1174 the caliph al-Mustadi' issued a decree granting Ibn al-Jawz**ī** special powers to identify and prosecute persons harboring heretical views. But the more Ibn al-Jawz**ī** read their literature – such as the works of the Asharis Al-Bayhaq**ī** (d. 1066) and Ibn F**ū**rak (d. 1015) - the more he was impressed by their anti-anthropomorphist interpretations of the scriptures until in 1175 and forward Ibn al-Jawz**ī** ceased his public opposition to the governmentally recognized heretics, the Ashariyya and the Mu'tazila. He began publicly employing their interpretations and issuing their negative judgments against the Traditionalist (**Ḥ**anbalī) Sunnism of his day, particularly in his works ***Daf ' shubah al-tashbih*** and ***Kitāb al-Akhbar al-Ṣifāt*** ("Book Regarding the Scriptural Divine Attributes"), angering the overwhelming majority of his **Ḥ**anbalī colleagues who condemned him. See for example the open letter written to him by Ab**ū** 'l-Fa**ḍ**l al-'Althī, a **Ḥ**anbalī contemporary. Al-'Althī says in part:

---

[40] See below.

You should know (Ibn al-Jawzī) that men of learning and virtue in various lands have become increasingly critical of your perverse pronouncements regarding the Divine Attributes. They have exposed the 'crack' in your arguments and report that you refuse to accept council given in good faith. You have made statements that do not accord with the Sunna…From where did you receive these heretical doctrines and embellished expressions?...It is amazing that one who [used to] subscribe to the doctrines of the Pious Ancestors (*Salaf*) and who disapproved of delving into philosophical theology (*kalam*) should [now turn around and] take up the study of what he originally disapproved, saying: 'When we use such and such expression, it actually means thus and so'…How can you go back on your [original] pledge and teaching...?...You reject the Attributes which (God) saw fit to ascribe to Himself and which have been duly reported in the most reliable prophetic traditions, [claiming]: 'Perhaps [that] is the correct interpretation, ' or 'Perhaps [that] is'… Statements concerning God and His attributes are not trivial matters that can be left to supposition…You maintain that the Companions of the Prophet were confused on the question of the Divine Attributes, but in fact you yourself are more deserving of censure than they. Clearly the Sunna does not suffice you…You and your ilk…have declared war on the sound traditions of the Prophet. Those who transmit them, in fact, transmit the Divine Law of Islam (*Shara'i' al-Islam*)…
I come to you (Ibn al-Jawzī) as spokesman for the people, the ulema and the hadith scholars (*huffaz*). If you renounce these (heretical) doctrines and recant in good faith as others before you have done, [well and good, but if you do not,] they will bring your case to the attention of the public and will spread the word of it to other lands, and they will demonstrate [for all to see] the shallowness of your pronouncements![41]

---

[41]Ibn Rajab, ***Kitāb al-dhayl 'alā ṭabaqāt al-Ḥanābila***. Edited by Muḥammad al-Fiqī (Cairo: Maṭba'at al-Sunna, 1952) 2:205ff.

As admitted by pro-Ibn al-Jawzī scholar Merlin Swartz, al-'Althī's position "represented the majority point of view."[42] Al-Althi's threat was realized. In 1194 a coalition which included Ibn al-Jawzī's own son, Abu'l Qasim, arrested him and exiled him to Wasit where he remained under house arrest for five years. Ibn al-Jawzī was publicly humiliated and his spirit almost broken.

There is absolutely no way one can present Ibn al-Jawzī and his metaphorical interpretations found in his ***Daf ' shubah al-tashbih*** as representing the Sunnism of his day. He may resonate strongly with modern Sunni Muslims who are far removed – in space, time, and theology – from the Sunni Islam of the Classical period, but one cannot anachronistically claim that Ibn al-Jawzī had the same appeal on his contemporaries as he does on moderns. His tragic history proves otherwise. Al-Dhahabī said it well: "May Allah have mercy on him and forgive him! Would that he had not probed metaphorical interpretations of the Scriptures (*ta'wīl*) nor diverged from his imam (i.e. Imām Aḥmad)." Al-Dhahabī quotes the judgment of Ibn Nuqta: "I never saw anyone who is relied upon in his religion, knowledge and reason, who approved of Ibn al-Jawzī."[43]

What did Ibn al-Jawzī's Sunni contemporaries believe? What was their doctrine that he rejected? He says they believed that:

> He (God) is on the Throne in His essence in the sense of being in contact with it, that when He descends [from His Throne, that descent] entails movement from place to place. They maintain that His essence has limits, and that it has measure and extent...They insist that one who descends must do so from above, and so they construe His descent in terms of sense experience, i.e. that kind of descent by which bodies are described. These anthropomorphists are persons who describe

---

[42] Merlin Swartz, ***A Medieval Critique of Anthropomorphism: Ibn al-Jawzī's* Kitāb Akhbār aṣ-Ṣifāt, *a Citical Edition of the Arabic Text with Translation, Introduction and Notes*** (Leiden: Brill, 2002) 283.

[43] Al-Dhahabī, ***Siyar a'lām al-nubalā'***, 15:483ff.

> the Divine Attributes in terms required by sense experience...and they represent Him as a physical person (*shakhṣ*) whose beauty exceeds all beauty...[44]

This was the view of the Orthodox (Traditionalist) Sunnism of Ibn al-Jawzī's day. He was but a heretical voice crying in an anthropomorphist wilderness – but that anthropomorphism was orthodox.

6. *The Affair of al-Qāḍī* ***Abū Ya'lā***

One of Ibn al-Jawzī's targets in his book was **Muḥammad b. al-Ḥusayn b. Muḥammad b. al-Farrā'** (990-1066), better known as al-**Qāḍī Abū Ya'lā,** undoubtedly 'the major leader and prime mover of the Hanbalite movement' in his day and clearly a leading influence on Traditinalist Sunnism for a good part of the eleventh century.[45] As recognized i**mām of the** Baghdad **Ḥanābila,** al-**Qāḍī Abū Ya'lā** was well respected by the pro-Sunn**ī** caliphs al **Qādir** (r. 991-1031) and al-**Qā'im** (r. 1031-1075). The latter beseeched him repeatedly to be chief judge (*qāḍī*) of the caliphal palace, a post **Abū Ya'lā** reluctantly assumed. **Abū Ya'lā** the theologian is said to have had a recognizable influence on the Caliph al-**Qā'im,** a claim supported by the Caliph's handling of the 'affair of al-**Qāḍī Abū Ya'lā.**'

The 'affair of al-**Qāḍī Abū Ya'lā**' can be said to have begun with the publication of his now lost ***Ibtāl al-ta'wīlāt li-akhbār al-ṣifāt*** ("The Invalidation of the Metaphorical Interpretations of the Reports on the Divine Attributes") circa 1040. The outcry from the local Sh**āfi'ī**-Ash'**arī**'s who condemned the book as "pure anthropomorphism" reached the Caliph who requested

---

[44] ***Tablīs Iblīs*** **(Cairo: Dār al-Ḥadīth,** 1995) 87.

[45] On al-**Qāḍī Abū Ya'lā see *EI*[2]** 3:765-766 s.v. Ibn al-Farr**ā'** **by H. Laoust**; Wadi Z. Haddad, "Al-**Qāḍī Abū Ya'lā Ibn al-**Farr**ā': His Life, Works and Religious Thought. Muslim Jurisconsult and Theologian, Died in Baghdad in** 458/1066" **(Ph.D diss. Harvard University,** 1969).

the writing from al-Qāḍī **Abū Yaʿlā**. After reading it himself the Caliph returned the book with an endorsing "thank you."[46] Shortly thereafter the Caliph summoned the city's **ʿulamā**ʾ and witness notaries to his palace where he proclaimed the traditionalist **Qadirī** Creed (***Iʿtiqād Qādirī*** or *al-Risāla al-Qādiriyya*), the doctrinal proclamation of his father. The gathered notables had to sign the proclamation. [47] The **Qadirī** Creed proclaimed by Caliph al-**Qāʿim** is apparently an epitome of the several edicts promulgated by his father, Caliph al-**Qādir,** between 1017 and 1029.[48] This creed has been likened to the creeds of the two **Ḥanbalī** leaders contemporary with the two caliphs, Ibn **Baṭṭa** (d. 997) and al-**Qāḍī Abū Yaʿlā** (d. 1065).[49] George Makdisi thus called it a traditionalist-**Ḥanbalī** profession of faith,[50] its proclaimation making **Ḥanbalism** "the 'official credo' of the state."

The gathering in 1040 called by Caliph al-**Qāʿim** likely had the purpose of putting an end to the controversy over al-**Qāḍī Abū Yaʿlā**'s book on the Divine Attributes.[51] Part of the proclamation reads: "Only those Attributes should be ascribed to Him which He has Himself ascribed or his Prophet has ascribed to Him. Further, each Attribute He or the Prophet have ascribed to Him is a real attribute (***ṣifa ḥaqīqīyya***), not metaphorical

---

[46] Ibn **Abī Yaʿlā**. ***Ṭabaqāt*** *al-Hanābila*. Edited by Mu**ḥ**ammad **Ḥāmid** al-F**ī**q**ī**. 2 vols. (Cairo: Maṭbaʿat al-Sunna al-Mu**ḥ**ammadīya, 1952) 2:197; Haddad, "Al-Qāḍ**ī** **Abū Yaʿlā,**" 86-7; al-**Qadī Abū Yaʿlā, *Kitāb al-Muʿtammad fī uṣūl al-dīn.*** Edited by Wadi Z.Haddad. (Beirut: Dar El-Machreq Éditeurs, 1974) 25.

[47] Ibn al-Jaw**zī**, ***al-****Muntaẓam* ***fī tāʾrīkh al-mulūk wa****ʾl-umma* (ed. Krenkow; Haydaraba**̄d: Dāʿirat** al-Maʿ**rif**, 1357/1938-1359-/1940) 8:109-11; Ibn A**bī** **Yaʿlā, *Ṭabaqāt*,** 2:197.

[48] On these edicts see George Makdisi, ***Ibn ʿAqīl: Religion and Culture in Classical Islam*** (Edinburgh: Edinburgh University Press, 1997) 8-9.

[49] According to Laoust, *Ibn Ba****ṭṭa*,** xcvi, xcvii the principles of the Q§dirÊ Creed were essentially identical with those of Ibn **Baṭṭa. Haddad** (*Kitāb* ***al-****Muʿ**tammad*, 26), on the other hand, identifies the Creed as "the doctrine of Ab**ū** **Yaʿlā**." The Qāḍī's son, Ibn Ab**ī** **Yaʿlā,** already identified the Creed with the essence of his father's creed. ***Ṭabaqāt*,** 2:197-8.

[50] **Makdisi, *Ibn ʿAqīl et la résurgence***, 308.

[51] Haddad, "Al-Qā**ḍī** **Abū Yaʿlā,**" 87.

(***lā majāzīyya*).**"[52] Wadi Haddad's suggestion that the proclamation of Caliph al-Q**ā**ʿim was a "vindication of Ab**ū** **Yaʿlā**'s doctrine and an exoneration of him,"[53] has support from the Arabic sources. According to Ibn Ab**ī** **Yaʿlā,** al-Q**āḍī** **Abū** **Yaʿlā** son, the ascetic shaykh Ibn al-Qazwin**ī** **(d.** 1050) looked at al-Q**āḍī** Ab**ū** **Yaʿlā** after the signing of the proclamation and said, "Just as your soul desired."[54] The **Qāḍī** responded**:** "Praise be to God for his graciousness in manifesting the truth."[55] Ibn al-Qazwin**ī** then said to the **Qāḍī:** "I shall not be satisfied until I go to the Man**ṣūr** Mosque[56] and dictate the reports of the Divine Attributes." The ascetic shaykh fulfilled his word and went to mosque each Friday dictating *akhb**ār al-ṣifāt*** in support of al-Q**āḍī** Ab**ū** **Yaʿlā.**[57]

What was the **Qāḍī**'s doctrine of the ***Ṣifāt*** that was made part of the 'official credo of the state'? Ibn Taym**īya** (d. 1328) provides one of the few excerpts from al-Q**āḍī** **Abū** **Yaʿlā**'s lost ***Ibtāl* in his *Majmūʿat al-rasāʾil al-kubrā*.** The **Qāḍī** declares:

> The traditions (concerning the Divine Attributes) cannot be rejected, nor can one be preoccupied with their metaphorical interpretation. They must be taken literally (ʿ***alā ẓāhirihā***) and that they are the Attributes of God. They are not to be likened to the same attributes in creation.[58]

What are some of these ***Ṣifāt*** that must be taken literally? In his critique of **Ḥanbalī** anthropomorphism - a critique that

[52] Ibn al-Jaw**zī,** ***al-**Muntaẓ**am,*** 8:110-11.
[53] Haddad, "Al-Q**āḍī** **Abū** **Yaʿlā,**" 87.
[54] Accepting Haddad's reading of the Arabic ***kamā fī nafsika*.** **Haddad,** "Al-Q**āḍī** **Abū** **Yaʿlā,**" 90.
[55] Ibn **Abī** **Yaʿlā,** ***Ṭabaqāt*,** 2:198.
[56] The main Sunn**ī** **cathedral mosque in West Baghdād.**
[57] Ibn **Abī** **Yaʿlā,** ***Ṭabaqāt*,** 2:198; Haddad, "Al-Q**āḍī** **Abū** **Yaʿlā,**" 90.
[58] Ibn Taym**īya**, ***Majmūʿat al-**rasā**ʾil al-kubrā*** **(Cairo:** al-Sharafiyya**,** 1905) 1:145.

often targeted al-**Qāḍī Abū Yaʿlā** himself – Ibn al-Jawz**ī** quotes the **Qāḍī** from an unidentified work that Merlin Swartz's believes is likely the ***Ibtāl.***[59] In one of those quotes the **Qāḍī** identifies some of these Divine Attributes:

> Terms such as 'young man' (*sh**ābb***), 'beardless' (*amrad*), 'short, curly' (***jaʿad wa qaṭaṭ***), 'moths' (*fir**āsh***)[60] 'sandals' (*maʿ**lān***)[61] and 'crown' (***tāj***)[62] have all been established as designations that apply to God, although we do not claim to know their precise meaning [when used for this purpose].[63]

All of these "established" Attributes come from reports of the Prophet's Vision of God, specifically ***aḥādīth al**-sh**ābb*** or reports according to which he saw Him in the form of a young man (see below). In his ***Kitāb al-Muʿtamad fī uṣūl al-Dīn* Abū Yaʿlā** affirms that **Muḥammad** saw God with his eyes during his Nocturnal Journey and with his heart (i.e. in a dream-vision) on some other occasion.[64] The most beautiful form of God, ***ṣūra,*** seen by **Muḥammad** in his vision was God's real form, though a form unlike forms.[65] **The Qāḍī** cites the ***ḥadīth al-shābb*** on the authority of Umm al-**Ṭufayl** as proof that God can be seen in a dream-vision.

Wadi Haddad has argued that al-**Qāʿim**'s proclamation of the **Qādirī** Creed and his support of al-**Qāḍī Abū Yaʿlā** in this controversy "reveal the creedal position of the Caliph".[66]

---

59 ***A Medieval Critique***, 136.

60 From the ***ḥadīth al shābb* on the authority of Umm Ṭufayl reading *farāsh min dhahab,*** 'moths of **gold**' over the youthful god's face rather than *fir**āsh min dhahab,*** "veil of gold."

61 The youthful God of ***ḥadīth al shābb* on the authority of Umm Ṭufayl wears sandals of gold.**

62 According to *a**ḥādīth al**-ru'**ya*** on the authority of Mu'**adh b. 'Afrā' and Ibn 'Abbās Muḥammad saw his Lord wearing a crown.**

63 Ibn al-Jawz**ī, *Kitāb*** *Akhb**ār al-Ṣifāt,*** 49 (Eng. 183).

64 Al-**Qāḍī Abū Yaʿlā, *Kitāb al**-Mu'**tamad fī uṣūl al**-D**īn***, 151.

65 Ibid., 58.

66 Haddad, "Al-**Qāḍī Abū Yaʿlā,**" 90.

Christopher Melchert and Steven Judd have both likewise argued that the doctrinal tendency a particular Caliph promoted can be discerned by examining the tendencies of the men he appointed to be judges (***qāḍīs***).[67] The official support given to traditionalist Sunnism (**Ḥanbalism**) by the two caliphs al-**Qādir and al-Qā'im** in general and the latter's support for al-Qāḍī **Abū Ya'lā** in particular suggests therefore that both popular Sunnism and state-sponsored Sunnism during the later part of the tenth and much of the eleventh century was a Sunnism that affirmed that God could appear to his servants in anthropomorphically. This was a part of the Sunni creed as constructed by Imām Aḥmad b. Ḥanbal and as championed by his followers for three centuries. This was the orthodoxy of the Black Sheep.

---

67 Christopher Melchert, "Religious Policies of the Caliphs from al-Mutawakkil to al-Muqtadir, A.H. 232-295/A.D. 847-908," ***Islamic Law and Society*** 3 (1996): 316-42; Steven Clark Judd, "The Third Fitna: Orthodoxy, Heresy and Coercion in Late Umayyad History" (Ph.D diss. University of Michigan, Ann Arbor, 1997).

Chapter II
Formless and Invisible?

The claim is that Allah (God) cannot be a man or come in the person of a man because He is a formless and invisible being (or *non*-being). This claim, however, finds no support at all from the Qur'**ā**n and Sunna. The verses routinely offered as proof-texts of this invisible and formless Allah actually offer no warrant for this doctrine.

1. *Formless and Immaterial?*

According to al-Ghazz**ālī** and those who defer to him in matters of *'aqīda*, God is not a *body*; he is formless and immaterial. The pivotal verse wherein God's incorporeality is most forcefully and (it would seem) clearly articulated is ***al-Shūrā*** 42:11: ليس كمثله شيء *Laysa kamithlihi shay'*, "There is none like Him." This verse is said to reject "all anthropomorphism." [68] If 'none is like' God, the argument goes, then God can't possess a form or body, because His creatures possess form and body, and this would make the Creator and his creatures alike. But this reading of this passage is unwarranted and in fact violates the philology of the text. What's more, the earliest Traditionalist Sunni theological text that we posses, Im**ā**m A**ḥ**mad's *Al-Radd 'ala 'l-Zanādiqa wa 'l-Jahmīya* ("The Refutation of the Heretics and the Heretical Followers of Jahm b. Safwan") explicitly rejects this reading. According to Ibn **Ḥanbal** Q 42:11 was from among the ***mutashābihāt*** or ambiguous verses thereby requiring explanation,[69] and a proper explanation did not preclude an anthropoid deity. It was, says Ibn **Ḥanbal, Jahm**

---

[68] Abdoldjavad Falaturi, "How Can a Muslim Experience God, Given Islam's Radical Monotheism," in ***We Believe In One God: The Experience of God in Christianity and Islam*** ed. Annemarie Schimmel and Abdoldjavad Falaturi (New York: Seabury Press), 78.

[69] **Aḥmad b. Ḥanbal**, ***Al-Radd 'ala 'l-Zanādiqa wa 'l-Jahmīya*** (Cairo, 1393 H) 20.

b. Safwān (d. 746) who first used this verse in an anti-anthropomorphist manner.

The Arabic of ***al-Shūrā*** 42:11 could be read in two ways. The most obvious reading is to take the comparative particle *ka* (***ka-****mithlihi*) as a non-expletive, thus: "There is nothing like (*ka*) His likeness (*mithlihi*)." *Mithlihi* is actually *mithl* = like or likeness, joined to the possessive pronoun *hi* (his). As Ibn al-Jawzī noted, "taken literally (***ẓāhir***) these words indicate that God has a *mithl,* likeness, which is like nothing and like which there is nothing." [70] In other words, the apparent meaning of this passage is not that God is formless, but that he actually possesses a likeness or form which is incomparable. *Mathal* is a model, pattern, exemplar and *mith**āl*** is a synonym of ***ṣūra*** = form.[71] Ibn al-Jawzī therefore cites this verse as one of the proof-texts relied upon by the Ḥanbalīs and other Sunnis who affirmed a human form for God.

Even when we take the comparative particle *ka* as a syndetic relative cause **(*ṣila*)** added for emphasis, "There (really) is nothing like Him," or simply as an expletive, "There is nothing like Him," such a reading does not preclude anthropomorphism, for in the Arabic Qur'ānic context a denial of 'likeness' is not necessarily a denial of morphism (from *morphē* = form). For example, *Surat al-Ahzab* [33]:32, "O wives of the Prophet, you are not like (*lastuna ka-*) any other women." In distinguishing the Mothers of the Faithful from all other Muslim women the same grammatical construction in used (*laysa ka-*) as used in *Surat al-Shura* [42]:11 to distinguish Allah from His creation. Certainly no one would assume that one of the differences between the wives of the Prophet and the other women is that the wives have no forms! Why then, in the absence of any such statement in the Qur'ān, would one assume that the construction as used in *Surat al-Shura* [42]:11 attributes 'formlessness' to Allah? Similarly, *Surat al-Fatir* [35]: 19, "the blind and the seeing are unalike [*mā yastawī*]." The 'unlike-ness' between those who see (the truth of

---

70 Ibn al-Jawzī, ***Kitāb Akhbār al-Ṣifāt,*** 29 (Ar.)

71 Edward William Lane, ***Arabic-English Lexicon*** (London: Williams & Norgate 1863) s.v. **ṣūra.**

revelation) and those that don't is real, but it does not involve formless-ness vs. form. A denial of *tamthīl* (or *tashbīh*, *siwan*, *ka*, *kufu'*) "likeness" to God is therefore not *de jure* a denial of anthropomorphism, God in the form of a man. God could have a human form but still be unlike man. The same expression ('there is none like him') was used for anthropomorphic deities prior to the Qur'ānic revelation. It was found already in ancient Egyptian temple inscriptions of the Ptolemaic period.[72]

At the heart of this semantic issue is the nature and degree of the 'likeness' posited or prohibited: absolute likeness vs. only relative likeness. While Muslims of all stripes held *tashbīh* or "likening God to His creation" as a theological crime, Taqī ad-Dīn Aḥmad b. Taymīyya (d. 1328) rightly pointed out that the term *tashbīh* "likening" can denote a properly acknowledgeable degree of likeness between Creator and created (i.e. relative likeness), and it can also denote an improper degree of similarity (absolute likeness) whose disavowal is mandatory.[73] This nuance is most clearly articulated by the **Ḥanafī *qāḍī* Ibn Abī al 'Izz** (d. 792/1390) in his ***Sharh al-'aqīda al-Ṭaḥāwīya*.** **Ibn Abī al 'Izz** begins by noting that the term ***tashbīh*** had become with the people rather vague (*lafẓ mujmal*).[74] He too suggests that there is an improper ***tashbīh*** prohibited by the Qur'ān wherein an identity is posited between Creator and created, and a proper or allowable *tashbīh* wherein only a general or limited correspondence is posited. Whoever denies the latter is as guilty as he who affirms the former:

72Ederhard Otto, ***Gott und Mensch nach den agyptischen Tempelinschriften der griechich-romischen Zeit*** (Heidelberg, 1964) 11ff.

73 Ibn Taymīyya ***Dar' ta'āruḍ al-'aql wa al-****naql*, 115f, 248f. See also Sherman Jackson's discussion, "Ibn Taymiyyah on Trial in Damascus," *JSS* 39 (1994): 51ff [art.=41-84].

74 Ibn **Abī al 'Izz, *Sharh al-'aqīda al-Ṭaḥāwīya*,** ed. **'Abd Allāh b. 'Abd al-**Mu**ḥsin,** 2 vols (**Beirut,** 1408/1987), I:57 (=*Commentary on the Creed of aṭ-* ***Ṭaḥāwī by Ibn Abī al-'Izz***. Translated by Muhammad **'Abdul-**Haqq Ansari [Riyadh, Saudi Arabia, 2000] 23).

> It is clear...that the Creator and the created are similar in some respects and differ in others (***ittifāquhumā min wajhi wa ikhtilāfuhumā min wajh***). And whoever denies what is common between them is a negator and is surely mistaken. On the other hand, whoever makes them homogeneous (***mutamāthilayn***) is a *mushabbih* and is equally mistaken. And Allah knows best. That is because, even though they are called by the same name, they are not *identical* (***mā ittafaqā fīhi***).[75]

Ibn Abī al 'Izz demonstrates this correspondence by citing Qur'**ā**nic verses wherein man is called by the names of God (e.g. 30:19, ***ḥayy*;** 51:28**,** ***'alīm***, ect.). He argues that these are not mere homonyms, such as *mushtar**ī*** (which means both buyer and the planet Jupiter), similar in name only; the attributes of God and man share a common element denoted by the term.[76] They differ in that God's are attributes of perfection (***Ṣifā**t al-Kam**ā**l*), whereas man's comprise imperfections.[77]

Understanding Q 42:11 to prohibit only absolute likeness, but allow for relative likeness between Creator and creature, allowed one to both disavow *tamth**ī**l/tashb**ī**h* and affirm an anthropoid form for God. This is the significance of the words of Mu**ḥ**ammad b. Sa'dun, better known as Ab**ū** 'Am**ī**r al-Qurayshī, the famous Andalusian theologian who died in Baghdad in 1130, who said:

> The heretics (who deny God's anthropomorphism) cite in evidence the Qur'**ā**n verse 'Nothing is like Him,' but the meaning of this verse is only that nothing compared to God in His divinity. In form, however, God is like you and me.

Q 42:11 therefore does not "reject all anthropomorphism," but affirms *transcendent anthropomorphism*. This point is most

---

[75] Ibn **Abī al 'Izz, *Sharh*,** I:62 (=*Commentary*, 27).
[76] Ibn **Abī al 'Izz, *Sharh*,** I:63 (=*Commentary*, 28).
[77] **Ibn Abī al 'Izz, *Sharh*,** I:93ff (=*Commentary*, 44ff). The definite article used with God's attributes is probably germane here, e.g. *Al-'**Amīn*** **(God) vs. *'amīn* (the Prophet).**

eloquently articulated by Muḥammad b. **Isḥāq** b. Khuzayma (d. 924), the most prominent **Shāfiʿī** in Nishapur at the time. Born in **Nīshāpur**, Ibn Khuzayma would later be described as the "chief of the **ḥadīth** scholars (***ra's al-muḥaddithīn***)."[78] Many eminent scholars (***fuḥūl al-ʿulamā'***) heard from him, including al-**Bukhārī,** "the Commander of the Faithful in **ḥadīth.**" A **Shāfi'ite** ***faqīh*** (jurisprudent), he was ***salafī al-ʿaqīda,*** that is to say he understood the Qur'**ā**nic and Prophetic statements about God according to their apparent meaning, without metaphorical interpretation of the ambiguous verses (***ẓāhirihā bi-dūn ta' wīl li-mutashābihihā***) and without alteration of their apparent meaning (***lā taḥrīf li-ẓāhirihā***).[79] Ibn Khuzayma's most important work is his ***Kitāb al-tawḥīd wa-ithbāt ṣifāt al-Rabb*** ("Book on the Unity of God and the Affirmation of His Attributes"), a collection of **ḥadīth** reports touching on the various Attributes of God. According to Muḥammad Khalīl **Harrās,** editor of this work, ***Kitāb al-tawḥīd*** enjoyed great respect among the traditionalists of his day, almost being dubbed "***Ṣaḥīḥ*** **Ibn Khuzayma.**" It even nearly surpassed the two ***Ṣaḥīḥ*****'s.**[80] Some scholars preferred "***Ṣaḥīḥ*** **Ibn Khuzayma**" to ***Ṣaḥīḥ Bukhārī*** **and** ***Ṣaḥīḥ Muslim.*** In his ***Kitāb al-tawḥīd*** Ibn Khuzayma takes up the charge that the **ḥadīth** scholars and Traditionalist Sunnis were "likeners (*mushabbiha*)" because they affirmed the literal meaning of the revealed attributes of God (***Ṣifāt*** *al-****Akhbār***). Discussing their affirmation that God truly has a face (*wajh*), against the "ignorant Jahmiyya" who claim that God's face in the Qur'**ā**n is really His essence (*dhāt*), Ibn Khuzayma writes:

> His face is that which He described with splendor (*jalāl*) and venerability (*ikrām*) in His statement, "The face of you Lord remains, possessor of Splendor, Venerability." (God) denied

[78] Muḥammad Khalīl **Harrās, ed. of Ibn Khuzayma**'s ***Kitāb al-tawḥīd***, "alif".
[79] Ibid., "**ḥā'.**"
[80] Ibid., "**ẓā**""

> that it perishes (*nafy ʿanhu al-halāk*) when His creatures perish. Our Lord is exalted above anything from His essential attributes (*min* ***ṣifāt dhātihi***) perishing…God has affirmed for Himself a Splendid and Venerable face, which He declares is eternal and non-perishable. We and all scholars of our *madhhab* (school of thought) from the Hijaz, the Tihama, Yemen, Iraq, Syria, and Egypt affirm for God (the) face, which He has affirmed for Himself. We profess it with our tongues and believe it in our hearts, without likening (*qhayr an nashabbiha*) His face to one from His creatures. May our Lord be exalted above our likening Him to His creatures…Listen now, O you who understand what we mentioned regarding the manner of speaking common among the Arabs (*jins al-lugha al-****sā****ʾira bayn al-ʿarab*): Do you apply the name *mushabbiha* to the **ḥadīth** scholars and followers of the Sunna? We and all our scholars in all our lands say that the one we worship has a face…And we say that the face of our Loud (radiates) a brilliant, radiant light (*al-****nūr*** *wa al-****ḍiyā****ʾ wa-bahā*ʾ) which, if His veil is removed the glory of His face will scorch everything that sees it. His eyes are veiled from the people of this world who will never see Him during this life...The face of our Lord is eternal …
>
> Now God has decreed for human faces destruction and denied them splendor and venerability. They are not attributed the light, brilliance or splendor (*al-****nūr*** *wa al-****ḍiyā****ʾ wa-bah****ā****ʾ*) that He described His face with. Eyes in this world may catch human faces without the latter scorching so much as a single hair...Human faces are rooted in time (*muḥdatha*) and created...Every human face perishes…Oh you possessors of reason (***dhawā al-ḥij****an*), could it ever really occur to any one with sense and who knows Arabic and knows what *tashbīh* (means) that this (transient and dull human) face is like that (splendidly brilliant face of God)?[81]

Ibn Khuzayma here adamantly argues for God's possession of a true face, but one dangerously radiant and non-perishable, in contrast to man's perishable and dull face: transcendent anthropomorphism. He asks, in short, 'Can one who

[81] Ibid., 10f, 22f.

acknowledges these differences be charged with *tashbīh*?' Certainly not according to the language of the Arabs! We have here both the affirmation of anthropomorphism and the disavowal of *tashbīh*. This is no doubt the context of Sura 42:11.

2. ***Sūrat al-****Ikhlāṣ and Islam's Corporeal God*

One of the most oft-repeated verses of the Qur'ān is *Al-Ikhlāṣ*: The Unity (Sura 112).

Qul: huwa llāhu aḥad
Allāhu l-ṣamad
Lam yalid wa-lam yulad
Wa-lam yakun lahu kufu'an aḥad

1 Say: He Allah is One
2 Allah is *aṣ-ṣamad*
3 He begets not, nor is He begotten
4 And none is equal to Him.

Sura 112 is reckoned the single most important chapter in the Qur'ān as it defines Islam's attitude toward Allah.[82] It is no question *al-Ikhlāṣ*, along with *al-Shūrā* 42:11, which is cited most often as proof of the completely non-anthropomorphic nature of God. But as in the latter case, this is an unwarranted reading of this passages. In fact, ***Sūrat al-****Ikhlāṣ* can be read as a clear statement of the Qur'ān's corporeal deity. In verse two, God is referred to as *aṣ-ṣamad*. While the precise sense of the epithet was debated in the Classical Arabic literature and is still in Western scholarship,[83] by at least the time of al-Ṭabarī (d. 923) a popular reading equated *ṣamad* with ***muṣmat,*** "solid, of even

---

[82] Gordon Newby, "*Surat Al-'Ikhlas*," ***Orient and Occident*** 22 (1973): 127.
[83] See e.g. Al-Tabarī, ***Jāmi' al-bayān 'an ta'wīl āy al-Qur'ān*** **(Cairo,** 1321) XXX: 196ff; Uri Rubin, 'Al-Ṣamad and the High God: An Interpretation of *sūra* CXII,' ***Isl*** 61 (1984): 187-217; Franz Rosenthal, 'Some minor problems in the Qur'an,' in ***The Joshua Starr Memorial Volume*** (New York, 1953) 67-84.

composition, massive, compact, or not hollow (i.e. without a stomach cavity)." Al-Ash'**ar**ī in his *Maqalāt al-Islāmīyīn* observed: 'Many people say, "He (God) is solid," interpreting the word of God *ṣamad* to mean solid, i.e., not hollow.'[84] Some of the greatest of the *Sahaba* (Companions) and the *Tabi'un* (Successors) attached this meaning to the word: Ibn Abbas, al-Hasan, Sa'id b. Jubayr, Mujahid, ad-Dahhak, Sa'id b. al-Mausayyib, Ikrimah. In fact, this interpretation goes back to the Prophet himself (see Tabari, ad 112).

But this is not all. The Arabs used *aṣ-ṣamad* in pre-Islamic times to designate their tribal chief and the High God who was thought to resemble this human tribal chief.[85] Most importantly, the pre-Islamic High God was called Allah.[86] The grammarian Abū 'Ubayda, in his *Majāz al-Qur'ān* (2, 316), noted: "*aṣ-ṣamad* is he towards whom one directs himself, and no one is above him. This is how the Arabs call their nobles (*ashrāfahā*.)" This clearly demonstrates that *aṣ-ṣamad* does not imply a non-anthropomorphic deity, for the Arabs commonly used the term for both God and men.

Verse 3 describes God as one who begets not and is Himself unbegotten. This of course, on the surface, appears unmistakable in its rejection of anthropomorphism. Again, analyzing it in its historical context proves otherwise. Four hundred Lihyanite and Dedanite inscriptions dating back to the fifth century BC were found in the area of al-Ulah in Northern Arabia. In these inscriptions are pre-Islamic invocations to Allah. One of the names applied to the pre-Islamic Allah, which distinguished him from the other deities acknowledged and worshipped by the idolatrous Arabs, was '*abtar*' which means he had "no offspring."

---

[84] Al- Ash'**ar**ī, *Maqalāt*, 34.

[85] Rubin, "Al-Ṣamad," 200ff.

[86] F. Winnet, ***A Study of Lihyanite and Thamudic Inscriptions*** (Toronto: University of Toronto Press,1937); idem., "Allah Before Islam," ***The Moslem World*** 28 (1938), pp. 239-259.

O Allah, God without offspring, greeting…
O Allah, God without offspring, knower of men…

F.V. Winnet, in his article, "Allah Before Islam," observes:

> Looking back over the texts given above, we find nothing distinctive in the appeals addressed to Allah…But there is one epithet applied to Allah which is not applied to any other god in north Arabic inscriptions and that is '*abtar*' (without offspring). It evidently denotes a quality that was regarded as peculiar to Allah alone; it thus forms our chief key to the Allah-theology of the pre-Islamic Arabs.[87]

'Abtar' denoted the quality of not producing offspring. Julian Baldick has shown that the 'Black God' of ancient South Arabia was characterized by this abnormal sexual behavior, i.e. the refusal to beget offspring.[88] This clearly demonstrates that the attributing to a god such a refusal need not indicate a non-anthropomorphic nature. The two descriptions of Allah found in *Al-Ikhlāṣ* – God as *aṣ-ṣamad* and as one who begets not – therefore connects the God of the Qur'ān with the god of pre-Islamic Arabia,[89] the proto-Semitic Black God called ***Ala*** who was human in form and black.[90]

87 Winnet, "Allah Before Islam," 244.
88 Julian Baldick, ***Black God. The Afroasiatic Roots of the Jewish, Christian and Muslim Religions*** (Syracuse University Press, New York. 1997) 65.
89 Newby, "*Surat Al-'Ikhlas,*" 130; Rubin, , "Al-Ṣamad," 206
90 See Muhammad, ***Black Arabia***, 81-87.

Nor does the fact that the God of the Qur'ān *lam yulad* ("is not begotten") preclude His being anthropomorphic. The Creator-god in ancient Kemet (Egypt), Min (see photo), was an anthropomorphic black god called *Kamu-tef*, "Bull of His Mother" or "He Who is His Own Father." This epithet indicates that this god is *self-created*, i.e. *unbegotten*. This, again, clearly demonstrates that ***Sūrat al**-Ikhlāṣ* does not unambiguously or necessarily describe an incorporeal deity.

Does the description of God as *aḥad*, "One" mean that He can't be a divine man, or even anthropomorphic, because the human form with all its parts is a multiplicity? Not according to the Islam of Imām Aḥmad.

> By saying that Allah was ever existing in all His qualities, are we not truly describing the one God in all His qualities? We gave the following example: Tell us about the palm tree, we said. Is it not made of stump, stem, fibre, foliage, leaves and pitch, and for all its attributes has it not one name? Likewise, Allah, who is to be compared to what is loftiest, is one God in all His qualities...And again, Allah referring to an infidel called al-Walid b. al-Walid b. al-Mughira al-Makhzumi, said: "Leave me to deal with him who I created, one (*waḥid*) (Q 74: 11)." The one so named had eyes, ears, a tongue, lips, hands, feet and many members, and is yet named *waḥid*, all his qualities notwithstanding. Likewise, Allah, who is to be compared to what is loftiest, is with all His qualities one God.[91]

[91] ***Al-Radd***, 116-117

Just as man has various body parts and still can be described as *one*, so too can Allah. There is thus nothing in ***Sūrat al-Ikhlāṣ*** that demands the incorporeal god of al-Ghazz**ālī** and most of the Muslim world.

3. *Deus Invisibilis in the Qur'**ān**?*

A.] *Surat al-An'**ām*** [6]: 103

> ***lā tudrikuhu 'l-abṣār wa huwa yudrik 'l-abṣār***

> "(Physical) vision (*al-ab**ṣār***) comprehends Him not (***lā*** *tudrikuhu*) and He comprehends vision."

It is commonly assumed that this verse indicates that Allah is an invisible being. But as the Classical Sunni *mufassirun* or Qur'**ā**nic exegetes saw, this is not actually a denial of God's visibility, *ru'ya*. It is a denial that this seeing of God (*ru'ya*) can afford man a full comprehension (*idr**āk***) of God. As they pointed out, the *idr**āk*** here denied (i.e. ***lā*** *tudrikuhu*) has the meaning of *i**ḥāṭ**a*, "encompassment, encirclement,"[92] implying a full, thorough comprehension. Thus al-Nawaw**ī** (d. 1278) declared: "*idr**āk*** is *i**ḥāṭ**a* and Allah Most High is not encompassed by vision (*ru'ya*). Hence, the text (6:103) furnishes a denial of encompassment (*idr**āk***). The non-encompassing *ru'ya* is not necessarily denied here."[93] See also Ibn Hajar (d. 1449), who stated: "the intent of the verse is the denial of encompassment (*i**ḥāṭ**a*) of Him by means of seeing Him (*ru'ya*), not the denial of the theoretical basis (*aṣl*) of seeing Him."[94] Ibn **Abī al-'Izz**

---

[92] See e.g. **Abū Manṣūr al-Māturīdī,** ***Kitāb al-Tawḥīd,*** **ed. Fathalla Kholeif (Beirut: Dar El-Machreq** Éditeurs, 1970) 3-14, 81; Ibn Hajar al-'Asqal**ānī,** ***Fatḥ al-Bārī bi-sharḥ Ṣaḥīḥ al-****Bukh**ārī*** (**Beirut: Dār al-**Kutub al-'**Ilmīya,** 1989) 8:607.

[93] Al-**Nawawī,** ***Sharḥ Ṣaḥīḥ Muslim*** 11 vols. (**Cairo: Dār** al-**Ḥadīth,** 1994) 2:11.

[94] Ibn Hajar al-'Asqal**ānī,** ***Fatḥ al-Bārī***, 8:607.

explained that "One can see Allah but cannot grasp (*idrāk*) Him, just as one can know Him but cannot comprehend Him."[95]

This interpretation is said to go back to the *Tarjumān al-Qur'ān* (Interpreter of the Qur'ān) himself, the famed Companion and cousin of the Prophet, 'Abd Allāh b. Abbās, as narrated by 'Ikrima, Ibn Abbās's *mawla* and famed Successor:

> Ibn Abbas said, "He saw Him descend another time (53:13), " meaning the Prophet saw his Lord. A man said to ['Ikrima]: "Didn't He say, 'Vision comprehends Him not and He comprehends all vision'." 'Ikrima said to him: "Do you see the sky?" He said yes. He said, "[Do] you see *all* of the sky[?]"[96]

The point of *Surat al-An'ām* 103 is therefore not that God can't be seen. The point is that seeing God with the eyes is not tantamount to comprehending His divine fullness.

B.] *Sūrat al-Baqarah* [2]: 55-56 and *Sūrat al-Nisā'* [4]: 153:

> And remember you (Israel) said: "O Moses! We shall never believe in thee until we see God openly (*jahrat^{an}*)." So the lightning (*ṣāʿiqah*) overtook them as they looked on. Then We raised you up after your death that you may be grateful. (2:55-56)

> The People of the Book ask thee (Muḥammad) to cause a book to descend to thee from heaven; indeed they asked Moses for an even greater (miracle), for they said: "Show us God openly (*jahrat^{an}*)." So lightning (*ṣāʿiqah*) overtook them on account of their ***ẓulm***. Then (*thumma*) they worshipped the calf after clear signs had come to them. We pardoned this. And We gave Moses clear authority. (4:153)

---

[95] ***Sharh***, 1:57.

[96] Al-Tabari, ***Jam' al-bayan***, 27:52; Ibn Abī **'Āṣim.** ***al-Sunna.*** 2 vols. (Riyāḍ: **Dār al-Ṣ**umay'**ī,** 1998) 1:307.

It is assumed that these passages too present us with an invisible deity. The argument is that the Qur'**ā**n puts the blasphemous request to see the invisible God in the mouth of rebellious Jews as a sort of "verbal golden calf". This impossible request is branded as ***ẓulm*** or wrongdoing, for which the blasphemous Jews are punished. This, we have shown, is an unlikely reading of these passages.[97]

Classical Qur'**ā**nic exegetes saw that these passages must be read in the context of *Surat al-A'**rāf*** [7]:143:

> And when Moses came at Our appointed time and his Lord spoke to him, he said: "My Lord, show Yourself to me that I may look upon You." [God] said: "You can't see Me (*lan taranī*); but look at the mountain. If it remains in its place then you will see Me. So when his Lord appeared (*tajall**ā***) to the mountain He made it crumble and Moses fell dumbstruck on account of the lightning (***ṣa'iq**[an]*). Then when he recovered, he said: Glory to You! I turn to You, and I am the first of the believers!

This last passage is an account of an actual theophany or visible appearance of God. The Arabic is clear and unambiguous: *fa-lamma**ā** tajall**ā** rabbuhu lil-jabali.* The verb *tajalla* is Form V of the root j-l-w, "to appear, become manifest." It also carries the meaning "He manifested His *Jal**ā**l* (luminous Majesty)." The ***ṣa'iqa*** or 'lightning' is the destructive radiance emanating from God's *Jal**ā**l*, as the Maliki *faqih* (jurist) al-Qayraw**ānī** (d. 996) noted: "God...appeared to the mountain and it became leveled at His Majesty (*Jal**ā**l*)." As al-**Qāḍī** 'Iy**ā**d (d. 1149) says as well in his classic text, *al-Shif**ā***, 104:

> This verse...means that Moses saw Allah and that is why he fell down in a swoon...His manifestation to the mountain was His appearance to Moses so that, according to the statement (Q 7:143), he actually saw Him"

97 See Williams, "*Tajall**ī** wa Ru'ya,*" 92-99.

God in the Qur'ān (39:69; 22:35; 55:27) and in the Sunna has a brilliantly radiant person which is destructive if it is unveiled to humans. Thus, for our protection He keeps it veiled. As it is narrated from the Prophet: "His (God's) veil is light. If He would remove it, the august splendor of Allah's Face would burn everything of his creation to which his glance reaches."[98]

It is reported on the authority of Ibn Abbas that, "When Allah decides to put fear in the hearts of His creatures, He manifests a part of Himself to the earth and it quakes; but when He wishes to destroy a people He manifests Himself [fully] to it." This partial manifestation designed to invoke fear is illustrated in *Surat al-A'raf*. Ibn Kathir reported that God manifested to the mountain only a part of His *Jalal*, the equivalent of His 'little finger.'[99] On the other hand, the full, genocidal manifestation is illustrated in Surat al-Baqarah [2]: 55-56 and Surat al-Nisa' [4]: 153.

In order to properly understand these passages we must be aware of the history alluded to here by the Qur'ān. It is the story of Israel at Sinai three months after leaving Egypt (Exodus 19). There God appeared to Israel to initiate the Covenant but for Israel's protection His morphic Glory (*kavod/jalal*) was veiled by a thick cloud. Israel was not satisfied with this mediated theophany and presumptuously requested, demanded even, to see God openly This is the meaning of the Arabic word *jahrat*[an] in the Qur'ān ("Show us God openly (*jahrat*[an])." It is likely this presumption that is the *ẓulm* or wrong doing for which they were struck. To punish them for this presumption and arrogance God granted their request and allowed them to suffer the consequences: death (*Exod. Rabbah* 29:4). Afterwards God restored them. This is what the Qur'ān alludes to. It thus says "So the lightning (**ṣa'iqa**) overtook them as they looked on (*tanẓurūna*)." The **ṣa'iqa** is the destructive radiance that emanates from God's *jalal* when He exposes it to view. While in

---

[98] Muslim, ***Sahih***, 79, 343; Ibn Majah, ***Sunan***, 1:110 195.
[99] ***Tafsir***, ad *surat al-A'raf.*

Moses' case there was only a partial manifestation which leveled the mountain and knocked Moses into swoon, in this case Israel is given the full, genocidal visual manifestation.

None of these passages therefore are evidence against God's visibility. Just the opposite. God is visible, but seeing Him is dangerous in our current state of sinfulness and weakness. As Ibn Abi al-'Izz noted: "We don't see Him in this life because our eyes are incapable of that, not because He cannot be seen. If someone tries to see the sun, he cannot, not because it cannot be seen but because our eyes are too weak."[100]

The God of the Qur'**ā**n is a visible God. Moses saw Him, as did Mu**ḥ**ammad. It is recorded in *Sūrat al-Najm* (53): 1-18

> In the name of Allah, the Beneficent, the Merciful
> By the star when it sets
> Your companion errs not, nor does he deviate
> Nor does he speak out of desire
> It is indeed revelation that is revealed
> One mighty in power has taught him
> Possessor of a beautiful form *(dhū mirra)*, He sat upright (on the Throne, *istiwā*)
> While He was on the uppermost horizon.
> Then He drew near, drew nearer still
> Until He was the measure of two bows or closer
> Then He revealed to His servant what He revealed.
> His (Muhammad's) heart did not lie concerning that which he saw.
> Do you then dispute with him over what he saw?
> He indeed saw Him in another descent
> At the Lote-tree of the Boundary
> Near it is the Garden of Repose
> When that which covers covered the Lote-tree.
> The eyes turned not aside, nor did they exceed the limit
> Certainly he saw of the greatest signs of his Lord.

---

[100] Ibn **Abī al 'Izz, *Sharh*, I:**127.

Imam Nawawī pointed out that "The view of the majority (*al-jumhūr*) of the exegetes is that the intention (of the verse) is that Muḥammad saw his Lord."[101] The claim that the object of the visions here recorded is actually the angel Jibrīl is a secondary development that is unsupported by the text itself.[102]

There is nothing in the Qur'ān that indicates that Allah is an invisible being. He can be seen – and Moses and Muḥammad did see Him – but it is dangerous to do so. While Moses was a 'victim of the theophany', Muḥammad not only survived it unharmed but he would be distinguished from all prophets by virtue of his visual encounter with God.

4. *The Qur'ān's Morphic God*

The Qur'ān therefore fails to substantiate the existence of a formless and invisible god. On the contrary, the Qur'ān describes Allah with vivid anthropomorphism. Against the philosophic notion of the immaterial "no-thing" or non-being, Allah is specifically described as a شيء *shay'* "thing." "Say: What thing (*shay'*) is mightiest in testimony? Say: Allah. (6:19)." *Shay'* literally means "thing,"[103] but in the theological context meant "being."[104] The God of the Qur'an is a being. A *shay'* by definition is a delimited and circumscribed entity, not a formless abstraction. **Abū Sa'īd 'Uthmān b. Sa'īd al-Dārimī**, a leading traditionalist of Harāt (d. 895), pointed out:

> Every one without exception is in agreement concerning the term *shay'*, namely that a *shay'* cannot exist with neither limit

[101] ***Sharh Sahih Muslim*** 2:12
[102] See Williams, "*Tajallī wa Ru'ya,*" Chapter V.
[103] Hans Wehr, ***Arabic-English Dictionary*** ed. J. M. Cowan (Ithaca: Spoken Language Services, Inc., 1994) 579 s.v. *shay'*
[104] R.M. Frank, "The Neoplatonism of Gahm Ibn Safwan," ***Le Museon*** 78 (1965), 399.

nor attribute (*hadd wa-ṣifa*) and that there is no *shay'* which has neither limit nor attribute.[105]

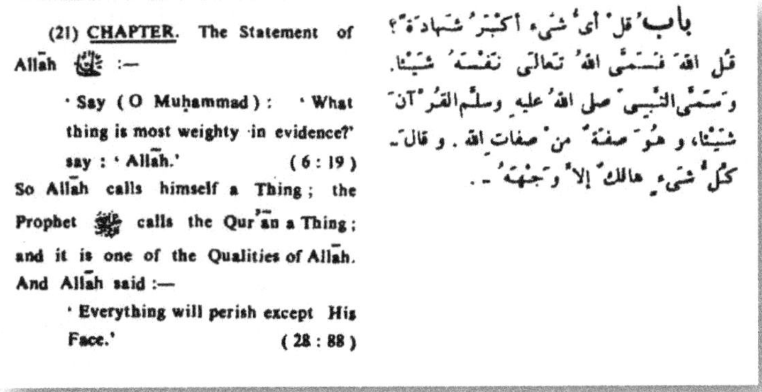

باب قل أى شىء أكبر شهادة؟
قل الله فسمى الله تعالى نفسه شيئا.
وسمى النبى صلى الله عليه وسلم القرآن
شيئا، و هو صفة من صفات الله . و قال
كل شىء هالك إلا وجهه .

(21) CHAPTER. The Statement of Allāh ﷻ :—

'Say (O Muḥammad): 'What thing is most weighty in evidence?' say: 'Allāh.' (6 : 19)

So Allāh calls himself a Thing; the Prophet ﷺ calls the Qur'ān a Thing; and it is one of the Qualities of Allāh. And Allāh said :—

'Everything will perish except His Face.' (28 : 88)

Sahih Bukhari, *kitab al-tawhid*

According to **al-Dārimī** it was Jahm b. Safwan who introduced into Islam the uncircumscribed deity, a fact pointed out by Imam Aḥmad as well. In his ***Radd 'alā Bishr,*** **al-Dārimī** argues:

> the obstinate heretic (Jahm) further alleges that God has no boundary (*ḥadd*), no limit, and no term; this is the foundation on which Jahm built all his errors and from which he derived all his falsehoods and is a statement in which, so far as we know, none preceded Jahm...Allah certainly has a limit... and so has His place, for He is on His Throne above the heavens, and these are two limits. Any person who declares that Allah has a limit and that His place has a limit is more knowledgeable than the Jahmis.[106]

---

105 **Al-Dārimī**, ***Radd 'ala Jahmiyya*** ed. Gosta Vitestam, ***Kitab ar-radd 'ala l-gahmiya des Abu Sa'id b. 'Uthman b. Sa'id ad-Darimi*** (Lund/Leiden, 1960), 62.

106 **Al-Dārimī**, ***Radd 'ala Bishr*** (Cairo 1358 H), 23.

Allah is thus a *shay'* or being with some physical limit (though not necessarily with any metaphysical limits). This was the position of Imām Aḥmad and the Traditionalist Sunni scholars of the 9th century.[107] **Ḥ**arb b. Ismā'īl al-Kirmānī (d. 893), one of Ibn **Ḥ**anbal's students, reports concerning this fact of God being ***maḥdūd*** or delimited:

> This is the *madhhab* of the people of knowledge, the people of the transmissions, the people of Sunnah, those who hold fast to its (i.e. the Sunnah's) roots, are known by it, and by whom, one can follow [the Sunnah]; and I have known the scholars of Iraq, Hijaz and Shams and others to be in support of it. Hence, whoever opposes any part of these *madhāhid*, or refutes and finds fault with anyone who endorses it, is an innovator and outside the community, a deviant from the way of the Sunnah and the true path.[108]

As a delimited being God possess a face (*wajh*, 55:26) with eyes (20:39; 11:37); two hands (*yadayya*, 38:75; 5:64), a leg (*sāq*, 68:42), side (*janb*, 39:56) a soul (*nafs*, 3:28, 5:116) and a spirit (***rūḥ***, 66:12); He is in the heavens (67:16) established (*istawā*) on his throne (7:54). From there he will "come" to earth (2:210). The qur'anic God also has some human behaviors: he gets angry (1:7, 2:61, 3:112 and 162, 4:93, etc.); he is cunning (3:54, 8:30, 10:21, 13:42, etc.); he pokes fun (2:15).

---

[107] Ibn Abi Ya'la, ***Tabaqat***, 1:267 reports: "Muhammad b. Ibrahim al-Qaysi said: I said to Imam Ahmad b. Hanbal: It is quoted from Ibn al-Mubarak that it was said to him: How do we know our Lord - the Mighty and Majestic? He said, "Above (fi) the heaven, upon ('ala) His Throne with hadd (limit, demarcation)." So Ahmad said, "This is how it is with us". Imam al-Dhahabi, *al-Uluww* (p.152 of its *Mukhtasir*) affirms: "This is *sahih* (authentic) from Ibn al-Mubārak and Ahmad, may Allah be pleased with him."

[108] Harb b. Isma'il al-Kirmani, ***al-Sunnah wa 'l-Jama'ah*** in ***Masa'il al-Imam Ahmad ibn Hanbal wa Ishaq ibn Rahwayh***, 1:355

Chapter III
The Man-God of the Sunnah

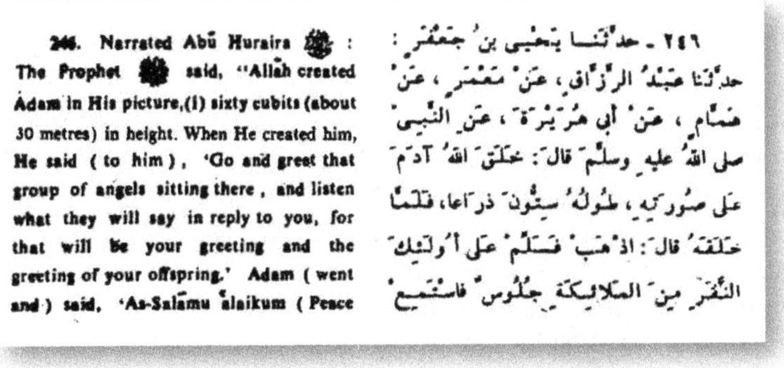

246. Narrated Abū Huraira ﷺ: The Prophet ﷺ said, "Allāh created Adam in His picture,(1) sixty cubits (about 30 metres) in height. When He created him, He said (to him), 'Go and greet that group of angels sitting there, and listen what they will say in reply to you, for that will be your greeting and the greeting of your offspring.' Adam (went and) said, 'As-Salāmu 'alaikum (Peace

٢٤٦ - حدّثنا يحيى بن جعفر: حدّثنا عبد الرزّاق، عن معمر، عن همّام، عن أبي هريرة، عن النبي صلى الله عليه وسلّم قال: خلق الله آدم على صورته، طوله ستون ذراعاً، فلمّا خلقه قال: اذهب فسلّم على أولئك النفر من الملائكة جلوس فاستمع

Bukhari, ***Sahih***, vol. 8, book 74 #246

1. *The Sunnah's Morphic Deity*

The Qur'**ā**nic description of God in no way supports the claim made by today's Ghazz**ā**lian orthodox. The Qur'**ā**n nowhere precludes an anthropomorphic deity. Nowhere does it declare that He lacks a body or form. It is also true that the Qur'**ā**n nowhere explicitly and unequivocally attests to an anthropomorphic deity. If the Qur'**ā**n alone is taken as the criterion of the faith, the most that could be said is that THEM's *tafsir* or interpretation of the Qur'**ā**n is one legitimate option among many and in no way puts him outside the pale of Islam.

The Sunnah of the Prophet was said by the early Muslims (*Tabi'un* [Successors to the Companions] and the *Tabi at-Tabi'in* [Successors to the Successors]) to explain and clarify the Qur'**ā**n.[109] The Qur'**ā**n, in particular the qur'**ā**nic description of God, can be understood only with the aid of the reliably transmitted word of the Prophet. And the Sunnah is

---

109 Ibn Hanbal argued "the Sunnah explains and clarifies the Qur'an." ***Usul us-Sunnah*** *apud* Ibn **Abī Ya'lā**. ***Ṭabaqāt*** 1:294.

unbelievably clear. Whereas the Qur'**ā**n has both clear and ambiguous verses, making the qur'**ā**nic description of God equivocal on the surface, the Sunnah suffers from no such ambiguity. The hadith literature is literally flooded with anthropomorphic descriptions of God.[110] What is most astonishing is that there are no abrogating or mitigating hadith that would serve to balance out or tone down this blatantly anthropomorphic presentation of deity. The Ash'arite theologian and scholar al-Suy**ūtī** unwittingly demonstrates this most convincingly in his ***Tafsīr al****-Durr al-manth****ūr,*** a commentary of the Qur'**ā**n by the hadith. He reports on each verse all of the relevant traditions. But lo! The passage concerning Q 42:11, "There is none like Him," is *desperately empty.*[111] This is astonishing because al-Suyuti himself completely rejected anthropomorphism. What is more, there are no exegetical traditions for this verse from the first generation of qur'**ā**nic exegetes.[112] Tabari doesn't cite any, nor does Qurtubi in his ***al-Jami' li-ahkam al-Qur'an***.

According to a ***ṣaḥīḥ*** (sound) report Adam's human form is a likeness of the divine form.

> God created Adam according to His form (*khalaqa llahu Adama 'ala suratihi*), his size being of sixty cubits. Then, once He created him, He said to him: "Go greet this group of angels seated [over there], and listen well in what way they will respond to you. Because such will be [in what follows] your way of greeting—yours and your descendants." [Adam] went, and said [to them]: *as-salamu 'alaykum*. They answered [him]:

---

[110]See especially Daniel Gimaret, ***Dieu à l'image de l'homme: les anthropomorphismes de la sunna et leur interprétation par les théologiens*** (Paris: Patrimoines, 1997). For different treatments of the anthropomorphisms in the Qur'**ā**n and Sunnah see: Ibn Khuzaymah, ***Kitāb al-tawhīd wa-ithbāt ṣifāt al-Rabb*** and Ibn al-Jawz**ī**, ***Kitāb Akhbār al-Ṣifāt.***

[111] Al-Suy**ūtī**. ***Tafsīr al-Durr al-manthūr fī al-tafsīr al-māthūr*** **(Beirut: Dār al-**Fikr, 1983).

[112] Claude Gilliot, "Muq**ā**til, Grand Exégete, Traditionniste Et Théologien Maudit." ***Journal Asiatique*** 179 (1991): 57 [art.=39-84].

> *as-salamu 'alayka wa rahmatu llah.* They had thus added: *wa rahmatu llah.* All those who will enter into Paradise will have the same form as Adam, their size [theirs also] will be sixty cubits. [But here below,] after [Adam], [the size of] creatures have up to this day not ceased to diminish.[113]

God thus has a form similar to that of Adam's, though different in some respects. Those scholars who preferred an incorporeal deity used various devices to interpret the 'form' away from God. Some for example read the possessive pronoun "His" (*hi*) of "His form" as "his," *viz.* Adam's form. That is to say that God created Adam in Paradise in the same form that he, Adam, had when he was sent to earth. In other words Adam wasn't a giant in Paradise and then shrunk as some had claimed. The traditionalist Sunni doctors were bitterly opposed to such tricks, however (even al-Ghazzālī rejected these: *Imla'*, 1:219ff; *Ihya'*, 4:205). According to Ibn Taymīyah,

> There was no disputation among the Salaf of the first three generations that the pronoun (hi/His) refers to Allah, and it is narrated via many isnads from many Companions. The contexts of the hadith reports all indicate this...(B)ut when the Jahmiyya became widespread in the third Islamic century a group began to say that the pronoun refers to something other than Allah...They were denounced by the imams of Islam and other ulema.[114]

The famous hadith scholar Abū Muḥammad b. Qutayba (d. 889) declared:

> That Allah should have a form is no stranger than His having two hands, fingers and eyes...[115]

---

[113] **Bukhārī, *Ṣaḥīḥ*, *isti'dhān*,** 1; Muslim, ***Ṣaḥīḥ*, *birr***, 115; **Aḥmad b. Ḥanbal, *Musnad*** 6 **vols. (Cairo,** 1313 **H) II:** 244, 251, 315, **etc.**

[114] ***Naqd al-Ta'sīs***, 3:202.

[115] Abu Muhammad b. Qutayba, *Kitāb **ta'wīl mukhtalif al-ḥadīth.*** **Translated into French by G**érard Lecomte in *Le Traité des Divergences du Ḥadīṯ d'Ibn Qutayba*. Damas: Institut Français de Damas, 1962) 221.

God possesses an actual form, though it is not like other forms, and He fashioned Adam after it.[116]

This was the position of that paradigmatic black sheep, Imām Aḥmad Ibn Ḥanbal. He states in one of his creeds, "God created Adam with His hand and in His form,"[117] and in another the Imām argues: "Adam was created in the form of the Merciful (i.e. God), as comes in a report from the Messenger of God..."[118] Ibn Ḥanbal rejected the exegetical devices that read 'his form' rather than 'His form.' When asked about a contemporary's statement that "he (Adam) is according to the form of Adam, He is not according to the form of the Merciful," Ibn Ḥanbal reportedly responded: "He who says that God created Adam according to the form of Adam is a *Jahmi* (disbeliever)."[119]

2. *The Prophet's Vision of God*

It is reported on the authority of '**Abd Allāh b. Ḥārith:**

Ibn '**Abbās** met Ka'b (**al-Aḥbār**) at 'Arafat and asked him concerning a certain thing. Then he said, 'God is great,' until the mountains returned the echo. Then Ibn 'Abb**ā**s said, "We belong to the Ban**ū** H**ā**shim. We say: Verily, Muhammad saw his Lord twice." Ka'b replied,

---

[116] Quoted by Ibn al-Jawzi, ***Kitāb Akhbār al-Ṣifāt.*** 175 (Eng.)

[117] Ibn Hanbal, *'Aqīda* I, *apud* Ibn **Abī Ya'lā**, ***Ṭabaqāt*** I:29. I use here Henry Laoust's classication of Ibn **Ḥanbal**'s creeds found in Ibn **Abī Ya'lā**'s ***Ṭabaqāt***. See Henry Laoust, "Les Premières Professions de foi Hanbalites," in *Mélanges Louis Massignon*, PIFD, 3 (Damas: Institut Francais De Damas, 1957), 12ff.

[118] Ibn Hanbal, *'Aqīda* I V, *apud* Ibn Abi Ya#la ***Tabaqat***, I:313. From the report of Ibn 'Umar: "Don't make your face ugly, because Adam was created according to the form of the Merciful." Ahmad b. Hanbal, ***Kitab al-Sunna,*** ed. 'Abd Allah b. Hasan b. Husayn (Mecca: al-Matba'at al-Salafiyya, 1349 H) 56. See also idem, *Musnad*, 30 vols. ed. Shu'ayb al-Arn**ā**'ut (Beirut: Mu'assasat al-Ris**ā**lah, 1993; hereafter *Musnad*[2]) 12:275, #7323; 12:382, #7420; 15:371, #9604.

[119] Ibn Abi Ya'la, ***Tabaqat***, I:309.

> "Verily God Most High divided His vision and His conversation between Muḥammad and **Mūsā**. He spoke to **Mūsā** twice; and Muḥammad saw Him twice."[120]

According to a great number of reports deemed sound by the hadith scholars, God came to Muhammad in a vision and Muhammad saw and even felt His form. The above report is most interesting because it claims that affirming the Prophet's Vision of God is characteristic of the Banū Hāshim, i.e. the black sheep *par excellence*. We will encounter this theme again. One of the most popular of these Vision narratives is reported on the authority of the Companion of the Prophet, **Muʿadh b. Jabal:**

> [**Muʿadh**] narrates: One morning, the Messenger of God took a long time to come join us for the dawn prayer, until the moment where we were on the point of seeing the sun come up. The Prophet then came out hurriedly. They did the second call to prayer, and the Messenger of God did the prayer, but his prayer was short. When he had pronounced the final salutation, he shouted to us: "Remain in rows as you are!" Then he turned towards us and said: "I am going to tell you what made me late this morning. I got up last night [to pray]. I did the ablution, I prayed what destiny wished that I pray; then while I was praying, sleepiness took me, and I fell asleep. And there, in front of me, was my Lord, under the most beautiful form (*fī ahsani ṣūrati*). He said [to me]: 'Oh Muḥammad!' –'[Yes] Lord, here I am!' He said [to me]: 'Over what does the Exalted Council dispute?' –'I do not know, Lord,' I responded. He posed

---

[120] Al-Tirmidhī, ***Jāmiʿ** al-Ṣaḥīḥ*, *apud* **al-Mubārakfūrī, *Tuḥfa al-aḥwadhī bi sharḥ jāmiʿ al-Tirmidhī*,** 10 vols. (Damascus: Dār al-Fikr, 1979), 9: 166, #3332; **ʿAlī b. ʿUmar** al-Dāraquṭnī, ***Kitāb al-ruʾya*, ed. Ibrāhīm Muḥammad al-ʿAlī and Aḥmad Fakhrī al-Rifāʿī. Zarqāʾ (Jordan:** 1411/1990) 308 # 226; al-Suyūṭī, ***Tafsīr al-****Durr al-manthūr*, 7: 247.

[to me] again two times the same question. Then I saw Him putting His palm between my shoulder blades, to the point that I felt the coolness of His fingertips (*anāmilihi*) between my nipples, and from that moment everything became evident and known to me," etc.[121]

The God of M**uḥ**ammad is beautiful, we are told in another **ḥadīth,** and he loves beauty.[122] We here learn that this includes paramount morphic beauty. Such a theophany offended the sensibilities of the anti-anthropomorphist theologians who subjected the report to de-anthropomorphizing interpretations. The **Ashʿarite Ibn Fūrak**, for example, recounts in his ***Mushkil al-ḥadīth wa bayānuh*** several interpretations advanced by the theologians: either the 'most beautiful form' refers to the Prophet who saw God while in this state, or it refers to a created form used by God to communicate to his Prophet, or even the form of an angel in which God inheres.[123] The ***aṣḥāb al-ḥadīth*** or Traditionalist Sunni scholars polemicized violently against these hermeneutics. **Abū Saʿīd ʿUthmān b. Saʿīd al-Dārimī** argued in his ***Naqḍ ʿalā al-Marīsī*:** 'Woe to you! It is not possible that this is Jibr**ī**l, or M**īkā**'l, or **Isrāfīl; it** is not possible that this (form) is other than All**ā**h.'[124] See also Ibn **Ḥ**anbal's interpretation, as reported by his son 'Abd All**ā**h

---

[121] Ibn **Ḥanbal,** ***Musnad¹***, 5:243; al-Tirmidh**ī**, ***Jāmiʿ al-Ṣaḥīḥ,*** *apud* **al-Mubārakfūrī,** ***Tuḥfa***, 9: 106ff, #3288; al-Suy**ūtī,** ***Tafsīr al-Durr al-manthūr,*** 7:203.

[122] Fudayl b. '**Amr al-**Fuqym**ī** < Ibr**āhīm** al-Nah**ā**'**ī** < '**Alqama b. Qays** < '**Abd Allāh b. Masʿūd:** "The Messenger of God answered: God is beautiful (*jamīl*). **He loves beauty.**" Muslim, ***Ṣaḥīḥ, imān*** 147; Ibn Khuzayma, ***Kitāb*** *al-taw**ḥīd,*** 384.

[123] **Abū Bakr b. Fūrak,** *Mushkil al-**ḥadīth wa-bayānuh*** (Cairo, 1979?), 70f. For a discussion of this **ḥadīth see Daniel Gimaret,** ***Dieu*** *à l'image de l'homme*, 143ff; idem, « Au Cœur du *MIʿ**RĀǦ***, **un Hadith Interpolé**, » in *Le Voyage Initiatique en Terre D'Islam*, ed. Mohammad Ali Amir-Moezzi (Louvain-Paris, 1991) 67-82.

[124] '**Uthmān b. Saʿīd** al-D**ārimī,** ***Naqḍ al-imām Abī Saʿīd ʿUthmān b. Saʿīd ʿalā al-Marīsī al-Jahmī al-ʿanīd,*** 2 vols (**Riyāḍ,** 1998)**,** II: 737. See also Ibn **Ḥ**anbal, *Kitāb al-Sunna*, 159.

> ['Abd Allāh said]: My father (Ibn Ḥanbal) reported to me...from 'Abd al-Raḥmān b. al-'A'ish from some of the companions of the Prophet: "He came out to them one morning while in a joyous mood and a radiant face. We said [to him]: 'Oh Messenger of God, here you are in a joyous mood and a glowing face!' --'How could I not be?' he answered. 'My Lord came to me last night under the most beautiful form, and He said [to me]: "'O Muhammad!'..." And my father (Ibn Ḥanbal) reported to us, 'Abd al-Razzāq from Ma'mar from Qatāda [from the Prophet], "Allah created Adam according to His form." My father reported to us, 'Abd al-Razzāq from Ma'mar from Qatāda, "'in the best stature *(fī aḥsani taqwīmin)*' meaning 'in the most beautiful form *(fī aḥsani ṣūratin)*'." Ibrāhīm b. al-Hajjāj reported to us, Hammād (b. Salama) reported to us...that the Prophet said, "Allāh is beautiful and He loves beauty."[125]

The implication of this collection of traditions is unmistakable. The "most beautiful form" is first identified with that form of God according to which Adam was created. This identification is further supported by the Imām's interpretation of *Sūrat al-Tīn,* "Surely We created man in the best stature *(fī aḥsani taqwīmin)* (95:4)." Ibn Ḥanbal accepts the *tafsīr* or exegesis of Qatāda identifying man's "best stature" with God's "most beautiful form."[126] Because Adam was created according to God's own form, this identification is logical. It is then affirmed that God is physically beautiful.[127]

Other anti-anthropomorphist scholars tried to impugn the authenticity of the **ḥadīth,**[128] but the traditionalists generally

---

125 Ibn Ḥanbal, *Kitāb al-Sunna*, 159.

126 'Abd Allāh, *Kitāb al-Sunna*, 2:490.

127 On the hadith, "God is beautiful..." Daniel Gimaret notes: "the sense of the word *jamīl* is unequivocal: it is about beauty, and of physical, material beauty." *Dieu à l'image*, 260. Ibn Hanbal, *Musnad*², 28:437f, #17206.

128 The Ash'arite Al-Bayhaqī (d. 1066), *Al-Asma' wa* ***al-Ṣifāt***, ed. 'Abd Allah b. Muhammad al-Hashidi, 2 vols (Jidda, 1993) II:79 declared 'all of [the reports]

accepted it as sound. This report and its variants is narrated on the authority of 12 Companions: **Mu'adh b. Jabal,** Jābir b. Samura,[129] Abū Hurayra,[130] Anas b. Mālik,[131] **Abū Umāma,**[132] Abū 'Ubayda b. al-Jarrāḥ,[133] 'Abd al-Raḥman b. 'A'is,[134] Thawbān, ***mawla rasūli llah,***[135] 'Abd **Allāh** b. 'Umar,[136] Abū **Rāfi'**,[137] 'Abd al-**Raḥman b. Sābiṭ,**[138] **and** 'Abd Allāh b. 'Abb**ās.**[139] **Ḥadīth** scholars such as Ibn **Ḥanbal,** Al-Tirmidhī, **Abī Ya'lā al-Mawṣilī (d.** 919), 'Abd Allāh b. 'Abd al-**Raḥmān** al-**Dārimī** (d. 869), **'Uthman** al-**Dārimī** (d. 895)[140] Ibn **Abī 'Āṣim (d.** 900), **al-Ṭabarānī** (d. 971), Al-Lālikā'ī (d. 1027), **Nūr al-Dīn al-**Haythamī (d. 1405), Ibn Ḥajar al-**'Asqalānī** (d. 1449), and al-Suyūṭī **(d.** 1505) all reported the

---

are *ḍa'īf* (weak)' and Ibn al-Jawzī said, 'It is not sound' (***Daf' shubah al-tashbīh bi****-akaff al-tanzīh* ('Ammān, 1991)149.

129 Al-Suyūṭī, ***Tafsīr al-Durr al-manthūr***, 7:203, *sūra* ***Ṣad.***

130 Al-Lālikā'ī. *Sharḥ* ***uṣūl i'tiqād ahl l-sunna wa l-jamā'a.*** 2 vols. (Riyāḍ, 1985) 2: 520; al-**Suyūṭī,** ***Tafsīr al-Durr al-manthūr,*** 7: 203.

131 Al-Suyūṭī, ***Tafsīr al-Durr al-manthūr,*** 7: 204.

132 Al-Suyūṭī, ***Tafsīr al-Durr al-manthūr,*** 7: 204; **Nūr al-Dīn al-**Haythamī, ***Kitāb majma' al-baḥrayn fī zawā'id al-mu'jamayn*** **(Riyāḍ: Maktabāt al-Rushd,** 1992), 370; Ibn Abī **'Āṣim,** *al-Sunna.* 2 vols. (**Riyāḍ: Dār al-Ṣ**umay'ī, 1998) 1: 326, #475.

133 **Khaṭīb** al-**Baghdādī,** ***Ta'rīkh Baghdād,*** 14 vols. (Cairo, 1931), 8: 151; **Al-**Suyūṭī, ***Tafsīr al-Durr al-manthūr,*** 7: 205.

134 Ibn Ḥanbal, ***Musnad²***, 27: 171, #16621; 'Abd Allah b. 'Abd al-**Raḥmān** al-**Dārimī,** ***Sunan al-Dārimī,*** 2 vols. **(Cairo: Dār** al-Ḥadīth, 2000), 1: 606f; Al-Lālikā'ī, ***Sharḥ uṣūl*** 2: 514; Al-Bayhaqī, ***Al-Asma' wa al-Ṣifāt***, 2: 63; Ibn **Abī 'Āṣim,** ***al-Āḥād wa al-mathānī*** **(Riyāḍ,** 1991), 5: 48; al-Haythamī, ***Kitāb majma'***, 366.

135 Ibn Abī **'Āṣim,** ***Al-Sunna***, 1: 328, #479; al-Suyūṭī, ***Tafsīr al-Durr al-manthūr,*** 7: 205; **al-**Haythamī, ***Kitāb majma'***, 367.

136 **Al-**Haythamī, ***Kitāb majma'***, 369, #11743.

137 Al-**Ṭabarānī,** ***Al-Mu'jam al-kabīr*** **(Baghdād: al-**Dār **al-**'Arabīyah **lil-Ṭibā'ah**, 1978) (hereafter ***Al-Mu'jam¹***), 1: 296, #938.

138 **Ibn Abī Shaybah,** ***al-Kitāb al-muṣannaf fī al-aḥādīth wa-al-āthār*** (Beirut: Dār al-Kutub al-#IlmÊya, 1989), 7:424.

139 Ibn Ḥanbal, ***Musnad¹***, 3:437, #3483; Al-Tirmidhī, ***Jāmi' al-Ṣaḥīḥ,*** *apud* **al-Mubārakfūrī,** ***Tuḥfa***, 9:101ff, #3286; Abū **Ya'lā al-Mawṣilī,** ***Musnad Abī Ya'lā al-Mawṣilī,*** **ed. Ḥusayn Salim Asad (Damascus: Dār al-Ma'**mūn **lil-Turāth,** 1984-), 4: 475, #281.

140 Al-Dārimī, ***Naqḍ***, 2: 733ff.

ḥadīth. **Khaldūn Aḥdab** declared, "The ***ḥadīth* is *ṣaḥīḥ*.** It was reported by a group of Companions, among them: **Muʿādh b. Jabal, Ibn ʿAbbas, ʿAbd al-Raḥmān b. ʿĀ**'is, **Ibn ʿUmar, Abū Hurayra, and Anas,** may God be pleased with them."[141] Ibn Mandah, in his ***Al-Maṣdar al-Sābiq*** said also: "This ***ḥadīth*** is reported from ten (sic) Companions of the Prophet; and the Imāms of the countries, from the people of the east to the west, relayed it from them."[142] Ibn Hajar confirms:"(There is) no discrepancy over it [the hadith] among the hadith scholars and the text is indisputable."[143] Al-Tirmidhī judged it ***ḥasan ṣaḥīḥ*** and said: "I asked Muḥammad b. Is**māʿīl** (al-**Bukhārī**) about this ***ḥadīth*** and he said: ***hadhā ṣaḥīḥ*** ("This is sound")."[144] Ibn Ḥanbal judged it ***ṣaḥīḥ***[145] **and** Muḥammad b. ʿAbd Allāh Ḥākim al-Nīsābūrī (933-1014) declared the ***isnād*** **of** Ibn 'A'is ***ṣaḥīḥ* in his *al-Mustadrak*.**[146] Al-'Awzāʿī[147] **and Mukḥūl**[148] transmitted the report. Maʿ**mar, ʿAbd al-Razzāq,** Ayyub al-Sikhtiy**ānī (d.** 748)**, Muʿāwiyah b. Ṣāliḥ** (d. 775),[149] **in short, the *muḥaddithūn* or ḥadīth** scholars generally accepted the **ḥadīth** as sound. The Prophet saw Allah, who came to him in a most beautiful form.

---

141 **Khaldūn Aḥdab**, ***Zawāʾid Tārīkh Baghdād ʿala al-kutub al-sittah*** (**Damascus: Dār al-Qalam**, 1996)**,** 6: 253.

142 *Apud* Al-D**ārimī,** ***Naqḍ***, 2:734.

143 ***al-Isaba fi tamyiz al-sahaba***, 2:397

144 Al-Tirmidhī, ***Jāmiʿ al-Ṣaḥīḥ,*** *apud* **al-Mubārakfūrī,** ***Tuḥfa***, 9: 106ff, #3288.

145 ʿAbd Allāh b. ʿAbī, ***Al-Kāmil fī ḍuʿafāʾ al-rijāl***, 7 vols. (Beirut: Dār al-Fikr, 1984), 6: 2344.

146 See. Al-Bayhaqī**,** ***Al-Asmaʾ wa al-Ṣifāt***, 2:74.

147 Al-Bayhaqī**,** ***Al-Asmaʾ wa al-Ṣifāt***, 2:73ff.

148 Al-Baghawī**,** ***Tafsīr al-****Baghawī* **(Multān: Idārat Tālīfāt Ashrafiyah,** 1988) 4:69; Ibn Abī **ʿĀṣim,** ***Al-Sunna***, 1: 326.

149 Ibn Abī **ʿĀṣim,** ***Al-Sunna***, 1: 328, #479; al-Suy**ūtī,** ***Tafsīr al-Durr al-manthūr,*** 7: 205.

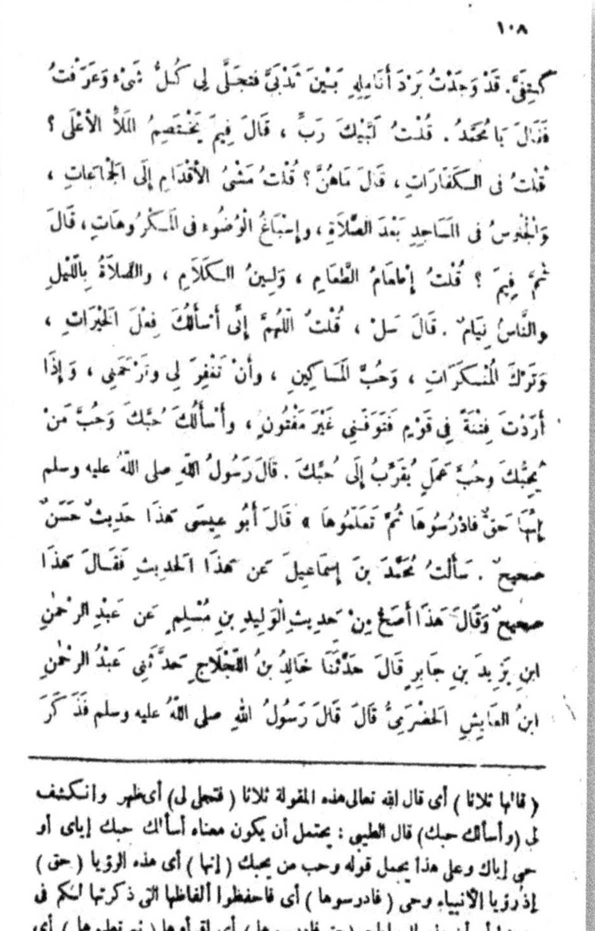

كتفي. قد وجدت برد أنامله بين ثديي فتجلى لي كل شيء وعرفت فقال يا محمد. قلت لبيك رب، قال فيم يختصم الملأ الأعلى؟ قلت في الكفارات، قال ما هن؟ قلت مشي الأقدام إلى الجماعات، والجلوس في المساجد بعد الصلاة، وإسباغ الوضوء في المكروهات، قال ثم فيم؟ قلت إطعام الطعام، ولين الكلام، والصلاة بالليل والناس نيام. قال سل، قلت اللهم إني أسألك فعل الخيرات، وترك المنكرات، وحب المساكين، وأن تغفر لي وترحمني، وإذا أردت فتنة في قوم فتوفني غير مفتون، وأسألك حبك وحب من يحبك وحب عمل يقرب إلى حبك. قال رسول الله صلى الله عليه وسلم إنها حق فادرسوها ثم تعلموها » قال أبو عيسى هذا حديث حسن صحيح. سألت محمد بن إسماعيل عن هذا الحديث فقال هذا صحيح وقال هذا أصح من حديث الوليد بن مسلم عن عبد الرحمن ابن يزيد بن جابر قال حدثنا خالد بن اللجلاج حدثني عبد الرحمن ابن العايش الحضرمي قال قال رسول الله صلى الله عليه وسلم فذكر

(قالها ثلاثا) أي قال الله تعالى هذه المقولة ثلاثا (فتجلى لي) أي ظهر وانكشف لي (وأسألك حبك) قال الطيبي: يحتمل أن يكون معناه أسألك حبك إياي أو حبي إياك وعلى هذا يحمل قوله وحب من يحبك (إنها) أي هذه الرؤيا (حق) إذ رؤيا الأنبياء وحي (فادرسوها) أي فاحفظوا ألفاظها التي ذكرتها لكم في ضمنها أو أن هذه الروايات (حق فادرسوها) أي اقرأوها (ثم تعلموها) أي معانيها الدالة هي عليها قال الطيبي: أي لتعلموها فحذف اللام. قوله (هذا حديث حسن صحيح) وأخرجه أحمد والطبراني والحاكم ومحمد بن نصر في كتاب الصلاة

Page from al-Tirmidhī's ***Jāmiʿ al-Ṣaḥīḥ*** quoting al-**Bukhārī**'s authentification of the 'hadith of the beautiful form'

The question still remains, what exactly did **Muḥammad see?** What does this "beautiful form" of God actually look like? Surprisingly, the **ḥadīth** corpus provides a rather detailed answer to this otherwise blasphemous question.

The important 10th century **ḥadīth scholar,** al-**Dāraquṭnī, in his *Kitāb al Ru'ya*** (Book concerning the Vision of God), reports a **ḥadīth** on the authority of the Companion Anas b. Mālik:

> [The Messenger of God said]: "I saw [my Lord] in His most beautiful form (*aḥsani ṣūratihi*) like a young man (***shābb*) with** hair to his earlobes (*muwaffar*), sitting on the Throne of Grace, around Him a gold carpet. He put His hand between my shoulders and I felt its coolness in my liver. He spoke to me etc.

Shābb is the intermediate stage between a boy before puberty (***ṣabī*,** 15-18 years old) and a mature man (*kahl*, 30-33 years old). Similar reports were narrated on the authority of Umm al-**Ṭufayl (wife of 'Ubayy b. Ka'b, d.** 642),[150] Mu'adh b. **'Afrā',**[151] **Ibn 'Umar,**[152] **Ibn 'Abbās,**[153] **and even 'Ā'isha.**[154] Most important is the report by the Prophet's cousin and famed "Interpreter of the Qur'ān," **'Abd Allāh b. 'Abbās:** "The Messenger of God said: 'I saw my Lord under the form of a young man (***shābb*)** beardless (*amrad*) with curly hair (*ja'd*) and

---

[150] Al-**Ṭabarānī, *Al-Mu'jam al-kabīr*** (Cairo: Maktaba Ibn Taymīyya, n.d) (hereafter ***Al-Mu'jam²***), 25: 143; Ibn Abī **'Āṣim, *Al-Sunna***, 1:328; al-Bayhaqī, ***Al-Asma' wa al-Ṣifāt***, 2:368; Al-**Suyūṭī**, *al-**La'ālī'** al-maṣnū'a **fī** al-aḥādīth al-**mawḍu'a*** (Egypt: al-Maktaba al-**Tijārīya** al-**Kubrā**, 196?) 28f; 'Alā' al-dīn al-Muttaqī al-Hindī, ***Kanz al-'ummāl fī sanan al-aqwāl wa 'l-af'āl***, 18 vols. (Haydar Abād al-Dakan: Dā'irat al-Ma'ārif al-'Uthmāniya, 1945), I:58; **al-**Haythamī, ***Kitāb majma'***, 370.

[151] Al-**Suyūtī**, ***Al-La'ālī'***, 30; Ibn Fūrak, ***Mushkil al-ḥadīth***, 387.

[152] Al-Bayhaqī, ***Al-Asma' wa al-Ṣifāt***, 2: 361f, #934; Ibn Fūrak, ***Mushkil al-ḥadīth***, 386.

[153] Ibn 'Adī, ***Al-Kāmil***, 2:677; Al-Bayhaqī, ***Al-Asma' wa al-Ṣifāt***, 2:363; **Khaṭīb** al-**Baghdādī, *Ta' rīkh Baghdād***, 11: 214; al-**Suyūtī**, ***Al-La'ālī'***, 29f; al-Muttaqī, ***Kanz***, I:58.

[154] Al-**Suyūtī**, ***Al-La'ālī'***, 30.

clothed in a green garment (***ḥulla***)."[155] This ***ḥadīth*** introduces more elements to the beauty of God. In stark contrast to the elderly creator-deity of Judaism and the ancient Near East, white haired and gray bearded, the youthful God of Islam is beardless. Now the Islamic morale advocates wearing a beard. The people of Paradise, however, are beardless, except **Mūsā.**[156] Adam, too, was created beardless. It was his sons who grew beards due to their father's sin.[157] The beard is thus the mark of the fall of man; beardlessness the mark the of righteous in the Hereafter.

The ***isnād*** or chain of transmitters of this report is **Ḥammād b. Salama (d.** 784) < **Qatāda d. Di'āma (d.** 735) < **'Ikrima (d.** 724) < **Ibn 'Abbās.** While this **ḥadīth** would become very controversial later, particularly with those who were offended by the explicit anthropomorphism of the text, it gained wide acceptance by the **ḥadīth** scholars and was even invoked in creeds. Ibn **Ḥanbal,**[158] **'Abd Allāh b. Aḥmad,**[159] Ibn Ab**ī** **'Āṣim,**[160] 'Abd Allah b. **'Adī,**[161] **al-Ṭabarānī,**[162] **al-Lālikā'ī,**[163] **and** Abū **Bakr al-'Ajurī**[164] reported it in full or ***mukhtaṣar*** **(abridged). Aḥmad Muḥammad Shākir (d.** 1958**),** editor of Ibn **Ḥanbal**'s ***Musnad*** and clearly the "greatest traditionalist of his time,"[165] declared: "the **ḥadīth** in

---

[155] **Ibn 'Adī**, ***Al-Kāmil***, 2:677; Al-Bayhaq**ī**, ***Al-Asma' wa al-Ṣifāt***, 2:363; **Khaṭīb** al-**Baghdādī,** ***Ta' rīkh Baghdād***, 11: 214; al-**Suyūtī**, ***Al-La'āli'***, 29f; al-Muttaq**ī**, ***Kanz***, I:58.

[156] Al-Tirmidh**ī**, ***al-Jāmi' al-ṣaḥīḥ, janna*** 8 and 12.

[157] *V.* C. Shöck, ***Adam im Islam*** (Berlin, 1993), 121f.

[158] Ibn **Ḥ**anbal, ***Musnad***[2], 4:350f, #2580.

[159] **'Abd Allāh,** ***Kitāb al-Sunna***, 2: 484, 503, #'s 1116, 1117, 1168.

[160] Ibn Ab**ī** **'Āṣim,** ***Al-Sunna***, 1:307, #442.

[161] Abd Allah b. 'Ad**ī**, ***Al-Kāmil***, 2:677.

[162] **Al-Ṭabarānī,** ***Kitāb al-sunna***, *apud* al-Muttaq**ī**, ***Kanz***, I:58.

[163] Al-L**ālikā'ī**, ***Sharḥ uṣūl*** 2**:** 512.

[164] Ab**ū** **Bakr** al-'**Ajurī**, ***al-Sharī'a*****, ed. Muhamma Hāmid al-Fiqī (Cairo:** 1950), 491f.

[165] G.H. A. Juynboll, "**Aḥmad Muḥammad Shākir** (1892-1958) and his edition of Ibn **Ḥ**anbal's ***Musnad***," ***Studies on the Origins and Uses of Islamic Ḥadīth*** (Brookfield, Vt.: Variorum, 1996), 222.

its essence is **ṣaḥīḥ**."[166] It was primarily the heretical Mu'tazila and later Ashariyya, influenced as they were by Greek philosophic ideas, who rejected this report. Ab**ū** Bakr b. **Ṣ**adaqa reported hearing Ab**ū** Zur'a al-R**ā**z**ī** (d. 878) say: "The **ḥadīth** of Qat**ā**da from 'Ikrima from Ibn 'Ab**ā**ss in the Vision is sound (***ṣaḥīḥ***). Sh**ā**dh**ā**n and 'Abd al-**Ṣ**amad b. **Kaysān and** Ibr**ā**h**ī**m b. Ab**ī** Suwayd reported it and none denies it except the Mu'tazila."[167] **Aḥmad b. Ḥanbal** likewise argued in his ***'Aqīda III*** that one of the fundamental principles of the Sunnah (***uṣūl al**-sunna*) is:

> To have faith in the Beatific Vision on the Day of Judgment...and that the Prophet has seen his Lord, since this has been transmitted from the Messenger of God and is correct and authentic. It has been reported from Qat**āda,** from '**Ikrima,** from Ibn '**Abbās**...And the **ḥadīth**, in our estimation, is to be taken upon its apparent meaning (***'alā ẓāhirihi***), as it has come from the Prophet. Indulging in *Kal**ām*** with respect to it is an innovation. But we have faith in it as it came, upon its apparent meaning, and we do not dispute with anyone regarding it."[168]

In his ***'Aqīda V*****, Aḥmad** argued that, "Belief in that (***ḥadīth** al-sh**ābb*** or the report of the Young Man) and counting it true is obligatory" for Muslims. [169] The general acceptance of this **ḥadīth** among the **ḥadīth** scholars is therefore well attested. Consequently, the description of God found therein had a significant effect on the community's ideas of God at that time. The Mu'**tazilī Qāḍī 'Abd** al-**Jabbār** noted that this report (***ḥadīth** al-sh**ābb***) along with "God created Adam according to Him Form," was the basis of the doctrines of the

---

[166] **Ibn Ḥ**anbal, ***Musnad*****, ed. Aḥmad Muḥammad Shākir (Egypt: Dār al-Ma'ārif,** 1949-.; hereafter ***Musnad³***) 4:201, #2580, 2634.

[167] Al-Suy**ūtī**, ***Al-La'āli'*****,** 30.

[168] **Ibn Ḥanbal,** ***'Aqīda III***, *apud* Ibn **Abī Ya'lā,** ***Ṭabaqāt*** 1:246.

[169] **Ibn Ḥanbal,** ***'Aqīda V***, *apud* Ibn **Abī Ya'lā,** ***Ṭabaqāt*** 1:312.

anthropomorphists popular even at his time.[170] But who were these *mushabbiha* or anthropomorphists? The Zaydī imām and scholar al-Qāsim b. Ibrāhīm (d. 860), who wrote several treaties against the *mushabbiha*, noted in his ***Kitāb al-Mustarshid***:

> The Muslims (lit. those who pray) have agreed with us that the glances will not perceive God, except for a group of the *Rāwafiḍ*, and the *Ḥashwīya* which agree with them. They said the Prophet had seen his Lord white-skinned and dark-haired. They related in another way that He had been seen in the form of an adolescent whose hair was cut off. Some of them claimed that this seeing was with the heart, and some others claimed that it was with the eyes.[171]

For al-Qāsim, "*ḥashwīya*" denoted the pro-Umayyad **ḥadīth** scholars who accepted Aḥmad b. Ḥanbal as their principle authority.[172] Binyamin Abrahamov, editor of al-**Qāsim**'s works, translates the term "*ḥashwīya*" as "scholars of the masses," indicating the general acceptance of these ideas among the community.[173] The Muʿtazilite essayist al-**Jāḥiẓ** (d. 869), writing around the same time, describes the same doctrinal trend among the early (proto-)Sunnis. He characterizes Ibn **Ḥanbal**'s supporters as ***Nābita,***[174] that is "contemptible, suddenly powerful, irritating sprouters on the scene."[175] According to al-

---

[170] **Qāḍī ʿAbd** al-**Jabbār, *Faḍl al-iʿtizāl*, ed. Fuʾād Sayyid (Tunis,** 1974**),** 149.

[171] Al-Qāsim b. Ibrāhīm, ***Kitāb al-Mustarshid***, 133.

[172] Al-Qāsim b. Ibrāhīm, ***Kitāb al-Dalīl al-Kabīr***, ed. and trns. by Binyamin Abrahamov in ***Al-Kāsim B. Ibrāhīm on the Proof of God's Existence*** (Leiden: E.J. Brill, 1990), 188; Abrahamov, ***Anthropomorphism and Interpretation***, 133, n. 160.

[173] Op. cited.

[174] Ch. Pellat ***EI***, *s.v.* "Nābita," 7:843.

[175] Wadad al-Qadi, "The Earliest 'Nābita' and the Paradigmatic 'Nawābit'," ***Studia Islamica*** 78 (1993), 59. **On the *nābita/ḥashwīya v.* also** A. S. Halkin, "**The Ḥashwiyya**" ***JAOS*** 54 [1934], 1-28): *EI, s.v.* "Ḥashwiyya," by ed., 3:269; G. van Vloten, "Les Hachwia et Nabita," ***Actes du Onzième Congrès International des Orientalistes, Paris, 1897*** Paris, 1899, 99-123; M. Th. Houtsma, "Die Ḥashwiya," ***Zeitschrift für Assyriologie*** 26

Jāḥiẓ the *Nābita* insisted that God "is a body, and they ascribed a form (***ṣūra***) and limits to Him and declared anyone who believes in *al-Ru'**ya*** (Seeing God) without ***tajsīm*** (ascribing a body to God) and ***taṣwīr*** (ascribing a form to God) to be a ***kāfir*** (disbeliever)."[176] The ***ṣūra*** that the ***Nābita*** attributed to God was undoubtedly that of a ***shābb,*** "young man," judging from al-Qāsim's contemporary report and from later polemics against the group.[177] Al-**Jāḥiẓ** informs us that, because of Ibn **Ḥanbal** and the concurrence with him of "the masses, the pious recluse, the jurists, and the **ḥadīth** people,"[178] the prevailing trend (***ghālib***) of the community was anthropomorphism and determinism.[179] Ninth century Sunnism, that is to say earliest Sunnism, was therefore characterized by belief in an anthropomorphic deity, a belief based in part on ***ḥadīth al-shābb*** (the report of the Youthful God) as championed by **Imām Aḥmad.**[180]

3. *A Real Vision?*

Did the Prophet see God in a physical vision during a wakened state or in a dream-vision? No consensus developed on

---

(1912), 196-202; Fritz Steppat, "From *'Ahd Ardasir* to Al-Ma'mūn: A Persian Element in the Policy of the Miḥna," in ***Studia Arabica et Islamica: Festschrift for Ihsan 'Abbas***, ed. Wadad al-Qadi (Beirut: American University of Beirut, 1981), 451ff; Ch. Pellat, "La 'nābita'de Djahiz," ***Annales de l'institut d'études orientales*** (Alger), 10 (1952): 302-325; I. Alon, "Farabi's Funny Flora: al-Nawābit as 'Opposition'," ***Journal of the Royal Asiatic Society*** 37 (1988), 222-25; W. Madelung, ***Der Imam al-Qasim ibn Ibrahim*** (Berlin: Walter De Gruyter & Co., 1965), 223ff.

176 Al-Jāḥiẓ, ***Risāla fī al-Nabīta, apud*** Al-Jāḥiẓ ***Rasā'il al-Jāḥiẓ,*** 4 vols., **ed. 'Abd al-**Salam Mu**ḥammad Harūn (Cairo: Maktabāt al-**Khanjī, 1964-1979), 2:18.

177 *See* for example the rescript of the Caliph al-Rāḍi in 935.

178 Al-Jāḥiẓ, ***Kitāb fī khalq al-Qur'ān***, *apud* al- Jāḥiẓ, ***Rasā'il al-Jāḥiẓ***, 3:297

179 Al-Jāḥiẓ, ***Risāla fī al-Nābita, apud* al-Jāḥiẓ, *Rasā'il al-Jāḥiẓ***, 2:20.

180 On anthropomorphists trends within 9th century Sunni movements *v.* also Wesley Williams, "Aspects of the Creed of Ahmad Ibn Hanbal," 450ff; Nimrod Hurvitz, "Miḥna as Self-Defence," ***Studia Islamica*** 92 (2001): 98ff.

this issue. Abd Allah b. Abbas reported that the Prophet saw Him in a dream vision on a night which had nothing to do with the nocturnal journey. He suggested that the vision occurred *fi l-manam*, "during the sleep." In the report of Mu'ad we find the Prophet setting the stage of the vision with *fa-statqaltu*, "then I fell asleep." In the version found in Ibn Hanbal's ***Musnad***, on the other hand, there is the explicit statement to the contrary: *hatta stayqaztu fa-ida ana bi-rabbi*, "then I woke up, and there in front of me was my Lord." Al-Nawawī claimed that the "preponderant view" with "most of the **'ulamā**'" is that the Prophet saw God with his eyes during his Night Journey. This was the position of **Qāḍī 'Iyād (d.** 1149)[181] and al-**Qāḍī Abū Ya'lā (d.** 1065)**,**[182] and the mystic Sheik of **Shirāz Ibn Khafīf (d.** 982) affirmed the same.[183] On the other hand al-**Lālakā'ī (d.** 1027),[184] **al-Māturīdī (d.** 944)**,**[185] **al-Ash'arī** (d. 935),[186] al-**Dārimī (d.** 895),[187] and others affirmed a *ru'**ya bi** 'l-qalb* or dream-vision.[188]

That Mu**ḥammad's** vision of God occurred during his sleep in no way mitigated the force of the theophany as far as the ***muḥaddithūn*** or **ḥadīth scholars** were concerned.[189] Some

---

[181] *Al-Shifa*, 101.

[182] ***Kitāb al-****Mu'****tamad***, 151.

[183] Abū **l-Ḥasan**-i. Daylamī, ***Sīrat****-i. shaykh-i.* ***kabīr Abū 'Abd Allāh Ibn****-i. Khafīf* ***Shirāzī*** (**Tehran: Intishārāt**-i. **Bābak,** 1984), 296.

[184] *Sharḥ*, 2:512f.

[185] ***Kitāb al-Tawḥīd,*** 80.

[186] Ibn **Fūrak** ***Mujarrad maqālāt al-Ash'arī,*** 342ff.

[187] ***Naqḍ,*** 2:738.

[188] Ibn **Abī 'Āṣīm,** ***al-Sunna***, 1: 324; Ibn Taymīya, ***Al-Qawl al-Aḥmad fī bayān ghalāt man ghaliṭa 'alā al-Imām Aḥmad*** (Riyāḍ: Dār al-**'Āṣimah**, 1998), 133; **Ibn Qayyīm al-Jawzīya,** ***Zād al-ma'ād***, 3:28f; al-Haythamī, ***Kitāb majma'***, 366f. On the vision of the heart (*ru'ya bi-l-qalb*) as a dream-vision see al-Taftazani, ***Sharh al-aqa'id al-Nasafiyya***, 135): "As far as the vision of Allah in sleep is concerned, it is something that has been related from many of the Salaf. And there is no doubt that this is a type of vision of the heart rather than the eye."

[189] The anti-anthropomoprhists of course took a different position. For them the Vision was an imaginary dream. Ibn **Fūrak** quotes the saying of one exegete: (The theologians) say that the dream is an imaginary vision (*wahm*) that God creates in the one sleeping to signify to him a thing which will be or which

have suggested that this dream-vision was like those granted to Yusuf, such as when he saw his brothers as stars prostrate before him (*Sura Yusuf*, 4). Just as Yusuf's brothers appeared in this dream as stars and not in their true form, the assumption is that if God appeared in the Prophet's dream in a human form, this was not His true form any more than the stars in Yusuf's dream were his brothers' true form. As Yusuf's dream was symbolic and required an interpretation so too would the Prophet Muhammad's dream-vision.

Those who make this claim do so only because they are unfamiliar with Islamic onierocriticism (dream-criticism and interpretation). Muslim onierocriticism, like the onierocriticism of the whole ancient Near East, distinguishes between literal message dreams that do not require interpretation, and symbolic dreams that do. The literal message dreams are the *ru'ya haqiqa*, "Truthful Dreams." As Ibn Khaldun says in his *al-Maqaddama* (80, 81):

> There are three kinds of dream-visions. There are dream-visions from God, dream-visions from the angels, and dream visions from Satan. Dream-visions from God are those that are (self)-evident and need no explanation. Dream visions from angels are true dreams that require interpretations. And dream visions from Satan are confused dreams.

Abdul Mun'im Hashmi, in his ***Ru'ya al-anbiya' wa al-salihin*** ("Dream Visions of the Prophets and the Righteous") notes further that these truthful dreams from God that are not symbolic and require no interpretation include visions in which one sees God. Hashmi cites Ibn Abbas's and Mu'adh b. Jabal's reports of the Prophet's seeing God in His most beautiful form as examples of this truthful dream-vision that requires no interpretation (pages 82-83). This is especially true regarding the form of God seen in the vision. As **Qāḍī 'Iyād** says:

---

was, by means of interpretation of dreams. Now the imaginary visions (*awh**ām***) can represent the imagined otherwise than it is in reality." Ibn **Fūrak**, ***Mushkīl al-ḥadīt***, 23.

> As far as seeing Allah Most High while asleep, there is no difference of opinion regarding its occurrence and truth, for Satan cannot take the form of Allah Most High like he cant take the form of the Prophet.[190]

Thus *ahl al-Sunna* declared that even though the Prophet's vision was a dream-vision, it was a true vision. When asked concerning this matter, Ibn **Ḥanbal** responded: "Yes, he saw Him in reality ***(rā'hu ḥaqqan),*** for the visions of the prophets are real."[191] For al-Ash'**arī** too the Vision was a ***ru'ya ḥaqīqa*** (true vision), not a dream delusion (*takhayyul*).[192] This is explained by **Abū 'l- Ḥāsan al-**Wā**ḥidī** (d. 1075):

> 'He (Mu**ḥ**ammad) saw his Lord with his heart' is a sound vision (***ru'ya ṣaḥīḥa***) and it is that All**ā**h Most High placed [**Muḥ**ammad's] eyes in his heart or created for his heart eyes so that [his seeing] his Lord is sound just as he saw with his eyes.[193]

More recently Gibril Fouad Haddad, in his short study on "The Vision of Allah in the World and the Hereafter" correctly notes:

> On the whole, the scholars' interpretation of the Prophets (s) vision show that whether it took place in his dream or in a wakeful state, 'with the eyes of the heart' or 'with the eyes of the head, ' does not change the fact that he saw Him in the real sense, as the Prophet's dream-vision or heart-vision (s) is by far

---

[190] al-Bajuri, ***Tuhfat al-murid 'ala jawharat al-tawhid***, 118)."

[191] **Ibn Qayyīm** al-**Jawzīya,** ***Zād al-ma'ād***,3:29.

[192] **Ibn Fūrak,** ***Mujarrad,*** 86.

[193] Al-Nawaw**ī,** ***Sharḥ Ṣaḥīḥ Muslim,*** 2:12; **Qārī al-Harawī,** ***Mirqāt al-mafātīḥ,*** 9:626. See also al-Qur**ṭubī,** ***al-Jāmi' li-aḥkām al-Qur'ān,*** 17:92: "All**āh Most High placed his eyes in his heart so that he saw his Lord, Most High, and Allāh made that a (true) vision.**"

sharper, more accurate, and more real than the visions of ordinary people.[194]

4. *'Ā'isha's Denial and Sunnism's Affirmation*

While the Prophet's vision of God is reported on the authority of a great multitude of Companions (19+), the solitary witness against it is **'Ā'isha**, the Prophet's favorite wife.[195]

> (**Masrūq** said): I was sitting back in **'Ā'isha's** house when she said: 'O **Abū 'Ā'isha**, there are three things, whoever says any of which, he is lying about All**āh** in the most hateful manner. I asked: 'Which things?' She said: [First,] whoever tells you that Muhammad saw his Lord, he is lying about All**ā**h in the most hateful manner.' I was sitting back, so I sat up and said: 'O Mother of the Faithful! Give me a moment and do not rush me. Did not All**ā**h Almighty say "Surely he beheld him on the clear horizon (53:7)?"' She replied: 'I was the first in the entire community to have asked All**ā**h's Messenger about this, and he said: "It is but Gabriel, I did not see him in the actual form in which he was created other than these two times. I saw him alighting from heaven, covering it all. The magnitude of his frame spans what lies between the heaven and the earth."' Then she said: 'Did you not hear All**ā**h say: "Vision comprehends Him not, but He comprehends all vision. He is the Subtle, the Aware (6:103)?" Did you not hear All**ā**h say:

194 Gibril Fouad Haddad, "Appendix 3: The Vision of Allah in the World and the Hereafter," in al-Bayhaqi, *Allah's Names and Attributes (al-Asma' wa al-Sifat), Excerpts*, trans. Dr. Gibril Fouad Haddad (Islamic Doctrines and Beliefs Vol. 4;Damascus, 1998) 74-75.

195 It is sometimes stated that, along with the Mother of the Faithful, ***ru'yat Allāh*** was likewise denied by **Abū Hurayra and 'Abd Allāh b. Mas'ūd (*V.*** for example Haddad's, "The Vision of Allah in the World and the Hereafter," 78). There is, however, no evidence that either denied Mu**ḥammad**'s vision of God. This claim is probably based on the fact that both are recorded as interpreting ***sūrat al**-Najm* as visions of Gabriel. But this hardly precludes an affirmation of a vision, say, on another occasion. Ab**ū Hurayra** in fact explicitly affirmed a Vision of God by the Prophet according to certain reports. See **al-**L**ālikā'ī**, ***Sharḥ uṣūl,*** 2:520; al-Suy**ūtī, *Tafsīr al-Durr al-manthūr,*** 7:203.

"And it is not (vouchsafed) to any mortal that Allāh should speak to him except by revelation or from behind a veil, or (that) He sends a messenger to reveal what He will by His leave. Lo! He is Exalted, Wise (42:51)?"' She continued: '[Second,] whoever claims that Allāh's Messenger concealed any part of Allāh's Book, he is lying about Allāh in the most hateful manner when Allāh is saying: "O Messenger, make known that which has been revealed unto you from your Lord, for if you do it not, you will not have conveyed His Message (5:67)."' She continued: '[Third,] whoever claims that he can tell what shall happen tomorrow, he is lying about Allāh in the most hateful manner, since Allāh is saying: "Say: None in the heavens and the earth knoweth the Unseen save Allāh [and they know not when they will be raised again (27:65)".'[196]

Sunnism between the nineth-eleventh centuries, generally speaking, affirmed Mu**ḥammad**'s vision of God. This is not to suggest that thereafter the Vision dropped out of the Sunnī profession of faith. **Al-Ghazzālī** in the twelfth century begrudgingly conceded that, in spite of his objections, "most **'ulamā'** are of the opinion that he saw Him"[197] and al-Nawawī **(d.** 1277) in the thirteenth century could still claim as well that "the preferred view (*al-rājiḥ*) with most of the **'ulamā'** is that the Messenger of God saw his Lord with the eyes of his head on the Night of Isrā'."[198] This begs the question: how could the Vision have become such an important, even at times defining, aspect of the Sunnī ***'aqīda*** in the face of the vehement denial from one of the pillars of Sunnism and the 'Beloved of Mu**ḥammad'? 'Ā'isha**'s nephew the famed *mu**ḥaddith*** **and** *Tābi'ī* Urwa **b. al-Zubayr** (d. 713), who is the main transmitter of her reports, affirmed the Vision and said that it was difficult for him whenever his aunt's denial was mentioned to him.[199] **Al-Ḥasan al-**Baṣrī (d. 728), "*the* outstanding representative of the

---

196 Muslim, ***Ṣaḥīḥ***, 1:111, #337.
197 ***Iḥyā' 'ulūm al-dīn*** 4:268
198 Al-**Nawawī,** ***Sharḥ Ṣaḥīḥ Muslim***, 2:11.
199 Ibn **Ḥajar,** ***al-Fatḥ al-Bārī***, 8:608.

earlier religious scholars"[200] and "the chief center of the religious life and movements of his time"[201] "swore by Allāh (***ḥalafa bi-llāhi***)" that Muḥammad saw his Lord.[202]

Traditionalist treatment of '**Ā'isha**'s denial varied. **Al-Dārimī** did "totally reject"[203] the ***ḥadīth al-shābb*** from Ibn '**Abbās** because he thought it is opposed by one version of the report of **Abū Darr** ("Light! How could I have seen Him?") and the denial of '**Ā'isha;**[204] but his "total rejection" was only of a physical vision during the Night Journey. Mu**ḥammad** did see God in a most beautiful form in his (**Muḥammad**'s) sleep on another occasion.[205] On the other hand, Ibn **Taymīyya** claimed that the "people of knowledge" reject as a lie this narration from '**Ā'isha.**[206]

Generally speaking the traditionalists did not go as far as Ibn **Taymīyya** in outright rejecting the '**Ā'isha**-report as a lie. They did, however, marginalize it. The Mother of the Faithful was generally dismissed in favor of Ibn '**Abbās** on this issue. '**Abd al-Razzāq b. Ḥammām** (d. 826) mentioned the **ḥadīth of** '**Ā'isha**'s denial to Ma'**mar b. Rāshid (d.** 770), the famous

---

200 W. Montgomery Watt, ***The Formative Period of Islamic Thought***. (Edinburgh: Edinburgh University Press, 1998) 64.

201 D.B. MacDonald, *Development of Muslim Theology*, 129.

202 '**Abd al-**Razz**āq b. Hammām al-Ḥimyarī,** ***Tafsīr 'Abd al-Razzāq b. Hammām al-Ṣan'ānī***, 3 vols. (**ed. Maḥūd Muḥammad 'Abduh; Beirut: Mansūrāt Muḥammad 'Alī Bayḍūn, Dār al-**Kutub al-'**Ilmīyah,** 1999) 2:253; Ibn Khuzayma, ***Kitāb al-tawhīd***, 200**; Ibn** Abī **al-Ḥadīd,** ***Sharḥ nahj al-balāghah*** **(Cairo: 'Īsā al-**Bābī **al-Ḥalabī,** 1959-), 3: 237; Ibn **Ḥajar,** ***al-Fatḥ al-Bārī***, 8:608.

203 **Al-Dārimī,** ***Naqḍ***, 2: 726.

204 **Al-Dārimī,** ***Naqḍ***, 2:726; idem, *al-Radd*, 53.

205 **Al-Dārimī,** ***Naqḍ***, 2:738, quoting the ***ḥadīth aḥsan ṣūra*** **on the authority of Thawbān.** To those ***mutakallimūn*** (speculative theologians) who tried to de-anthropomorphicize the report by various interpretations such as the "most beautiful form" refers to a created form used by God to communicate to his Prophet, or even the form of an angel in which God inheres, **al-Dārimī pronounces:** "Woe to you! It is not possible that this is **Jibrīl**, or Mīkā'l, or **Isrāfīl; it** is not possible that this (form) is other than Allāh." ***Naqḍ***, 2:237.

206 Ibn **Taymīya,** ***Minhāj al-sunna al-nabawīya***, 2: 511.

Yemenite *muḥaddith* who said, "'**Ā'isha** is not with us more knowledgeable (in this matter) than Ibn '**Abbās.**"[207] **Al-Marrūdhī** reported concerning Aḥmad Ibn **Ḥanbal:**

> I said to **Aḥmad:** "Some say that '**Ā'isha** said 'Whoever claims that Muḥammad saw his Lord lies greatly against God!' How should we respond?" (Aḥmad) said: "With the words of the Prophet, 'I saw my Lord.' His words are greater than hers."[208]

Here '**Ā'isha** is not just juxtaposed – to her detriment – to the Interpreter of the Qur'ān Ibn '**Abbās.** Her words are set in direct conflict with those of the Prophet himself. The way al-**Marrūdhī** posed the question to Ibn **Ḥanbal** may suggest doubt regarding the authenticity of the report: not "'**Ā'isha** said so and so" but "*Some say* that '**Ā'isha** said so and so." Al-**Ash'arī rejected** '**Ā'isha**'s denial in favor of **Ibn 'Abbās**'s and Umm al-**Ṭufayl**'s affirmation.[209] So too did Ibn Khuzayma, who wrote regarding '**Ā'isha**'s vehement denial:

> 'Ā'isha did not report from the Prophet (s) that he informed her that he did not see his Lord, May He be Exalted and Great. She simply recited [God's] words, "Visions comprehend Him not" and "It is not for man that Allah speaks to him except (through) revelation." (But) from the contemplation of these two verses and in accordance with attainment of the "Right," it is known that there is not in either of the two verses that which merits charging one who said that Muḥammad saw his Lord with lying against Allah.... the Tribe of Hāshim, collectively, contradict 'Ā'isha (m) in this matter and they, all of them, used to affirm that the Prophet (s) saw his Lord twice. The agreement of the Tribe of Hāshim is...more appropriate than 'Ā'isha's

207 '**Abd** al-**Razzāq,** ***Tafsīr,*** 2:252; **Ibn** Khuzayma, ***Kitāb*** *al-**tawḥīd,*** 229.
208 Al-Khall**āl,** ***Kitāb al**-Sunna, apud* Ibn **Ḥajar,** ***Fatḥ al**-Bārī,* 8:608-9; Andrea, *Dei Person,* 75 (who quotes Ab**ū Manṣūr** al-Baghd**ādī,** ***Kitāb al**-Sunna, apud* **al-Qasṭallānī,** ***al**-Mawāhid al-**ladunnīyya bi*** *'l-minah al-Muḥ**ammadīyya***).
209 Ibn **Fūrak** ***Mujarrad maqālāt al-Ash'arī,*** 342.

> isolated statement. Companions who are known did not follow her, nor did any woman from the wives/women of the Prophet, nor any of the female Successors.[210]

Again, the affirmation of **Ibn ʿAbbās,** Abū Dhar, Anas b. Mālik and the whole Tribe of Hāshim collectively is preferred to **ʿĀ'isha**'s isolated charge against those with whom she disagrees. **ʿĀ'isha**'s denial, Ibn Khuzayma claims, is not based on a denial relayed to her from the Prophet; it is based on her own incorrect interpretation of certain relevant passages from the Qur'ān. Her *tafsīr* can not impeach that of ***Turjumān al**-Qur'ān* himself, Ibn **ʿAbbās**; at least not here since his *tafsīr* is supported by a prophetic statement. We learn from al-Nawawī that this sentiment was still alive in the twelfth century:

> (Ibn **ʿAbbās** and others) affirm (the Vision) only due to the narrations (*bi 'l-samāʿ*) from the Messenger of God. This is from that (type of knowledge) which to doubt it is improper. **ʿĀ'isha** (r) did not deny the Vision with a transmission from the Messenger of God; if she had such a transmission she would have mentioned it. (Instead she relied on the apparent meaning of [the qur'ānic passages]. Other Companions disagree with her.[211]

The popularity of this sentiment must be the answer to the question posed above: the Vision became an important aspect of Sunnī doctrine despite **ʿĀ'isha**'s vehement denial because **ʿĀ'isha**'s qualifications in the matter were subordinated to those of Ibn **ʿAbbās.** Certainly her years as 'Favorite Wife' of Muḥammad privileged **ʿĀ**'isha's insight and qualified her as an important witness to and, thus, source of tradition. But she doesn't here transmit an explicit denial from the Prophet, it is argued. Rather, she does *tafsīr.* But **ʿĀ**'isha the *mufassira* could

---

[210] Ibn Khuzayma, ***Kitāb al-tawḥīd***, 225ff.

[211] Al-**Nawawī,** ***Sharḥ Ṣaḥīḥ*** *Muslim*, 2:11 (=Ibn **Ḥajar,** ***al-Fatḥ al-Bārī***, 8:607).

not rival the *Turjumān al-Qur'ān*, at least not on this issue.

5. *The Hon. Elijah Muhammad on the Prophet's Vision*

While the Prophet's vision of God may be comfortably situated in the history of Islamic dogma, its place in the teachings of THEM is, ironically, less obvious. THEM seemed to have categorically rejected the Prophet's vision of God. He stated in ***Our Savior Has Arrived***: "In fact Muhammad (the Prophet) never saw the God. Muhammad only Heard His Voice." [212] He goes on to say, "The Muhammad of the prophecy of the Holy Quran teaches and prophesies of a Muhammad who would get his Word from the Mouth of Allah (God) and not through visions of talking to Him and never seeing the Speaker." Relevant to these passages is one found in ***Message to the Black Man***. The Messenger says, "The Holy Qur'an refers to the Days of Allah, meaning in the years of resurrection, and it often repeats that the people will meet with Allah in person, *not in visions*"[213]

It appears that, according to THEM, there are two Muhammads: one who will experience Allah only in visions, and another who will experience Allah in Person. This latter will not be communicated to through the veil of visions. He will speak to God "face to face, as a man speaketh to his friend." Many of the Prophets experienced God. In fact, according to THEM, *all* of the Prophets saw God but only through the veil of a vision.

> the last Prophet…is not really a prophet in the sense of the word, but rather an apostle or messenger, for He is the Answer and End of the Prophets. His call is unlike the others before him, for *all of the Prophets* before the last one had their call and mission through inspirations and *visions*, for they saw not the *Person of Allah (God) in reality*-only in visions-but the last one is

---

[212] 135.

[213] Muhammad, ***Message to the Black Man***, 189.

Chosen and Missioned directly from the mouth of Allah (God) in person at the end of the world (emphasis added).[214]

THEM draws a distinction between the last Apostle (himself) and *all* of the prophets that went before him. The distinguishing mark is that while the latter (i.e. the prophets) saw God in a vision, the former (i.e. the Last Apostle) encounters the Person of God in reality and is commissioned directly from the mouth of God. This is consistent with scriptural history. Micaiah the prophet had a vision of God as reported in I Kings 22:19: "And he said, Hear thou therefore the word of the Lord; I saw the Lord sitting on his throne, and all the host of heaven standing by him on his right hand and on his left." Isaiah also reports a vision of God; "In the year that the king Uzziah died I saw also the Lord sitting upon a throne, high and lifted up (Isaiah 6:1)." Without a doubt, the most important is that reported by the Prophet Ezekiel. In his "Inaugural Vision" the priest-prophet reports, "And above the firmament (I saw) the likeness of a throne, as the appearance of a sapphire stone: and upon the likeness of the throne was the likeness as the appearance of a man above upon it…(Ez. 1:26)." These experiences that the prophets of old had are referred to in Hebrew as *Re'uyot Yahweh* or Visions of Yahweh. These prophets saw and experienced God only in a vision.

According to numerous reports Prophet Muhammad too experienced God in visions, as did the Hebrew prophets before him. He did not see God in the Person nor speak to Him "face to face, as a man speaketh to his friend." Thus, there is no conflict between THEM and Classical Arabic sources on this point.

---

214 Elijah Muhammad, "The History of Jesus," ***Pittsburgh Courier***, July 27 (1957): A6.

> (20) CHAPTER. The statement of the Prophet ﷺ "No person has more Ghira (1) than Allah."
>
> باب قَوْلِ النَّبِيِّ صلى الله عليه وسلّم : لا شَخْصَ أغْيَرُ مِنَ الله .

Ṣaḥīḥ Bukhārī

Al-Bukhari and Muslim report a hadith from the Prophet on the authority of the Companion Al-**Mughīra b. Shuʿba**: "No *shakhṣ* is more jealous (*aghyar*) than Allah; no *shakhṣ* is more pleased to grant pardon than He; no *shakhṣ* loves praiseworthy conduct more than He."[215] A *shakhṣ* is a corporeal person, a man.[216] The term connotes "the bodily or corporeal form or figure or substance (*suwād*) of a man," or "something possessing height (*irtifāʿ*) and visibility (*ẓuhūr*)," Ibn **Manẓūr** informs us in his ***Lisān al-ʿArab*** (7, 45, 4-11).[217] Ibn al-Jawzī, in his ***Kitāb Akhbār al-Sifāt*** 53-4 (Ar.), admits as well that "the term *shakhṣ* implies the existence of a body (*jism*) composed of parts, for one terms something a *shakhṣ* because it possesses corporeality (*shukhūs*) and height (*irtifāʿ*)." The Arabic syntax of this hadith suggests that God is a person with a physical body.

This is a sentence with a superlative (e.g. *aghyar*). In such a sentence, attention is drawn to one from a whole that is greatest at something that is characteristic of the whole. The noun described by the superlative (i.e. Allah) is one, though a remarkable one, of the whole or genus (i.e. *shakhṣ*). The

---

[215] **Bukhārī**, *Ṣaḥīḥ, tawḥīd,* 20:512; Muslim, *Ṣaḥīḥ, līʿān,* 17; Ibn Ḥanbal, *Musnad* IV:248; Nisāʾī, *al-Sunan, nikāḥ,* 37, 3.
[216] *Al-Mawrid,* 664
[217] See also Lane, ***Arabic Lexicon***, 2:1517.

sentence could thus be re-written: "Allah is the most jealous ***shakhṣ***." This is because the apparent meaning (*ẓāhir*) of the text presents us with an *istithnā' al-muttaṣil* or "joined exception", i.e. an exception from among likes. The excepted noun is joined to or of the same kind as the genus from which it is excepted.

- Genus = شخص *shakhṣ*
- Excepted Noun = Allah

Allah is thus an exceptional ***shakhṣ*.** However, those with an anti-anthropomorphist theology like Ibn al-Jawzī chose to read this as an example of ***istithnā' al-munqaṭi'*** or the "severed exception," in which the excepted noun (i.e. Allah) is severed from or of a wholly different kind than the genus.[218] But Ibn al-Jawzī confirms that the Traditionalist Sunni (Ḥanbalī) scholars against whom he was writing – that is to say the *orthodox* Ḥanbalīs - read the hadith according to its apparent meaning with an *istithnā' al-muttaṣil*, thus acknowledging Allah as a man.[219] He says of them:

> These anthropomorphists are persons who describe the Divine Attributes in terms required by sense experience…and they represent Him as a physical man (*shakhṣ*) whose beauty exceeds all beauty…[220]

No less of an authority than the leading orthodox Ḥanbalī, **al-Qāḍī** Abū Ya'lā', affirms this in his ***Kitāb al-Mu'tamad fī Uṣūl al-Dīn***.

> If it is said, "He is a person (*shakhṣ*) or form (*ṣūra*)," it (should be) said: The report from different routes on the night of the

---

[218] Ibn al-Jawzī, ***Kitāb Akhbār al-Sifāt***, 190-191 (Eng.). On *istithnā' al-muttaṣil* and ***istithnā' al-munqaṭi'*** see W. Wright, ***A Grammar of the Arabic Language*** 2vols. (3rd edition; Beirut: Librairie du Liban, 1996 [1974]) II, 335D-336A.

[219] Ibn al-Jawzī, ***Kitāb Akhbār al-Sifāt***, 189-191 (Eng.)

[220] *Talbis Iblis*, 87.

mi'rāj mentioned, "I saw my Lord in the most beautiful form"...And the application of that is not to be refused. Just as "soul" (*nafs*) not like souls and essence (*dhāt*) not like essences weren't denied Him. Likewise form unlike forms, for the *sharī'a* (uses it in this manner).[221]

It was thus well within Sunni orthodoxy as represented and championed by the **Ḥ**anbalīs, the school of the paradigmatic black sheep himself Im**ā**m A**ḥmad**, to refer to Allah as a man (***shakhṣ***) because according to the apparent meaning of a prophetic hadith the Prophet himself refered to Allah as man.

7. *The Coming of Allah*

In his ***Jesus and the Kingdom of God***, G.R. Beasley-Murray notes:

> The decisive element in the theophany descriptions of the Old Testament...is the concept of the coming of God; the descriptions of the accompanying phenomena in the natural order are to be viewed as parabolic...but the supremely important matter is that God 'comes' into the world...in the future.[222]

Georges Pidoux, in his treatment of the coming of God in the Old Testament, commences with a similar observation:

> The faith of the Old Testament rests on two certainties, equally profound and indissolubly bound together. The first is that God has come in the past, and that he has intervened in favor of his people. The other...is the hope that God will come anew in the future.[223]

---

[221] al-**Qāḍī Abū Ya'lā,** ***Kitāb al-Mu'tammad fī uṣūl al-dīn***. 58. Cf. 85.
[222] G.R. Beasley-Murray, ***Jesus and the Kingdom of God*** (Grand Rapids, Mich.: W.B. Eerdmans Pub. Co., 1986) 7
[223] Ibid.

Prophecies of the immanent coming of the Lord to judge man and raise the dead characterize both Old and New Testament theology.[224] Though we hear less of them today, descriptions of God's personal appearance on earth in the Last Days were widespread and numerous during the first centuries of Islam as well and were of marked importance for Sunni scholars. Like similar notions in Judaism, Islamic ideas of God's coming derived from scripture.

> Wait they for naught else than that Allah should come to them in the shadows of the clouds with the angels? (2:210)

> Your Lord shall come with the angels, rank on ranks. (89:22)

While current interpretations of these passages render the coming (*ityān*) of God metaphorically as the coming of God's 'order (*amr*)' to the earth, not God himself,[225] early Sunni scholars understood differently. Al-Dhahak, for example, read 89:22 as saying: "the angels ascend in ranks of separate lines, then the Exalted descends with Jahannam (Hell) next to him, on his left." Muḥammad b. al-**Ḥasan al-Shaybānī** reported from **Ḥammād b. Abū Ḥanīfa:**

> We said to (the heretics who deny Allah's coming): Do you consider the saying of Allah – the Mighty and Majestic: "And your Lord comes accompanied by the angels, ranks upon ranks" (89:22). They said: "As for the angels then they come, ranks upon ranks. But as for the Lord – the Most High – then we do not know what is meant by that and we don't know how he comes." So I said to them: We do not oblige you to know how he comes but we oblige you to have faith in his coming. Do you not consider that the one who rejects that the angels come, ranks upon ranks, what is he to you? They said: "A ***kāfr***

---

[224] On the NT cf. II Thessa. 2:9: "And then shall the wicked be revealed, whom the Lord shall consume with the spirit of his mouth, and shall destroy with the brightness of his coming: Even him, whose coming is after the workings of Satan with all power and signs and lying wonder…"

[225] See for example Ibn al-Jawzi, ***Daf' shubah al-tashbih***, 12f., 110.

(disbeliever), a *mukadhdhib* (rejecter)." I said: "Then likewise, the one who denies that Allah – theMost Perfect – comes is a ***kāfr***, a *mukadhdhib*.[226]

The affirmation of God's *coming* to and visible presence on earth was a part of the orthodox ' ***aqīda*** (creed). **Al Ash'arī** (d. 935) declared: "We believe that Allah will come on the Day of Resurrection, as he said, 'and thy Lord shall come and the angels, rank on rank" (***Ibāna*****,** 54). The famous **Ḥanbalī Ibn Baṭṭa** (d. 334/945) argued in his creed:

> It is necessary then to know that God, on the Day of Resurrection, will appear (*tajallī*) to those of His servants that believe. They will see Him and God will see them. God will speak to them and they will speak to Him. God will address them and salut (them). God will laugh…[227]

The Sunnah gives a number of accounts of God's coming. An important **ḥadīth** is found in Al-Bukhari, Muslim, and Ibn Hanbal in several versions narrated by Abu Said Al-Khudri:

> We said, "O Allah's Apostle! Shall we see our Lord on the Day of Resurrection?" He said, "Do you have any difficulty in seeing the sun and the moon when the sky is clear?" We said, "No." He said, "So you will have no difficulty in seeing your Lord on that Day as you have no difficulty in seeing the sun and the moon (in a clear sky)." The Prophet then said, "Somebody will then announce, 'Let every nation follow what they used to worship.' So the companions of the cross will go with their cross, and the idolators (will go) with their idols, and the companions of every god (false deities) (will go) with their god, till there remain those who used to worship Allah, both the obedient ones and the mischievous ones, and some of the

---

[226] Quoted from **Abū Uthman al Sābūnī,** ***'Aqīdat Salaf wa Aṣḥāb al ḥadīth*****,** 49.

[227] Ibn **Baṭṭa,** *al-****Ibāna.*** Edited and translated by Henry Laoust in ***La Profession de foi d'Ibn Baṭṭa*** (Damascus: Institut Français de Damas, 1958) 89.

people of the Scripture. Then Hell will be presented to them as if it were a mirage.

Then it will be said to the Jews, 'What did you use to worship?' They will reply, 'We used to worship Ezra, the son of Allah.' It will be said to them, 'You are liars, for Allah has neither a wife nor a son. What do you want (now)?' They will reply, 'We want You to provide us with water.' Then it will be said to them 'Drink,' and they will fall down in Hell (instead). Then it will be said to the Christians, 'What did you use to worship?' They will reply, 'We used to worship Messiah, the son of Allah.' It will be said, 'You are liars, for Allah has neither a wife nor a son. What (do you want now)?' They will say, 'We want You to provide us with water.' It will be said to them, 'Drink,' and they will fall down in Hell (instead).

When there remain only those who used to worship Allah (Alone), both the obedient ones and the mischievous ones, it will be said to them, 'What keeps you here when all the people have gone?' They will say, 'We parted with them (in the world) when we were in greater need of them than we are today, we heard the call of one proclaiming, 'Let every nation follow what they used to worship,' and now we are waiting for our Lord.' Then the Almighty will come to them in a form (***ṣūra***) other than the one which they saw the first time, and He will say, 'I am your Lord,' [They will say: "(God protects us from you!) We associate nothing with God!" (We will stay here until our Lord comes to us. When our Lord comes, we will recognize Him!")[228] And none will speak to Him then but the Prophets, and then it will be said to them, 'Do you know any sign by which you can recognize Him?' ["Yes!" they will say. "***So, a leg will be uncovered*** (68:42)."] and so Allah will then uncover His Leg whereupon every believer will prostrate before Him…"[229]

228 Ibn Hanbal, ***Musnad¹***, 2:275; idem, ***Kit§b al-Sunna***, 42.
229 Al-**Bukhārī**, ***Ṣaḥīḥ,*** *tawḥīd* 24/5; *tafsīr* 4/8; Muslim, ***imān*** 302; Ibn Hanbal, *Musnad¹*, 2:275.

God will thus appear on the Day of Judgment in a visible form (***ṣūra***)**,** but one that the believers don't recognize. It differs, we are told, from the form God had the 'first time' the people saw Him. The commentators tell us that 'the first time' is a reference to the Primordial Covenant (*mithāq*) alluded to in ***sūrat al ʿArāf*** 172. The pre-incarnate souls of humanity, prior to the creation of Adam's physical body, entered into a primordial covenant with their creator to serve him alone once they are sent to earth. The first time the people saw God, then, was prior to creation; they saw then God's true form. It is this divine form the people expected to see on the Day of Judgment. Instead, however, God shows up in a new, unrecognized form. Orthodox exegesis understood the point of this test (*imtiḥān*) as a means of distinguishing the true believers from the hypocrites and others.[230] The faithful are expected to recognize their Lord, the strange form notwithstanding.

The important question is, of course, what is the nature of these two forms? In a variant of this **ḥadīth**, it reads, "Then the Lord of the worlds will come to them under a more lowly form (***fī andā ṣūratin***) than that under which they had seen Him [before]."[231] It is not clear what makes this form "lowly" or how exactly it differs from the form God had the 'first time' the people saw him prior to creation. That this first form is God's true form is indicated in two versions of this hadith reported by **Ibn Ḥanbal**, where we find the words, ***yaʾtīhim Allāhu ʿazza wa jalla fī ṣūratihi,*** "God will (again) come to them in 'His form'," i.e. His true form.[232] This true form, the form that the people saw "the first time" or "before," is anthropomorphic; its sign is somehow marked on God's "Leg," his disclosure of which convinces the incredulous Muslims that this is God, however unrecognized his new form.

In other reports the form God will don in the Last days is specifically identified with that form of the Young Man (*shābb*)**.**

---

[230] See Gimaret, ***Dieu à l'image***, 139.

[231] Al-**Bukhārī**, *tawḥīd* 24/5.

[232] Ibn Ḥanbal, ***Musnad²***, 13:304, #7927 and 16:527, #10906.

God will, according to certain narrations, descend on the Day of Judgment in this form ridding a red camel, dressed in a *jubba* (long outer garment, open in front, with wide sleeves).[233]

8. *Literal or Metaphorical?*

The God of the Sunnah is unquestionably anthropomorphic. The Qur'ān and Sunnah speak of His eyes, ears, arms, legs, hands, feet, chest, elbows, loins, fingers, palms, etc. He is blatantly stated to have appeared to the Prophet "in the form of a young man" and is referred to as a man. The question undoubtedly raises itself, "Did the Prophet mean these descriptions literally?" Anti-anthropomorphists can offer absolutely no verse from the Qur'ān or report from the Prophet from the Six Books even suggesting that the Prophet intended these to be pure metaphor. Nowhere in these sources does the Prophet deny that God has a form, and all over the place in the Sunna he explicitly says God has a form. The Six Books give ample evidence of the Prophet's own interpretation of these anthropomorphic attributes indicating that, while they can be used poetically, they are rooted in literal reality.

In a tradition narrated by ʿAbd Allāh and found in Bukhari, the Prophet contrasts the two eyes of Allah with the one eye of *ad-Dajjal.* In the process and obviously for clarity purposes, he points to his eyes so the people will make no mistake as to what type of eye he is referring:

> Narrated by ʿAbd Allāh: Ad-Dajjal was mentioned in the presence of the Prophet. The Prophet said: "Allah is not hidden from you; He is not one-eyed," and pointed with his hand towards his eye, adding, "While Al-Masih Ad-Dajjal is blind in the right eye and his eye looks like a protruding grape."[234]

---

[233] Al-Faḍl b. **Shādhān,** ***Al-Īḍāḥ*** **(Tihrān,** 1972), 15f. See also Ibn al-Jawzī, ***Kitāb al-mawḍūʿāt***, 1:180; al-**Suyūtī**, ***Al-Laʿāliʿ*****,** 28.

[234] Al-**Bukhārī,** ***Ṣaḥīḥ*** 9:371

Another relevant **ḥadīth** is reported on the authority of Ab**ū** Hurayra and found in Ab**ū** D**ā**w**ū**d.

> [Abu Yunus] said: I heard Ab**ū** Hurayra recite the verse "Surely God commands you to make over trusts to those worthy of them, and that when you judge between people, you judge with justice. Surely God admonishes you with what is excellent. Surely God is ever Hearing, Seeing." Then he said: «I saw God's messenger [when he recited these last words] put his finger on his ear, and the next finger on his eye.» Ab**ū** Hurayra says: «I saw God's messenger, when he recited this [verse], he [so] put his two fingers. »[235]

Ibn Majah reports in his ***Sunan*** (vol. 1 # 198):

> Ibn Umar reported: "I heard Allah's Messenger (s) saying while he was on the pulpit, 'Allah the Compeller grasps His heavens and His earth in His Hand,' and the holy prophet closed his fist and began to close and open it."

These physical gestures made by the Prophet clearly suggest that his intent was for the descriptions to be taken in the physical sense. According to a tradition on the authority of Jubayr b. Mut'im and found in Ab**ū** D**ā**w**ū**d, Ibn Khuzayma, at-Tabarani and others, God sits on the Throne like a man sitting on a leather saddle and makes it creak.

> [Jubayr b. Mut'im] narrates: A Bedouin came to find the Messenger of God and said to him: "O Messenger of God, the men are all in, the women and the children perish, the resources are growing thin, the beasts are dying. Pray then to God in our favor so it rains! We ask of you to intercede for us alongside God, and we ask of God to intercede for us alongside of you." "Unfortunate one!" answered the Messenger of God, "do you know what you're saying?" Then he started to say

---

235 Abu Dawud as-Sijistani, ***as-Sunan***, ed. M. Muhyi d-din 'Abd al-Hamid, 4 vol., (Cairo, 1339/1920; repr. Beirut n.d.) 18, 4728; Ibn Khuzayma, ***Kitāb al-Tawḥīd*** 42, 16s.

> *subhana llah*, and did not stop repeating it so long as he didn't see his Companions doing as much. Then he said [to the Bedouin]: "Unfortunate one! One does not ask God to intercede alongside any one of His creatures! God is very much above this! Unfortunate one! Do you know who God is? (God is on His Throne, which is above His heavens, and heavens are above His earth,) like this"—and the Messenger of God put his fingers in the shape of a tent—*and it creaks under Him like the creaking of the saddle under the rider*."[236]

The Prophet compares Allah sitting on the Throne and making it creak to a man sitting on a saddled horse and making the saddle creak. The anthropomorphism is blatant. The Prophet's physical gesturing hardly allows us to see in this report anything other than a physical description of God's "establishment" on the Throne.

It was therefore a principle of Traditionalist Sunni Islam to affirm (*ithbāt*) the ***Ṣifāt** Khabariyyah* (Divine Attributes known only through revelation) without *tahrīf* (alteration of the meaning of the Attributes) or *ta'tīl* (divesting God of these Attributes or negating their reality) or *takyīf* (questioning them or disputing about them) or *tamthīl* (likening them to the same attributes in creation). Assuming anything other than the real (***ḥ**aqīqa*) and apparent or literal (*ẓāhir*) meaning of the word used is to alter the **Ṣ**if**ā**t (*tahrīf*). A**ḥ**mad b. **Ḥ**anbal affirmed that the **Ṣ**if**ā**t must be understood according to their literal meaning. In his ***A Description of the Believer From Ahl as-Sunnah wal-Jama'ah*** Ibn **Ḥ**anbal argued: "That he (the Believer) confirms everything that the Prophets and Messengers came with and that he believes in it resolutely, according to the apparent and manifest [meaning]." Yusuf b. 'Abd al-Barr (d. 1071) affirmed as well:

> *Ahl al-Sunna* are agreed in affirming all the Attributes which are related in the Qur'**ā**n and the Sunnah, having faith in them and

---

[236] Abu Dawud, ***as-Sunan***, 18 §4726; Ibn Khuzayma, ***Kitāb al- Tawḥīd*** 103: 6ff.

understanding them *'alā l- ḥaqīqa* (in the real sense), not *'alā l-majaz* (metaphorically).[237]

Al-Khattabi (d. 950) said "The way (*madhhab*) of the Salaf with regard to the **Ṣifāṭ** is to affirm them as they are *'alā ẓāhir* (with their apparent meaning), negating any *tashbīh* to them, nor ***takyīf*** (asking how)."[238] Under the influence of al-Qāḍī **Abū Ya'lā** in 1040 the Sunni, pro-**Ḥ**anbal**ī** caliph al-Q**ā'im** proclaimed the traditionalist **Qadirī** Creed (***I'tiqād Qādirī***) which affirmed in part: "Only those Attributes should be ascribed to Him which He has Himself ascribed or his Prophet has ascribed to Him. Further, each Attribute He or the Prophet have ascribed to Him is a real attribute (***ṣifa ḥaqīqīyya*), not metaphorical (*lā majāzīyya*)."**[239]

What exactly does it mean to take these **Ṣifāṭ** *'alā ẓāhir*? The authoritative Arabic dictionary *Al-Mawrid* by Dr. Rohi Baalbaki and published by Dar El-Ilm Lilmalayin (Beirut, 2001), page 736 reads:

> ظاهر : "apparent, visible, distinct, manifest, patent, plain, clear, obvious, evident, conspicuous; prima facie, external, exterior, outward, outside, outer…exterior, surface, face…letter, *literal meaning, external sense*".

See also Shaykh 'Abd All**ā**h bin **Ḥ**amid Ali's discussion of these two terms in the context of Classical Aqida:

> The second category of words is known as *zahir*, which means "apparent." The *zahir* meaning of a word or phrase is its apparent meaning. This type of word always has more than one meaning, but has an acknowledged original meaning. *Ẓahir* is similar to the word *haqiqa*, which means "reality, fact, or the literal/true sense of a word or expression." The *zahir* of a word is its *haqiqa*, which means the original linguistic

[237] ***at-Tamhid***, 7:145.

[238] ***Al-Ghuniyah 'an Kalam wa Ahlihi*** as quoted in ***Mukhtasir al-Uluww***, no. 137.

[239] Ibn al-Jaw**zī, *al-*Muntaẓ*am*,** 8:110-11.

meaning. An example of a *zahir* word in Arabic would be the word *yad*, which can be taken to mean a number of things such as "hand, favor, power or authority." The *zahir* of *yad* is "hand," because this is the first meaning that the Arabs understood it to refer to. The other meanings developed over time and were therefore considered to be the figurative uses of the word. When a word is used in its figurative sense, it is said to have been interpreted or reassigned a different meaning. This is where the term *ta'wil* comes from. *Ta'wil* is usually applied when the literal understanding of a word can no longer be taken. The Arab linguists express this by saying, "Predominance in speech is given to the literal sense.[240]

[240] 'Abd al-Rahman Ibn al-Jawzi, ***The Attributes of God***. Translation, Notes and Appendices by 'Abdullah bin Hamid Ali [Bristol, England, 2006] 6).

Conclusion

The Hon. Elijah Muhammad and the Islam of the Black Sheep

If THEM's Islamicity were to be judged on the basis of the Islam of the Black Sheep, how will he fair? British scholar of Islam Aziz Al-Azmeh, in his article on "Orthodoxy and Hanbalite Fideism," has observed:

> When asked whether one may transmit a *ḥadīṯ*...which related of the Prophet his statement that he saw God in the shape of a young man, Aḥmad b. Hanbal readily declared that one may, given the authority of the transmission...It comes (then) as no surprise to us that, given the interdiction of allegory and insistence on literalness, streetcorner religiosity purveyed an anthropomorphic Allah.[241]

This religiosity with its anthropomorphic Allah that dominated the street-corners of Classical Baghdad could have been found on street-corners in any of the seventy American cities where THEM established a temple. This observation problematizes Zafar Ansari's conclusion in his 1981 study:

> When all these various characteristics are pieced together in order to obtain an integrated view of the 'Nation of Islam's' concept of God, the concept that emerges does not even remotely resemble the one to which the Muslims all over the world subscribe.[242]

The irony here is that the concept of God as presented by the Muslim world today-that invisible, incorporeal deity-is foreign to Islam as laid down by the Qur'ān and Sunnah. It is an import from Greece via Persia. The Honorable Elijah Muhammad's God is closer to the God of the *Arabic* Qur'ān and Sunna and

---

[241] A. Al-Azmeh, "Orthodoxy and Hanbalite Fideism." *Arabica* 35 (1988): 264-265 [art.=253-266]

[242] Ansari, *art. cited,* 147.

the God of black sheep – those original Arab Muslims - than the current Muslim world is with their formless and invisible god. If Prophet Muhammad was not "un-Islamic" for saying God came to him in the form of a man, why then should Elijah Muhammad be condemned for saying the same? If Prophet Muhammad can refer to God as a man, why does such a claim make the Honorable Elijah Muhammad 'un-islamic'?

Appendix

Is THEM Guilty of Shirk? The Long Overdue Scholarly Dialogue Between Students of Imam W.D. Mohammed and the Honorable Minister Farrakhan

February - March 2011

In December 2010 a group of Sunni Muslims out of Philadelphia, the most Muslim of all cities, conducted a two-part blog-talk show entitled "The Deconstruction of Wesley Muhammad: The Shaytan (Satan) of This Age". These particular Muslims, who are not affiliated with the community of the late Imam W.D. Mohammed, took grave issue with my work demonstrating that the Teachings of the Hon. Elijah Muhammad (hereafter THEM), including the critical and controversial 'Point Number Twelve,' were consistent with the Arabic Qur'an and Sunna, at least as understood by the Arab Ummah before the Ummah and Islam became 'Aryanized' through the mass conversion of Persians, Byzantines and Turks; these brought with them into Islam a spook theology as well as an anti-black racism. On the show, the chief scholar among this group presumed to refute some of my claims. He several times indicated his desire to debate me on the subject of THEM's Islamicity. Because of the chatter that this show generated within the community, and agreeing that that particular discussion is long overdue, the Allah Team reached out to the scholar and invited him to engage me in a live, public debate on the question: "Is it Un-Islamic to claim that Allah appeared in the form of a Man". The scholar readily accepted the invitation, and we had hoped to hold the discussion in Philly in January 2011. However, in January the scholar backed out of the debate, claiming a concern over my safety (?!?!). We, the Allah Team and Muhammad Mosque No. 12, decided that we would make our case in Philly anyway, and on January 22, 2011 at the Freedom Center I delivered the lecture: "Are the Followers of the Honorable Elijah Muhammad Guilty of Shirk?"

This lecture was live-streamed to hundreds of viewers and through this medium I engaged the Muslim scholars whom I figured would be tuned in. A number of Imam W.D. Mohammed's students tuned in or watched the archive, including at least two of the three premier scholars among the Imam's community today, Imam Salim Mu'min and Mubaashir Uqdah. Imam Salim is Director of M.A.L.I. (Muslim American Logic Institute), and Mubaashir is the author of the important commentary of the creed of the Imam entitled, ***Applying the Teachings of W.D. Mohammed*** (2 vols.). In their online group (M.A.L.I.), Imam Salim and then, in February 2011, Mubaashir posted critiques of my lecture, the latter's quite extensive. This began an online dialogue between the three of us (primarily) that spanned several weeks. It was scholarly, as all three of us are able to engage the Islamic tradition in the original Arabic. It was also generally civil and brotherly, for the most part. I believe all three of us left this discussion with a much greater respect for the views of the other. I certainly have tremendous respect for and appreciation of Imam Salim and Bro Mubaashir.

Unfortunately, the dialogue did not end as cordially as it began and progressed. It was abruptly ended, much to my and others consternation and disappointment. I was advised that my contribution on this subject was no longer welcome in the M.A.L.I. discussion group. Nevertheless, the dialogue as a whole was, in my mind, a watershed moment in the history of Islam in America. The issue of Point Number Twelve and its Islamicity has always been the elephant in the room whenever members of the two communities (viz. the Imam's and the Minister's) come together. It was always necessary and inevitable that an open, scholarly dialogue on the subject with qualified individuals take place. It now has. I thank Bro Imam Salim and Bro Mubaashir for a wonderful and important dialogue, which I think the whole of the Muslim world could and should benefit from.

Below is the discussion as it progressed, with one omission. Prior to the abrupt termination of the dialogue, Bro Mubaashir had posted a two-part Final Response. I responded to Part I, but before I could respond to Part II, the dialogue was terminated. I have thus not included Mubaashir un-responded to Part II, but will post it and my response in the near future.

I pray that all who read this document and follow the discussion may increase in understanding. In Sha' Allah.

Peace

Wesley Muhammad, PhD

1.] Mubaashir Uqdah - Response to Dr Wesley Muhammad Lecture, "Are followers of Honorable Elijah Muhammad Guilty of Shirk?"

As Salaamu Alaikum!

As a student and follower of Imam Warith Deen Mohammed (IWDM), I watched the lecture by Dr. Wesley Muhammad with interest and can appreciate the intellectual effort he used. Dr. Muhammad put forth a case to prove that the followers of the Honorable Elijah Muhammad (HEM) are not guilty of shirk (joining partners with Allah) when they claim that Allah is a man (Master Fard Muhammad). He challenged Muslims to consider his arguments (scholarly, not cantankerous) and he welcomed feedback and responses.

I am submitting the following comments in the spirit of providing the requested responses to his case and feedback to the intellectual arguments he makes. I hope that Dr. Wesley and all who read this response will find some benefit in it, just as I have found benefit in watching Dr. Muhammad's presentation. It is a long post, so there are bound to be some mistakes. Please seek to understand the point I am making despite any mistakes I may make with my writing.

Before making my own comments, I would like to elaborate a bit on the point made by Imam Salim Mu'Min. Imam Salim, in his usual succinct, yet content-rich style, stated that Dr. Wesley presented a compelling argument which proves that the followers of the Honorable Elijah Muhammad (PBUH) are guilty of shirk, using the Qur'anic and linguistic definition of the word shirk. Imam Salim stated that the only way Dr. Wesley's case proves that the followers of the Honorable Elijah Muhammad (HEM) are not guilty of shirk is if he changes the definition of the word shirk to something other than what it means.

In other words, to argue whether or not someone is guilty of shirk assumes that we understand and agree on the definition of shirk. The linguistic meaning of shirk and the Qur'anic usage of shirk define this term as associating or joining partners with Allah.

Linguistically, reasoning from Lane's lexicon as the source, what is meant by associating partners is that one partner takes something away from another partner. As an example, if a business was owned by a single person, that person gets all of the profit and he distributes it as he pleases. But, if two partners own a business, they share the profits from that business and each one gives something up to the other. Hence, each takes something away from the other. One owner cannot do as he pleases, because he must give way and consideration to his partner.

So, if Prophet Jesus or Master Fard are referred to as some kind of manifestation of G-d, and they exist at the same time as Allah The G-d, then that is like referring to them as co-owners or co-G-d's with Allah. They would be Allah's partners. If you were to say that they were Allah Himself, then you would make them the sole owner and Allah would be discarded, leaving Jesus or Fard as the Creator who should be prayed to, not Allah.

As a note of humor, I wonder who would be The new Creator, Jesus or Fard? Now, that would be a battle. Although Allah says in Sura 5:17 that if He decided to kill Jesus, His mother (or Fard and his father), and everyone on earth, who could stop Him from doing so?

The Qur'an states in Sura 24:42 that to Allah belongs the dominion of the skies and the earth. Sura 2:165 states that there are men who take others besides Allah as equal to Him; they love them as they should love Allah. The verse goes on to say to Allah belongs all power.

So, if Allah, The Creator is the owner and someone thinks or calls Jesus or Fard or any other man The Creator, then they are saying that Jesus or Fard is the owner, not Allah. This would be associating these persons with Allah and having others focusing on those who are not the true owner. So, according to the linguistic meaning of the word shirk, most Christians and followers of HEM are committing shirk.

With respect to Qur'anic usage, there is an abundance. But, suffice the following. Allah says in Sura 9:31 that they have taken their Rabbis and Monks and Jesus as their lords instead of Allah. Yet they were commanded to serve only the One Allah.

The HEM says in his book, Our Savior Has Arrived, "All these scriptures show that He sees, hears, feels, tastes, smells, talks our language, walks, stands, sits, eats, drinks. Therefore, God must be a human being. He must be a human being, a man since we all refer to Him as being our Father." In his book, The Supreme Wisdom, in the section titled, The Coming of Allah, the HEM tells us that this human being came to us from the Holy City Mecca, Arabia in 1930 and that "He used the name of Wallace D. Fard, often signing it W. D. Fard."

Sura 5:73 says that those are misguiding others who say that Allah is one of three. In Sura 16:51, Allah says take not two gods, for Allah is One. Thus, by Qur'anic usage to refer to others as Allah is a joining or associating others with Allah (shirk) and Allah is against this practice.

It is ironic that the NOI, who brought to the attention of the black masses that it was crazy to believe in a 3 in 1 G-d, is defending the belief in a 2 in 1 G-d.

So, to Imam Salim's point, Dr. Wesley has proven that according to the linguistic and Qur'anic definition of shirk, the followers of the HEM are guilty of shirk. Imam Salim points out that for them not to be guilty of shirk, Dr. Wesley would have to have a different definition of shirk.

And in fact, this is precisely what Dr. Wesley attempts to do: reframe the definition or concept of G-d in order to claim that those who believe that G-d is not a man are the ones who are guilty of shirk and that those who believe that G-d is a man are actually following the Qur'an and the sunnah of prophet Muhammad.

The foundation of the majority of Dr. Wesley's case rests upon five arguments. I will restate the essence of the argument to demonstrate that I understand it and then respond to it with my own thoughts. I will take them one at a time.

ARGUMENT 1

First, Dr. Wesley refers to early Islamic history and he cites that there was a dispute between the early Muslims as to whether the Qur'an and Hadeeth references to Allah's characteristics should be read allegorically or literally. He references that there were Muslims of repute who believed literally that Allah had attributes such as a hand, foot, etc. The most well known of them all would be Imam Ahmad Ibn Hanbal, founder of one of the major madhabs, the Hanbali school. The Hanbalis are the literalists of the four major madhabs.

Dr. Wesley argues that if the Hanbalis and other literalists in Islamic history can be accepted as legitimate Muslims with a legitimate viewpoint, then why not the followers of the HEM? In fact, he argues that not only are these literalists accepted, they are the ones who are correct and those inclined to treat the words of Qur'an and Hadeeth as metaphorical are the ones who are misguided and guilty of shirk.

RESPONSE 1

The debates between the Mutazilites and the Asharites were not about whether Allah was a human being or not, they were about whether Qur'anic statements referencing Allah's hand, foot, etc. should be accepted on face value (literally) or understood as metaphorical.

So, Imam Hanbal and the others argued that Allah has a hand and a foot and a throne, but that no human's eyes can see His hand, throne, foot, etc. Imam Hanbal would argue that Allah has a hand, but His hand does not look like your hand. He would cite the hadith:

"Narrated Ibn 'Umar: Allah's Apostle said, "On the Day of Resurrection, Allah will grasp the whole Earth by His Hand, and all the Heavens in His right, and then He will say, 'I am the

King." Abu Huraira said, "Allah's Apostle said," Allah will grasp the Earth...' "

But, Imam Hanbal would tell us that Allah has a hand, but we can't see or comprehend Allah's hand that will hold the earth and skies and it is certainly not a human hand. The Mutazilite would argue that Allah does not have a hand at all; that this Qur'anic reference is a metaphor for Allah's power and control.

Imam Hanbal was concerned about preserving the integrity of the text of the Qur'an so that translators and interpreters would not substitute their interpretations for the actual words used. He was not trying to prove that Allah was a man or human being. If that was his point, he would have said so. He was a scholar, prolific muhadith, and teacher. Surely, he could have and would have made this clear. But, you cannot find anywhere where Imam Hanbal argued that Allah is a human being.

ARGUMENT 2

Secondly, Dr. Wesley points to the sayings of prophet Muhammad. He states that the prophet has referred to Allah as a physical being in Sahih (sound) hadeeth, not while he was dreaming, but while he was awake. He cites the following hadeeth as proof:

"Narrated 'Abdullah: Ad-Dajjal was mentioned in the presence of the Prophet. The Prophet said, "Allah is not hidden from you; He is not one-eyed," and pointed with his hand towards his eye, adding, "While Al-Masih Ad-Dajjal is blind in the right eye and his eye looks like a protruding grape."

"Narrated Anas: The Prophet said, "Allah did not send any prophet but that he warned his nation of the one-eyed liar (Ad-Dajjal). He is one-eyed while your Lord is not one-eyed, The word 'Kafir' (unbeliever) is written between his two eyes."

Here are some additional hadeeth that seem to support Dr. Wesley's point:

"Narrated Jabir bin 'Abdullah: when this Verse:--'Say (O Muhammad!): He has Power to send torments on you from above,' (6.65) was revealed; The Prophet said, "I take refuge with Your Face." Allah revealed:-- '..or from underneath your feet.' (6.65) The Prophet then said, "I seek refuge with Your Face!" Then Allah revealed:--'...or confuse you in party-strife.' (6.65) Oh that, the Prophet said, "This is easier."

"Narrated Abu Huraira: The Prophet said, "When Allah had finished His creation, He wrote over his Throne: 'My Mercy preceded My Anger.'

Dr. Wesley makes the point that in sayings like these it is reported that the prophet referred to Allah as having two Eyes like a man and the Dajjal had One. The additional hadeeth report the prophet as saying Allah has a Face, Feet, a Throne, He writes and gets emotional (Angry).

He then goes on to say that you cannot find the description of Allah in the Hadeeth that is put forth by Imam Ghazzali and those who teach that Allah is formless and invisible.

"Why didn't the prophet say Allah wasn't a body, not inside the universe, not in a location? It was easy enough for him to say," questions Dr. Muhammad.

On this basis, he asserts that the Allah prophet Muhammad taught about had a body and was a man, and that those who teach otherwise do not believe in the same G-d that prophet Muhammad believes in and therefore are not following the sunnah and are committing shirk themselves by associating a "spook" G-d with the real, physical Man G-d. "It is the teaching of the HEM that is following the sunnah," says Dr. Muhammad.

RESPONSE 2

As a follower of Imam Waarithud-Deen Mohammed, it is important that I point out that we have been taught that the Qur'an is the number one source of our guidance and is the criteria by which we judge the validity of all knowledge, including the reports (hadeeth) of what Prophet Muhammad said and the debates between scholars. I would also note that students of Imam Mohammed do not accept hadeeth at face value, even Sahih hadeeth, without first sifting them through the lens of the Qur'an.

With this in mind, just as Dr. Wesley asked the question, "Why didn't the prophet say that Allah wasn't a body, a man, or that he was unlimited or formless," I would ask the rhetorical question, "If Allah wanted people to think He was a man, would He have not said so in the Qur'an?"

Allah instructed Prophet Muhammad to tell the people, "I (prophet Muhammad) am a mortal man just like you." Couldn't He just as easily have instructed the prophet to say, "Tell them I, Allah, am a human being, just like them, but only the greatest one amongst them all."

Yes, Allah could have said that. But instead, in Sura 41:6 Allah instructs Prophet Muhammad to say this to the people, "Say thou: "I (Muhammad) am but a man like you: It is revealed to me by Inspiration, that your Allah is one Allah. So stand true to Him, and ask for His Forgiveness. And woe to those who join gods with Allah."
To those reading this response who really want to get the full impact and definitive commentary on this topic, please find a quiet place and take 30 minutes to think while reading Sura 6, the Cattle. It says it all. It gives you the full context and scope of Allah's argument on this topic. Read it and let your heart and mind tell you if Allah supports the idea of being thought of as a man or human being.

Sura 6:103 states clearly that no vision can comprehend or perceive Him, but He comprehends and perceives all things.

Now, let me make one more reference from the Qur'an and then talk about those hadeeth where the Prophet refers to Allah's hand, foot, etc.

Allah says in Sura 17:89, "And We have explained to man, in this Qur'an, every kind of comparison, similitude, parable: yet the greater part of men refuse (to receive it) except with ingratitude!" This, and many verses, tell us that you will find parables, comparisons in the Qur'an and that the purpose of these parables, similitudes, comparisons is to explain things to men and women.

If Allah uses parables and comparisons to teach, isn't it reasonable to recognize that His prophet would use parables and comparisons to try and teach the people also? That is common sense, isn't it?

When the Prophet tells his people that Allah will hold all of the heavens and the earth in His right hand, do you really think he is talking about Allah's human right hand? Do you really believe that Prophet Muhammad is suggesting that Allah's hand is a human hand like Master Fard's or his own and that He will use it to hold the skies and the earth? Isn't it more reasonable and intelligent to reason that he is making a parable to give the people an idea of the vastness and greatness and bigness of Allah, whom they cannot grasp with their vision? We can't see the bigness of Allah, so the prophet gives us a parable in terms the uneducated Arabs could understand.

Doesn't that explanation make more sense than trying to figure out how a human being standing on a corner in Detroit or Chicago is going to grow his hand so that it can hold the sky and earth while he is standing on the corner? Maybe he has to levitate into outer space and then grow his hand to hold the earth and sky. Which understanding makes better sense?

With respect to the prophet never referencing a G-d who you can't see. There is the well known report of the story of the incident when the angel Jibril questioned the prophet on his religion in front of his companions. I retell a portion of it below and I bring your attention to the last sentence:

"One day we were sitting in the company of Allah's Apostle (peace be upon him) when there appeared before us a man dressed in pure white clothes, his hair extraordinarily black. There were no signs of travel on him. None amongst us recognized him. At last he sat with the Apostle (peace be upon him) He knelt before him placed his palms on his thighs and said: Muhammad, inform me about al-Islam. The Messenger of Allah (peace be upon him) said: Al-Islam implies that you testify that there is no god but Allah and that Muhammad is the messenger of Allah, and you establish prayer, pay Zakat, observe the fast of Ramadan, and perform pilgrimage to the (House) if you are solvent enough (to bear the expense of) the journey. He (the inquirer) said: You have told the truth. He (Umar ibn al-Khattab) said: It amazed us that he would put the question and then he would himself verify the truth. He (the inquirer) said: Inform me about Iman (faith). He (the Holy Prophet) replied: That you affirm your faith in Allah, in His angels, in His Books, in His Apostles, in the Day of Judgment, and you affirm your faith in the Divine Decree about good and evil. He (the inquirer) said: You have told the truth. He (the inquirer) again said: Inform me about al-Ihsan (performance of good deeds). He (the Holy Prophet) said: That you worship Allah as if you are seeing Him, for though you don't see Him, He, verily, sees you...." (Sahih Muslim)

In this report the prophet tells us that you can't see Allah, but Allah sees you. This is consistent with the Qur'anic verse 6:103 that no vision can grasp Him, but His vision grasps all things.

ARGUMENT 3

Thirdly, Dr. Wesley addresses one of the challenges of the Qur'an, Suratul Ikhlas, where Allah states that He is One, He is the One on whom everything depends (As-Samad, which is sometimes translated as Eternal), He never had a child, He never was someone's child, and there is nothing equal to the One.

Dr. Wesley claims that the attribute or characteristic As-Samad doesn't mean eternal, but rather solid. This meaning of As-Samad would lead to the translation that Allah is One, a solid whole. So, according to Dr. Wesley Allah is a solid and for something to be solid it must be delimited, which means that it is limited by boundaries; finite. Hence, Allah is a material thing, not an immaterial thing; He is a limited, finite thing, not an unlimited, infinite thing.

He addresses the next verses; He gives not birth, nor is He born. The typical logic says, Men have fathers and they give birth to children, therefore how can Allah be a man? Dr. Muhammad responds to this challenge by referring back to ancient Kemet (Egypt) for a solution. He shows a picture of a man with a penis that is called G-d, the Creator. This G-d is referred to as "He who is His own Father." Thus, this G-d is self-created, having no Father. He then points out that a man does not have to have children. Dr. Wesley reasons that if previous scriptures can have a self-created G-d and that a man does not have to have children, then why can't the Allah of the Qur'an also be a Self-Created G-d who chose not to have children?

With these arguments, Dr. Muhammad believes he has defended the idea of G-d being a man against the statements of Suratul Ikhlas.

RESPONSE 3

First, a little about this word Samad. Like many words, it has several meanings associated with it. It's first and second meanings are to tend to something, to repair something, to reach or attain something. It's third meaning is to contend with someone in a fight. It's fourth meaning is to rest. It's fifth meaning is elevated ground, rugged ground. It also could mean a rock embedded in the earth. Another meaning is a she-camel.

Another meaning, and the one to which Dr. Wesley ascribes to Allah's attribute is a solid, not hollow.

The next meaning is associated with Allah, because the definite article Al or As is attached in front of the word Samad making it As-Samad. It means the One on whom all things depend and are in need of; the one whom all things get their existence and the one whose reach is over all things; the One who exists eternally and forever (we'll come back to this).

The reason that I have taken the time to list all of the possible meanings of the word Samad is to help us make it clear that you cannot just pick any definition you want to use for a word and say that is what it means, because you saw it in a dictionary. For example, the word 'Ran' has many meanings in English. "He ran the race." "He ran up the bills." "He ran the cable wire up to the second floor." You can't just pick any one of these meanings and fit it into a sentence and say that is what it means. You have to select the correct meaning of the word for the sentence that is being used.

While it is fair to argue or debate the meaning of a word, it is intelligent to choose the word that makes the most sense and is most likely the correct meaning of the word for the sentence you are talking about. So, the task before us is to consider which of these definitions most likely applies to Allah, The Creator of the skies, the earth, and every single thing within; including you and I and Dr. Wesley.

To save us all time, let us simply consider Dr. Wesley's choice of definition for As-Samad and the definition used by the majority of Muslims in the world.

Dr. Wesley argues that because one of the meanings of Samad is a solid, not hollow, this proves that Allah is a solid, physical thing; a delimited being, a finite, solid material being, yes a human being. By choosing this meaning of the word Samad, he declares that the Muslim scholars have mistranslated this word as eternal in order to support their own definition of a non-physical, non-material G-d.

Most other Muslims accept the definition of As-Samad that means the One upon whom everything else depends for its existence. They get this meaning from the definition of Samad that means to tend or repair or attain to something.

You see, all things are tended to (taken care of) by Allah. You could not tend to anything without using the gift of your body and mind Allah gave you. You couldn't tend to your garden without the water and sunlight. Everything that needs tending to or that wants to tend or take care of something is dependent upon Allah.

All things in need of repair depend upon what Allah has put here to help them repair. Whatever needs to be fixed depends upon the things Allah made and makes available to us for making the repair. We can't repair wooden things without the trees Allah gave us. We can't repair the streets without the body, knowledge, and skills we got from Allah. The sidewalk couldn't be repaired without Allah's creating the materials from which concrete is made. Everything is dependent upon Allah.

Anything that seeks to attain or acquire something depends upon what Allah has put here for them to use to try and attain it. In order to become a doctor or lawyer, you need air to breathe, you need eyes to read and ears to hear. Whatever seeks to attain or acquire, it needs Allah. Whatever exists needs Allah in order to exist, but Allah doesn't need anything to exist, He is independent of everything.

The reason that some translators use the word Eternal and Absolute for the word or attribute As-Samad is because if everything depends upon Allah for its existence, then Allah had to have been here before everything. If space owes its existence to Allah, and it does, then Allah's existence had to precede the existence of space.

You see, all things get there existence from Allah, including all solid things; all material things, all males and females, all human beings. Allah is not a limited solid, all solids get their existence from Allah, therefore Allah had exist before solids or materials could come into existence.

Now, consider the two explanations of this word, Dr. Wesley's and the one I've given, and choose which one you think is more correct in describing the G-d who created the Sun and the Moon and your brain.

Equally curious is the way that Dr. Wesley has tried to circumvent Allah's proof in the Qur'an that He (Allah) is not a human being. In Sura 4:1 Allah says "O men! Reverence Allah who created you and your mate from a single soul and from them scattered like seeds countless men and women."

Then Allah says in Suratul Ikh'las that He (Allah) has no father and He is not a father of any child. Thus, in these two verses Allah makes it plain that He created men and women, and that He is not a man (father or child). After understanding this verse and knowing that Master Fard had a father, Alfonso, how could you still teach that Allah is Master Fard, a human being?

But, what about Dr. Wesley's argument that Allah is a self-created human being and that Allah as a man is different from man as a man? Dr. Wesley offers proof of such a being by pointing to a picture of a man from ancient Egypt who is referred to as a G-d who created himself, thus indicating that he needed no father.

Dr. Wesley's proof that this self-created G-d had no children is a picture in someone's book which refers to a pre-Arabian black G-d named Allah who had sexual problems and therefore, did not have children. So these are the proofs for his claim that there is nothing in Suratul Ikh'las that negates the assertion that Allah is a man.

But, while Dr. Wesley seeks to prove his argument using the ancient Mystery system or other doctrines, Allah tells Muslims to judge all things by the criteria of the Qur'an. What Muslim would leave the proofs of the Qur'an and pick up another doctrine in an attempt to refute or avoid what the Qur'an clearly says? Sura 2:16 says they trade guidance for error, but they realize it not.

Think about it, what does it really mean to self-create yourself? First of all, if G-d is a man, a human being, where did he exist when he created himself? I mean, he would have to create himself, before he could create the universe and the earth with water and air so he could breathe. Did he float around in the abyss? I guess you could say that when he created himself, he created everything else at the same time. In this way, when he manifested, so did the earth, air, and water, so he had air to breathe and water to drink too.

To say "he" created "himself' implies that "he" existed before creating "himself." The act of creation is an action and an action must have an actor or doer. Action cannot exist in a vacuum. Therefore, if "he" created, "himself" as a man, "he" already existed in order to create "himself." So, there is always something prior to that which is created.

ARGUMENT 4

Fourthly, Dr. Wesley argues his case against the prevailing interpretation of Sura 42:11, which states that There is not like Him (Allah) any thing. He points us to the Arabic phrase, laysa ka-mithlihi shayun and asserts that the translators have also mistranslated this verse.

He argues that the comparative particle ka, which means 'like' and the noun 'mithli', which means likeness, parable, metaphor, allegory, indicates that Allah does have an likeness and therefore an image. He says the translation should be, There is not like, his likeness, a thing. To Dr. Wesley this means that if you say there is nothing like His likeness, then He must have a likeness and this likeness is what He looks like; His image. Thus, if He has an image and it is said that He has a hand, foot, face, and eyes, and that G-d created man in His own image, He must be a man.

He adds to his case by saying that the Qur'an's use of the word laysa, which means 'not' indicates that the negation is not necessarily absolute. He argues that if Allah wanted to make it perfectly clear that there is absolutely nothing like Allah, He would have used the emphatic negation Laa rather than laysa. So, to Dr. Wesley, the use of laysa means that there is some room for interpreting this phrase differently. He references the verse which says about the prophet's wives that they are not like any of the other women. The word laysa is used here and he retorts, "does this mean that the prophet's wives are not women?" Therefore, he reasons, when Laysa is used in 42:11 it does not necessarily mean that Allah is not like a man.

RESPONSE 4

Dr. Wesley's complaint here is with the translation of ayat 11. We have to ascertain whether his translation of this verse is more accurate than the translations of over 30 translators. Go to this website

http://www.islamawakened.com/Quran/42/11/default.htm

to see thirty different translations of this verse. None of them translate it the way Dr. Wesley does. Let me explain why.

Dr. Wesley correctly points out that 'Ka' is a particle of comparison in this phrase. So, Laysa Ka can be translated "there is not Like" or it could be translated "there is not a comparison" or "there is not a similar." The word Mathli comes from Mathalun, which means resemblance, likeness, similar.

So Laysa Ka-Mithli simply means "There is not like (ka) his resemblance (Mithli)" or "There is not a comparison (ka) of His resemblance (Mithli)" or as Dr. Wesley has said, "There is not like (ka) his likeness (mithli), meaning there is no thing like or that can be compared to Allah. This is why the translators translate, "There is nothing like Him or that can be compared to Him."

However, Dr. Wesley says that is exactly the point. That by saying nothing can be compare to Allah's likeness, tells us that Allah has a likeness, which is that He is like Himself, like His own image. To this we must reply....duh! That is the whole point. Allah is One, Unique, Like Himself Only, not like anything in His creation, not like the sun, moon, stars or a man. This is what Abraham discovered; that Allah is not like the stars, moon, or sun, and by extension, not comparable to a man either. Allah is like His own likeness (or image if you want) and we men and women can't see or comprehend Him, His likeness, or His image.

The second part of Dr. Wesley's argument is that the use of the verb Laysa rather than Laa is evidence that Allah did not really mean that there is nothing like Himself, because if He did mean that He would have used the particle Laa which is sometimes used to emphatically negate something beyond a shadow of a doubt and into future. Dr. Wesley questions why Laa was not used?

On the contrary, the emphatic Laa is used in many places in the Qur'an to make it clear that Allah is not a man or anything else in creation that a man would want to worship as G-d. In Sura 2:163 the emphatic Laa is used to say that Allah is One; not 2 or 3. In Sura 2:255 the emphatic Laa is used to establish that there is no Allah but Himself, the Ever-Living (Al-Hayyu), the Eternal (Al-Qayyuumu).

It is worth noting, that no man has always lived and will continue to live forever. If you say a man can, then you have changed the definition of a man. Why make a man into G-d, so you can worship a man? Why not just worship G-d? Secondly, while the meaning of the word Samad in Suratul Ikhlas is sometimes translated as Eternal (no beginning and no ending), it is more accurately translated as He is Independent, on whom all other things depend. But, the word used in 2:255 is Al-Qayyuum, which does mean Eternal. This same verse states that Allah does not sleep. Men sleep. The verse also says that no one shall obtain any of His knowledge, except as He wills. It says His throne extends over the skies and earth. This is not a big chair that sits over the universe. It is a metaphor indicating that His authority is over everything in the creation. And if it is a big chair, we can't see it anyway and we don't know what it's made out of, so it's a metaphor to us anyway.

When we read the Qur'an, we must consider verses in the light of other verses, because Allah tells us that He does not contradict himself. So, He uses the emphatic Laa many times. However, in Sura 42:11, He uses the perfect tense verb Laysa to tell us that He is not like anything you try to invent as a comparison to Him.

After so many uses of the emphatic Laa; Sura 3:2, 3:6, 3:64, and many more, there is no need to always use emphasis. It should be common sense or obvious to us by now.

ARGUMENT 5

The Fifth and last point of his case does not revolve around mainstream Islamic concepts, but rather a case to his own brothers and sisters in the NOI. He attempts to reconcile the case he has made on behalf of the NOI; namely that prophet Muhammad believed that G-d was a man and claims to have seen Allah in person, and the Honorable Elijah Muhammad statement that Prophet Muhammad never saw G-d, he only heard Him.

He tries to reconcile this by referring to a news article written in 1957 where the HEM states that all of the prophets saw G-d, but only in a vision. Dr. Wesley uses this news article as proof that he is not contradicting the HEM.

According to Dr. Wesley, if prophet Muhammad saw Allah in a vision, then he saw Him, but He really actually didn't see Him, he just saw a vision of Him, but it was a true vision. In this way, Dr. Muhammad claims to reconcile his case that claims Prophet Muhammad saw Allah in the person of a man and the Honorable Elijah Muhammad's statement that Prophet Muhammad did not see Allah, but only heard his voice.

Dr. Wesley's purported logic is, the prophet saw Allah as a man in a vision. The vision was a true vision and HEM said the prophet saw Allah in a vision, thus, my case agrees with the HEM. Yet, the prophet did not really, actually, physically see Allah in person, because it was a vision. Therefore, he is still consistent with the HEM's statement that the prophet never saw Allah.

RESPONSE 5

This was an interesting way to conclude the lecture. Dr. Wesley spent two hours making a tremendous effort to prove to us that prophet Muhammad saw and felt the physical touch of Allah, as a man, not in a dream, but while he was awake and aware and then in the last 15 minutes of the presentation contradicts his entire case in order to avoid contradicting the Honorable Elijah Muhammad's statement that Prophet Muhammad did not see Allah.

Dr. Wesley uses the 1957 news article which states that prophet Muhammad saw G-d in a vision (not in actual physical person), as proof that he is not contradicting the HEM's statement that prophet Muhammad did not actually see G-d, but saw a vision. Well, this contradicts Dr. Wesley's entire argument up to this point. Now, he appears to be conceding that Prophet Muhammad did not see Allah as a human being in the flesh.

If this is Dr. Wesley's position, why spend two hours trying to prove that the prophet saw and touched Allah, only to turn around and say, well no, he saw and touched him only in a vision?

Dr. Wesley states that the vision was an accurate portrait of Allah, but how would he know this if it was only a vision? He has nothing to compare the vision with in the real world, because he didn't see the physical Allah in the real world. For example, if I asked you to see my cousin who lives in France in a vision, you could have a vision of what you think is him, but you wouldn't know it, because you never saw my cousin. However, if you had seen him and then had a vision of him, you could tell me with conviction that you saw him in a vision, because you know what he looks like.

So, if Dr. Wesley accepts the HEM's position that the prophet never saw G-d, but only saw a vision of G-d, then perhaps he should have spent 2 hours trying to prove that the reports of the prophet's visions were true, not that the prophet actually saw and taught that Allah is a physical man.

In this effort to not contradict the HEM, I believe Dr. Wesley contradicts a large part of his own case; namely, that prophet Muhammad's words prove that he saw Allah as a man.

CONCLUDING ARGUMENT

Dr. Wesley Muhammad concludes his case by saying to the Muslim world at large, which concept of Allah will you choose? The belief in Allah as eternal, who cannot be comprehended with the eye, who has no form or shape like anything in the material world or the belief in Allah as a man, who has a shape, is limited, is like the material world, and can be seen with the physical eye and heard with the physical ear?

He concludes that those who don't believe in Allah as a man are the ones guilty of setting up partners with Allah (shirk) by making an invisible G-d, the G-d instead of the real Allah, who is a man.

CONCLUDING RESPONSE

Obviously, I disagree with Dr. Wesley Muhammad's viewpoint. Therefore, I conclude with a comment from my leader Imam W. Deen Mohammed and his leader the Holy Qur'an.

Imam Mohammed has said, "You can't put Allah on a slide so that you can examine Him...that is foolishness. You can't even see everything in the creation, how are you going to see Allah, who is bigger than the creation?" The Imam said, "You claim to comprehend Allah and you haven't even analyzed yourself; you can't even comprehend everything about yourself."

Each one of us has our own life and it is difficult to master. We don't even understand ourselves and the world we live in. Yet, we are going to define Allah and bring Him down to our level where we can see Him.

Let me end with Allah's words:

40:57 "Assuredly the creation of the heavens and the earth is a greater (matter) than the creation of men: Yet most men understand not."

9:31 "They take their priests and their anchorites to be their lords in derogation of Allah, and (they take as their Lord) Christ the son of Mary; yet they were commanded to worship but One Allah. there is no god but He. Praise and glory to Him: (Far is He) from having the partners they associate (with Him)." 28:88 "And call not, besides Allah, on another god. there is no god but He. Everything (that exists) will perish except His own Face. To Him belongs the Command, and to Him will ye (all) be brought back.

35:3 "O men! Call to mind the grace of Allah unto you! Is there a creator, other than Allah, to give you sustenance from heaven or earth? There is no god but He: How then are ye deluded away from the Truth?"

40:62 "Such is Allah, your Lord, the Creator of all things, there is no god but He: Then how ye are deluded away from the Truth!"

47:19 "Know, therefore, that there is no god but Allah, and ask forgiveness for thy fault, and for the men and women who believe: for Allah knows how ye move about and how ye dwell in your homes."

Sincerely,

Mubaashir Uqdah

2.] Dr Wesley Muhammad - Response to Brother Mubaasir Uqdah's Review: Part I

As-salaam Alaikum!

I would like to first thank Bro Mubaashir Uqdah for the time he has taken to carefully view my lecture and write an in-depth and reasonably fair review of it. I respect his scholarship and representation of our brother, the late Imam W.D. Mohammed. I have equal respect for the scholarship and representation of Imam Salim Mu'min and Imam Benjamin Bilal. These erudite brothers come to mind when I reflect on a recent experience I had with the Honorable Minister Farrakhan, whom I follow and of whom I am a student. This past July I was among those fortunate enough to join Brother Minister Farrakhan for dinner at the National House in Chicago, during which he shared with his guests, among other things, his desire to see his followers and the followers of Imām Wārrithuddīn come together as a unified community descendant from the spiritual loins of the Honorable Elijah Muhammad (hereafter THEM). The Minister acknowledged that our claim that God is a man is *the* obstacle to this unity. Because members of the Imām's community tend to be more learned in the Arabic Islamic tradition and frequently engaged the Qur'an and the Sunna of the Prophet Muhammad (s) in the Arabic, they are convinced with most of the Muslim world of the theological error of this aspect of THEM's teaching of Islam, believing it to be nothing less than shirk (as Bro Salim and Bro Mubaashir have both affirmed). Being trained in Classical Arabic myself, however, and being inspired to go behind the 'ulemaic' gate-keepers of Islamic tradition and straight to the Classical Arabic texts themselves, I happen to know that this conclusion by many in the Islamic world is based on a rather shallow engagement of the Classical Arabic sources and tradition. The theological interpretation of the Qur'ān and Sunna that is held up as the criterion by which

THEM's teaching is judged as shirk is in fact grounded less in the Arabic Qur'ān and Sunna themselves but rather in non-Arabic (and even non-Islamic) ideas and interpretations that have accreted within Islam over the last several centuries and which today, ironically, merely *pass* as 'true Islam'. At several points in his review of my lecture Bro Mubaashir exhibited and relied upon this same shallow engagement of the Arabic sources. I thus did not find his conclusion surprising at all. Nevertheless, I share Bro Minister Farrakhan's desire and believe that, if we can engage the Classical Arabic sources together as brothers (and sisters), we might just be able to remove that obstacle to our collective unity once and for all.

In his review Bro Mubaashir displayed honorable attention to and patience with the arguments I laid out in the lecture, shunning the emotionalism and acrimonious speech that often characterizes this particular dialogue. For this I am grateful and I pray that I am found equally attentive, patient and level-headed in this response. Bro Mubaashir hoped that I would find some benefit in his review; I certainly did. Despite the erudition exhibited in this review, however, there are three unfortunate trends that mar it and ultimately render his (counter-) arguments unpersuasive: 1.) the tendency to use straw-man arguments, where the straw-man is a mischaracterization of my position as articulated in that Philly lecture 2.) the tendency to juxtapose "Dr Wesley's claims" on behalf of the Qur'an with his claims, but passing the latter off as 'what the Qur'an actually says' rather than his own ideological, idiosyncratic reading of the Qur'an and 3.) this conflation of the Qur'an and his idiosyncratic reading of the Qur'an is supported by the tendency to man-handle and thus mistranslate and misrepresent Qur'anic verses and hadith statements. In these cases Bro Mubaashir tries to pass obvious eisegesis off as strict, non-sectarian exegesis (*tafsir*), which it simply is not 4.) Finally, there is in this review the noticeable tendency to misrepresent the Classical Arabic/Islamic Tradition in general in an attempt to claim prestigious precedent for his (and the Muslim world's today) very non-Semitic view of God. I cannot address every single point made by Bro Mubaashir- such a response would be long and tedious. I have to be selective (which even still may seem long and tedious). However, in Part II of this response I hope to address other matters, such as Surat al-Ikhlas [112] and Surat al-Shura [42]:11.

I.] *Misrepresenting the Classical Islamic Tradition*

Bro Mubaashir begins his review by echoing the sentiment of Bro Imam Salim Mu'min that "the only way Dr. Wesley's case proves that the followers of the Honorable Elijah Muhammad are not guilty of shirk is if he changes the definition of the word shirk to something other than what it means." This, Beloveds, is deflection. The problem is not at all our respective understandings of shirk: we three all agree that a mushrik is one who associates partners with Allah. The problem is our respective understandings of "Allah" to whom no partners may be legitimately associated. We who adhere to the Islam taught to us by the Honorable Elijah Muhammad understand that Allah is a man – a divine man rather than a mortal man, but a man nonetheless. In my most recent book, "Take Another Look: The Qur'an, the Sunna, and the Islam of the Honorable Elijah Muhammad," I demonstrate that this understanding of Allah is absolutely consistent with the Qur'an and Sunna when these are no longer read through the lens of al-Ghazzali and other non-Arab converts to Islam who rejected the Black Arabs to whom the message first came and their understanding of the religion. These non-Arab converts – particularly the Persians and Byzantines – introduced a new understanding of God and a peculiar way of reading the Qur'an so as to locate this new God therein. I introduced this history in Philly and identified there the great Imam Ahmad ibn Hanbal (d. 855) as the champion of the Islam of the original Black Arabs against those who tried to de-Arabize the religion by (among other things) replacing the Semitic God of the Qur'an with the Greek God of Hellenism. In my lecture (and book) I emphasized this Black Arab/White convert dichotomy in understanding Islam because the Prophet pointed it out.

> "Zayd b. Aslam related that the Prophet (s) saw a vision and told his companions about it. He said: "I saw a group of black sheep and a group of white sheep then mixed with them [until the white sheep became so numerous that the black sheep could no longer be seen in the herd of sheep.] I interpreted it to mean that [the black sheep are the Arabs. They will accept Islam and become many. As for the white sheep, they are the non-Arabs (i.e. Persians, Turks, Byzantines, ect.)] They will enter Islam and then share with you your wealth and your genealogy [and become so numerous that the Arabs will not be noticed amongst them.]" The Companions became surprised by what he (s) said. Then one said, "The non-Arab Persians will enter our land, O' Messenger of Allah?!" The Prophet (s) then said, "Yes. By He Who Has my soul in His Hand, if the religion was hanging on the distant star, men from the non-Arab Persians would reach it and the luckiest of them would be the people of Faris."

I have demonstrated that these 'Black sheep' who are the original recipients of the message of Islam are the Black Arabs and they and their Islam are best represented by Ahmad ibn Hanbal. I further demonstrated that the White sheep and their re-interpretation of Islam are best represented by the Persian *Hujjat al-Islam* al-Ghazzali.

It is in this context that Bro Mubaashir offers the following Argument:

> "The debates between the Mutazilites and the Asharites were not about whether Allah was a human being or not, they were about whether Qur'anic statements referencing Allah's hand, foot, etc. should be accepted on face value (literally) or understood as metaphorical. So, Imam Hanbal and the others argued that Allah has a hand and a foot and a throne, *but that no human's eyes can*

> *see His hand, throne, foot,* etc. *Imam Hanbal would argue* that Allah has a hand, but His hand does not look like your hand. *He would cite* the hadith:
>
> 'Narrated Ibn 'Umar: Allah's Apostle said, "On the Day of Resurrection, Allah will grasp the whole Earth by His Hand, and all the Heavens in His right, and then He will say, I am the King." Abu Huraira said, 'Allah's Apostle said, Allah will grasp the Earth..."'
>
> "But, Imam Hanbal *would tell us* that Allah has a hand, *but we can't see* or comprehend Allah's hand that will hold the earth and skies and *it is certainly not a human hand.* The Mutazilite would argue that Allah does not have a hand at all; that this Qur'anic reference is a metaphor for Allah's power and control. Imam Hanbal was concerned about preserving the integrity of the text of the Qur'an so that translators and interpreters would not substitute their interpretations for the actual words used. *He was not trying to prove that Allah was a man or human being. If that was his point, he would have said so.* He was a scholar, prolific muhadith, and teacher. Surely, he could have and would have made this clear. *But, you cannot find anywhere where Imam Hanbal argued that Allah is a human being.*" [End Quote; emphasis mine]

I must admit that I was taken aback after reading this. I can't believe that, had Bro Mubaashir been familiar with my published works, he would have advanced this particular argument. I am humbled to be one of those who are forcing a reevaluation of the Aqida of Imam Ahmad and its place within the development of Sunni Islam. I have three published articles in peer-reviewed academic journals on the subject, and I go into great detail regarding this matter in my doctoral dissertation, all of which are freely available at www.drwesleymuhammad.com. The fact of the matter is, Bro Mubaashir completely misrepresented the position of Imam Ahmad here. It is not his fault though: most Muslim scholars today do. Because the religion of the non-Arab converts dominates Muslim thinking today, it was found necessary to posthumously "convert" important early figures to this religion, including the proud Black Arab and staunch antagonist of this religion, Imam Ahmad ibn Hanbal. But of all of the Four Imams, his Aqida is best known to us because there is a wealth of material going back to Imam Ahmad himself. So we don't have to engage in such unwarranted speculation about what Imam Ahmad "would have said," as Bro Mudaashir felt free to do above. We need only quote Imam Ahmad himself. On the basis of this wealth of material we can make the following affirmations with no fear of contradiction: 1.) Imam Ahmad affirmed that Allah is a delimited (*mahdud*) being who literally has a human-like form, after which Adam's form was patterned 2.) This human form *can* be seen with human eyes and 3.) Allah appeared to the prophet in this human form as a man.

1. Imam Ahmad Ibn Hanbal affirmed that the God of Prophet Muhammad is physically delimited (*mahdud*), though His divinity, power, and knowledge know no limit. Ibn Abi Ya'la, in his important text on the Hanbali madhhab, ***Tabaqat al-Hanabila*** [I:267] reports: "Muhammad b. Ibrahim al-Qaysi said: I said to Imam Ahmad b. Hanbal: 'It is quoted from Ibn al-Mubarak that it was said to him: How do we know our Lord - the Mighty and Majestic? He said, "Above (*fi*) the heaven, upon (*'ala*) His Throne with *hadd* (limit, demarcation)." So Ahmad said, "This is how it is with us".' Imam al-Dhahabi in his *al-Uluww* (p.152 of its *Mukhtasir*) affirms: "This is *sahih* (authentic) from Ibn al-Mubarak and Ahmad, may Allah be pleased with him."

This physically delimited Allah according to Imam Ahmad has a human-like form. According to a sahih report, the Prophet declared: *khalaqa Allah Adam 'ala suratihi*, "Allah created Adam according to His form" (Bukhari, 8.74.246; Muslim, *birr*, 115; Ibn Hanbal, *Musnad*, II:244, 251, ect.) This report was controversial in Ibn Hanbal's day and beyond. Some scholars read the possessive pronoun "His" (*hi*) of "His form" as "his," *viz.* Adam's form. That is to say that God created Adam in Paradise in the same form that he, Adam, had when he was sent to earth. In other words Adam wasn't a giant in Paradise and then shrunk as some had claimed. On the other hand other scholars read "His form". The famous hadith scholar Abu Muhammad b. Qutayba (d. 889) explained: "God possesses an actual form, though it is not like other forms, and He fashioned Adam after it" (Quoted by Ibn al-Jawzi, *Kitab Akhbar al-Sifat*, 271). This was the position of Imam Ahmad. This hadith played a significant role in his Aqida. He reports it countlessly in his ***Kitab al-Sunna*** and invokes it in his published creeds. He states in his *Kitab al-Risalah li-Ahmad*, "God created Adam with His hand and in His form," and in *'Aqīda* IV the Imam argues: "Adam was created in the form of the Merciful, as comes in a report from the Messenger of God..." This is from the report of Ibn 'Umar: "Don't make your face ugly, because Adam was created according to the form of the Merciful." See: Ahmad b. Hanbal, ***Kitab al-Sunna*** (Mecca: al-Matba'at al-Salafiyya, 1349 H) 56; idem, *Musnad* (Beirut: Mu'assasat al-Risalah, 1993) 12:275, #7323; 12:382, #7420; 15:371, #9604. Imam Ahmad rejected the exegetical devices that read 'his form' rather than 'His form.' When asked about Abu Thawr's (d. 854) statement that "he (Adam) is according to the form of Adam, He is not according to the form of the Merciful," Ibn Hanbal responded: "He who says that God created Adam according to the form of Adam is a *Jahmi* (disbeliever)"(Ibn Abi Ya'la, ***Tabaqat***, I:309).

For the Imam of Baghdad, to deny that God truly had a human-like form is *kufr*. Thus, the "hand, foot, ect," *contra* Bro Mubaashir, was indeed a human-like hand that "looks like your hand," because it was part of Allah's human-like form after which Adam's was patterned.

2. Imam Ahmad affirmed, *contra* Bro Mubaashir, that this human-like hand and the human-like form to which it was attached can be seen with the physical eyes (*ta'ayana*; *bi-l-'absar*;

see his *Al-Radd 'ala l-Ẓanadiqa wa l-Jahmiya*, 20 and Ibn Abi Ya'la, ***Tabaqat***, 29). Listen to his words directed against the Jahmiyya and others who deny that Allah can be seen with the eyes:

> "Why do you deny that those in Paradise will look at their Lord? They (the Jahmiyya) replied: 'It is not proper for anyone to look at his Lord. A thing looked at is passible and qualified. Things are only seen by refraction.' [We replied:] 'Does not Allah say...*Looking at their Lord* (Q 75:22)?'...They replied, 'Allah is not seen in this world or the next,' quoting one of the ambiguous verses (*mutashabihat*) where Allah says *Vision comprehends Him not, but He comprehends all vision* (Q 6:103). But the Prophet, who knew what Allah meant, said: 'You shall surely see your Lord'. And Allah said to Moses: *You shall not see Me* (Q 7:139), but He did not say, 'I shall not be seen'. Who then is more deservedly followed: the Prophet who said, 'You shall surely see your Lord,' or Jahm (ibn Safwan) who said, 'You shall not see your Lord'?" (*Al-Radd 'ala l-Ẓanadiqa wa l-Jahmiya*, 112-113)

There is absolutely no warrant in the materials available attesting to Imam Ahmad's Aqida for Bro. Mubaashir's attribution to him of the belief that "no human eyes can see His hand, throne, foot, etc." Ibn Hanbal in several of his available creeds was adamant that Allah had a human-like form that can be and will be seen with human eyes.

3. And this visible, delimited God with a human-like form appeared to the Prophet as a man, according to Imam Ahmad. An important report for Imam Ahmad's understanding of Allah was the *hadith ahsan sura* or report of Allah's Beautiful form.

> Abu Amir < Zuhayr b. Muhammad < Yazid b. Yazid b. Jabir < Khalid b. al-Lajlaj < Abd al-Rahman b. 'A'ish < some of the Companions of the Prophet:

> One morning, the Messenger of God went out to them (his companions) in a joyous mood and a radiant face. We said [to him]: "Oh Messenger of God, here you are in a joyous mood and a glowing face!" "How could I not be?" he answered. "My Lord came to me last night under the most beautiful form (*fi ahsan sura*), and He said [to me]: 'Oh Muhammad!' –'Here I am, Lord, at Your order!' He said [to me]: 'Over what disputes the Exalted Assembly?' –'I do not know, Lord.' He posed [to me] two or three times the same question. Then He put His palm between my shoulder blades, to the point where I felt its coolness between my nipples, and from that moment appeared to me [all] that is in the heavens and on the earth...'" etc

Imam Ahmad reported the *hadith ahsan sura* in his *Musnad* with four different *asanid* or chains of transmission (I:368, IV:66, V:243, V:378). He left no room to doubt also that this *ahsan sura* of Allah in which he appeared to Muhammad was a human form. His son, Abd Allah Ibn Ahmad, quotes a very important piece of *tafsir* from his father, Imam Ahmad:

> "[Abd Allah said]: My father (Ibn Hanbal) reported to me...from Abd al-Rahman b. al-'A'ish from some of the companions of the Prophet: "He came out to them one morning while in a joyous mood and a radiant face. We said [to him]: 'Oh Messenger of God, here you are in a joyous mood and a glowing face!' --'How could I not be?' he answered. 'My Lord came to me last night under the most beautiful form, and He said [to me]: "'O Muhammad!'..." And my father (Ibn Hanbal) reported to us, 'Abd al-Razzaq from Ma'mar from Qatada [from the Prophet], "Allah created Adam according to His form." My father reported to us, 'Abd al-Razzaq from Ma'mar from Qatada, "'in the best stature (*fi ahsani taqwimin*)' meaning 'in the most beautiful form (*fi ahsani suratin*)'." Ibrahim b. al-Hajjaj reported to us, Hammad

> (b. Salama) reported to us...that the Prophet said, "Allah is beautiful and He loves beauty." (Ibn Hanbal, *Kitab al-Sunna*, 159)

The implication of this collection of traditions is unmistakable. The "most beautiful form" is first identified with that form of God according to which Adam was created. This identification is further supported by the Imam's interpretation of *Surat al-Tin,* "Surely We created man in the best stature (*fi ahsani taqwimin*) (95:4)." Ibn Hanbal accepts the *tafsir* or exegesis of Qatada identifying man's "best stature" with God's "most beautiful form." Because Adam was created according to God's own form, this identification is logical. It is then affirmed that God is physically beautiful (the sense of the word *jamil* is unequivocal: it is about physical, material beauty). Thus, God's most beautiful form, in which he came to the Prophet, is the beautiful human-like form after which Adam's best stature or shape was patterned.

But this is not all. According to Imam Ahmad, Allah came to the Prophet not just in a human-like form, *but as a man.* Important to Imam Ahmad was the *hadith al-Shabb* or report according to which Allah came to the Prophet as a young man. *Shabb* is a young man of intermediate age. This is reported on the authority of four companions, including the *Tarjuman al-Qur'an* himself, Abd Allah ibn Abbas. This latter is the one Imam Ahmad affirmed and made binding on a Muslim's faith. He affirmed the following report: "Qatada < Ikrima < Ibn Abbas < the Prophet: 'I saw My Lord Blessed and Most High as a young man, beardless, on him a red/green garment'." Imam Ahmad argued in his *Aqida III* that one of the fundamental principles of the Sunnah (*usl al-sunna*) is:

> To have faith in the Beatific Vision on the Day of Judgment…and that the Prophet has seen his Lord, since this has been transmitted from the Messenger of God and is correct and authentic. It has been reported from

> Qatada, from Ikrima, from Ibn Abbas…And the hadith, in our estimation, is to be taken upon its apparent meaning (*ala zahirihi*), as it has come from the Prophet. Indulging in *Kalam* with respect to it is an innovation. But we have faith in it as it came, upon its apparent meaning, and we do not dispute with anyone regarding it."

In his *Aqida V*, Imam Ahmad argued that, "Belief in that (*hadith al-shabb*) and counting it true is obligatory" for Muslims. Thus, the definer of early Sunni orthodoxy has made obligatory and a fundamental principle of the Sunna belief in the literal significance of the reports of the Prophet's encounter with Allah as a man. This is why in his madhhab "man (*shabb, shakhs*)" was an appropriate term for Allah, supported by the *Akhdar* or narrations from the Prophet. Thus, Bro Mubaashir's claim that "you cannot find anywhere where Imam Hanbal argued that Allah is a human being' is simply off the mark.

Imam Ahmad was the champion of the Islam of the "Black Sheep" or Black Arabs against the distortions of the "White Sheep" or Persian and Byzantine converts. The God of *this* Islam was unquestionably anthropomorphic and was indeed a man, just not the type of man that Bro Mubaashir and others assume to be defining for the category (see below). It is demonstrable that Bro Mubaashir is unfamiliar with Imam Ahmad's works and is therefore unqualified to speak on his Aqida. Yet he does just that, and with such authority as to give one pause. He even felt confident enough to tell us what the great Imam of Baghdad *would have said*! This diminishes credibility. While I still maintain that Bro Mubaashir is an excellent representative of Imam W.D Mohammed and his *tafsir*, he has proven incredible (i.e. un-credible) as a representative of the Classical Arabic/Islamic tradition.

II.] *Misrepresenting the Qur'an and Sunna*

Unfortunately, the same conclusion is forced upon us with regard to Bro Mubaashir's representation of the Qur'an and Sunna. He claims that both give "proof" that Allah can't be seen (is invisible) and is not a man. But when we examine the Arabic texts upon which his confidence is based, we find that they do not at all say what Bro Mubaashir has them say. But let me be clear: I don't blame Bro Mubaashir for these theological interpretations that infringe upon the philology of the Arabic texts. He is merely following the received or so-called orthodox reading. But therein lies the problem. This 'orthodox' reading of the Qur'an and Sunna is that of the White Sheep who introduced it into Islam long after the time of the Prophet. Just because it is 'orthodox' and popular today does not make it authoritative. We are demonstrating that the Islam of the Prophet and the other Black Sheep was fundamentally different from the Islam of al-Ghazzali (White Sheep) and those who defer to him in matters of aqida.

1. Invisible Allah?

Bro Mubaashir claims that "you can't see" Allah. He bases this claim on two pieces of evidence: his reading of Surat al-An'am [6]: 103 and the famous Hadith of Jibril. Regarding the first he says: "Sura 6:103 states clearly that no vision can comprehend or perceive Him, but He comprehends and perceives all things." Those who engage the Qur'an in Arabic and are sensitive to the philology of this text, know well that this is a very mischievous use and translation of it by our Beloved Brother (or those from whom he learned this use and translation). The Arabic reads: *Lā tudrikuhu 'l-absār wa huwa yudrik 'l-absār*, which literally translates as: '(Physical) vision [*al-absār*] comprehends Him not, and He comprehends vision'. The first bit of mischief is in the translation offered by Bro. Mubaashir: no vision can comprehend *or perceive* Him. Bro. Mubaashir (or whoever) added "*or perceive* Him" no doubt because they knew that the term used in the Qur'an, *adraka* (comprehend), does not make the point they want to make – that God can't be seen or perceived (*absara*) by the eyes (*al-absār*). The verse only denies that eyes *adraka* God, not that they *absara* Him. What does this mean?

The Arabic term *adraka/yudriku/idrāk* has the basic meaning 'to overtake, catch up with' and implies a sense of ultimacy (see Lane). This is why Classical Sunni *tafsir* equated *idrāk* in this verse with *ihāta*, 'encirclement, encompassment'. *Idrāk* is thus understood as a 'total seeing' versus *ru'ya* or *basar* which is understood as a general, limited seeing. Surat al-An'am [6]: 103 denies that the eyes can accomplish the former (*Idrāk/ ihāta*), not the latter (*ru'ya/basar*). Thus the Shafi'i scholar al-Nawawi (d. 1278) declared: "*idrāk* is *ihāta* and Allah Most High is not encompassed by vision (*ru'ya*). Hence, the text (6:103) furnishes a denial of encompassment (*idrāk*). The non-encompassing *ru'ya* is not necessarily denied here (*Sharh Sahih Muslim*, 2:11)." See also Ibn Hajar (d. 1449), who stated: "the intent of the verse is the denial of encompassment (*ihāta*) of Him by means of seeing Him (*ru'ya*), not the denial of the theoretical basis (*asl*) of seeing Him (*Fath al-Bar*i 8:607)." The Hanafi qadi Ibn Abi al-'Izz (d. 1390) explained that "One can see Allah but cannot grasp (*idrāk*) Him, just as one can know Him but cannot comprehend Him (*Sharh al-'aqida al-Tahawiya*, 1:57)." The point of Surat al-An'am [6]:103 is therefore not that God can't be seen. The point is that seeing God with the eyes is not tantamount to comprehending His divine fullness.

Nor does Bro Mubaashir's use of the Hadith of Jibril make out any better. The relevant part for our discussion is the exchange between the Prophet and the Angel about *Ihsan*. Bro Mudaashir quotes it thusly:

"Inform me about al-Ihsan (performance of good deeds). He (the Holy Prophet) said: That you worship Allah as if you are seeing

Him, for though you don't see Him, He, verily, sees you.... (Sahih Muslim)"

Bro Mubaashir concludes from this the following:

"In this report the prophet tells us that you can't see Allah, but Allah sees you. This is consistent with the Qur'anic verse 6:103 that no vision can grasp Him, but His vision grasps all things."

This conclusion is wrong both with regard to this report and, as we saw, with regard to the Qur'anic verse. Nowhere in this report does it say Allah can't be seen. The Arabic reads: *an ta'buda Allah ka-annaka tarāhu fa-in lam takun tarāhu fa-innhu yarāka.* This translates: "It is to worship Allah as though you see Him, *and if (fa-in)* you see Him not, He truly sees you." This is yet another example of philology overturning theology, and the issue is a tiny syntactical point. The particle *in* means "if" even when preceded by *fa (fa-in)* . Bro. Mubaashir translates it "*though you* don't see Him," as if the Arabic uses the conjunction *wa-in*, which means "although, even if". "Though (*wa-in*) you don't see Him" implies a negation of seeing Him (though not a categorical negation). "And if (*fa-in*) you see Him not" implies no such negation; it is simply a conditional phrase.

Thus neither of the two evidences adduced by Bro Mubaashir supports his claim that Allah is invisible or can't be seen. This claim is supported only by theologically man-handling the Arabic in both the Qur'an and the hadith and making them say what they don't naturally. Nowhere in the Qur'an or Sunna is a formless, invisible God affirmed. These sources are twisted out of shape in order to impose this god on them. But as I have demonstrated in my writings, these sources actually affirm an anthropomorphic and visible Allah who has a beautiful human-like form after which Adam's form was modeled.

2. *Qur'anic "Proof" that Allah is Not a Man?*

The Qur'an does not explicitly affirm or deny that Allah is man. Such clarification was left to Allah's Prophet, Muhammad ibn Abd Allah, who did just that (see below). However, Bro. Mubaashir claims that in the Qur'an "Allah makes it plain…that He is not a man…" He says further:

Equally curious is the way that Dr. Wesley has tried to circumvent Allah's proof in the Qur'an that He (Allah) is not a human being. In Sura 4:1 Allah says "O men! Reverence Allah who created you and your mate from a single soul and from them scattered like seeds countless men and women."

Sura 4:1 along with Surat al-Ikhlas (112) are the two "proofs" Bro Mubaashir alleges "makes plain" that Allah is not a man. I will address Surat al-Ikhlas in Part Two of this response.

The first verse of Surat al-Nisa' [4] reads: "O People (*Yā ayyuha al-nās*)! Reverence your Lord Who created you from a single Person/Soul (*nafs*) and created, of like nature, his mate and from these two scattered many men (*rijālan*) and women." Bro. Mubaashir apparently assumes this verse is a "proof" that Allah is not a man because here it is affirmed that Allah created *rijālan* (men) and *nās* (people). This is a very shallow engagement of the Qur'an that takes no account of its philological context.

Bro. Mubaashir is apparently unaware of the distinct connotations of the different words in Arabic for 'man'. To illustrate the relevance of this philological fact to our subject, allow me to cite the Biblical Hebrew example. Hebrew has five words (plus their derivatives) for man: *'îsh*, *geber*, *'ādhām*, *'enôš* and *mt*. The last two terms (*'enôš* and *mt*) connote human frailty and weakness and as such are never applied to God. It is a different story, however, with *'îsh* and *geber*. These two terms connote strength, kingship, and spirituality and the Hebrew Bible declares that God is this sort of man: Yahweh is an *'îsh* and *geber* or rather *gibbôr*, mighty man. The Book of Exodus states emphatically *YHWH ʿîsh milhāmāh*, "Yahweh is a man (*ʿîsh*) of war (15:3).

We find the same linguistic circumstance with Arabic. There are several terms for "man" or "human," each with distinct connotations. The general term for "mankind" or "human being" is *bashar*. This term derives from the verb *bashara* which means "to peal, scrap, shave off; to grate, shred." It also means "peal the hide or skin off". The noun *bashara* means external skin closest to the flesh (epidermis). It is thus a cognate of the Hebrew word *bāsār* "flesh". The Arabic term *bashar* thus indicates that human beings are 'fleshy' and it associates them with "scrapes". It also hints at humans as sexual beings: Form III of the verb means "to touch; to have sex with". We can understand why this term is never associated with God. In the Hebrew, God is a kingly, spiritual man (*ʿîsh/ gibbôr*) but He is emphatically disassociated from *bāsār* "flesh."

For related reasons the common term for man, *rajul*, would be disassociated from Allah, the Most High as well. The lexicons tell us that a *rajul* is specifically an adult male from among *bashar* or human beings (See Lane s.v.). The "lowness" of this designation is inherent, as it is related to "feet". The verb *rajala* means "to go on foot" and *rijl* is foot or (lower) leg. Those familiar with Arabic culture and the taboo associated with feet therein understand immediately why this term would be inappropriate as a designation for God. The term *nās* may be derived from *nāsa, yanūsu*, "to hang down; to be in a state of commotion." Like *rajul*, the term *nās* is applied to both humans and jinn, which alone makes them inapplicable to Allah. That *nās* implies creaturely weakness is indicated by its derivative, *insān*, "human, man, person". In the same Surat al-Nisa' [4]: 28 it is written: "Allah wishes to lighten your (difficulties), for He created man (*al-insān*) weak (*da'if*)."

So Bro Mubaashir is right on this point: It is inappropriate to call Allah a *rajul* or *insān*: He is not *that* type of man. What type of man is He then? According to *hadith al-shābb* which was authenticated by Imam Ahmad and many others (see my book, "Take Another Look"), Allah appeared to Muhammad as a *shābb*, which is a young man between the ages of sixteen and thirty-two. But the term has more connotations. The verb *shabba* means "he was raised or elevated", thus connoting height and elevation. *Shabba* means also "to kindle a burning fire" and "to appear bright and beautiful". All of these are appropriate for God and consistent with what we otherwise know of Allah.

Al-Bukhari, Muslim and Imam Ahmad report a hadith from the Prophet on the authority of the Companion Al-Mughira b. Shu'ba: "No *shakhs* is more jealous (*aghyar*) than Allah; no *shakhs* is more pleased to grant pardon than He; no *shakhs* loves praiseworthy conduct more than He." (al-Bukhari, ***Sahih, tawhid***, 20:512; Muslim, ***Sahih***, *li'an,* 17; Ibn Hanbal, ***Musnad*** IV:248). *Al-Mawrid* informs us that a *shakhs* is a "person, individual, man…" The term connotes "the bodily or corporeal form or figure or substance (*suwad*) of a man," or "something possessing height (*irtifa'*) and visibility (*zuhur*)." A *shakhs* is literally a man with a body and height. It too implies elevation, which is fitting for the Most High. The verb *shakhasa* means "He rose or became elevated." The Arabic syntax of this hadith indicates that God is a person or man with a physical body, but an elevated man.

Thus, *contra* Bro Mubaashir, Surat al-Nisa' [4]:1 in no way "proves" that Allah is not a man: it only suggests that He is not a *rajul* or *insane*. According to the Prophet, Allah is a *shakhs* and *shabb.*

III.] *Conclusion Part I*

This concludes Part I of my response to my Beloved Brother Mubaashir. He said so much in his review of my lecture that is worthy of note and engagement, but it will take me two parts to address the most important aspects. In Part II I hope to address his discussion of Surat al-Ikhlas (112) and Surat al-Shura [42]:11, along with some other matters.

What I hope was clearly demonstrated in this Part I is that, while Bro Mubaashir presumes to juxtapose and contrast my claims with the Qur'an itself, what he really did was juxtapose my claims with his own claims for the Qur'an, NOT the Qur'an itself. His reading of the Qur'an is *eisegesis*, not *exegesis*. He read his theology into the Qur'an and Sunna, but in order to do so he had to manhandle the texts, disregarding their philology. The Qur'an NOWHERE describes Allah as a formless, invisible something; nor does the Sunna. Nor do they offer ANY "proofs" that God is not a divine man. On the contrary, the Sunna – which we know *clarifies* the Qur'an – clearly and unambiguously presents Allah as a divine man with a divine human-like form. This was the God of those Black Arabs who first embraced the message of Islam. The God on whose behalf Bro Mubaashir is arguing – that formless, invisible god – is in fact the god of the White sheep – those non-Arab (Persian, Byzantine) converts who supplanted the position of the Black Sheep and changed the religion. Nevertheless, I love my Brother Mubaashir. Despite what I have said here, his erudition is undeniable. I have tremendous respect for his mind and an honored to be able to engage him on this most important subject.

To Be Continued

Salaam
Bro Dr Wesley Muhammad

3.] Dr Wesley Muhammad - Response to Bro Mubaashir Uqdah - Part II

I am sincerely thankful for this opportunity to dialogue in the best of manners over such an important topic – *tawhid* –

with such erudite and, most importantly, sincere and honorable brothers, Bro Mubaashir and Imam Salim Mu'min. I appreciate the cordial and non-accusatory spirit in which they welcome my views and engage them, even though not everyone viewing and commenting on this exchange shares this spirit. In this regard I must correct something I said in my previous post (Part I). When challenging Bro Mubaashir's presentation of Imam Ahmad's aqida, I suggested that he was 'misrepresenting' the Classical Arabic/Islamic Tradition. Likewise, in challenging his reading of the Qur'an and Sunna, I suggested that he was guilty of 'misrepresenting' these. 'Misrepresent' was an unfortunate choice of terms, as it implies the intent to mislead. I do not at all believe this term, with that implication, applies to my brother Mubaashir. I believe he sincerely represented these as best he could with what he has been blessed to know. The problem with the 'representation' of these sources that he provided is not him – he faithfully articulated the orthodox representation. The problem is with the authors of this orthodoxy; the ulema of Mecca and Medina, Cairo and Tehran, and throughout the Muslim world, many of whom have indeed consciously misrepresented the Tradition and its sources. I humbly apologize to my brother Mubaashir for this mischaracterization of his intentions.

I must, unfortunately, offer a second apology. I thought I could conclude my Response in two parts. However, as I re-read Bro Mubaashir's Review, there is just so much in it worthy of discussion, and more importantly there is so much there that compels a response. I therefore had to delay my response to his discussion of Surat al-Ikhlas (112) and Surat al-Shura (42):11 until Part III, because the arguments he presented in his Argument 2 section must be addressed.

With that being said, it appears that Bro Mubaashir failed to comprehend my arguments as laid out in that Philly lecture. This is evident, for example, in his "Argument 2,", where he suggests that the "basis" of my claim that Prophet

Muhammad's (s) God had a body and was a man was hadith reports mentioning God's hands, face, feet, throne, etc. This is not the case, however. While I do mention the *Ayat al-Sifat* or Qur'anic verses that make mention of Allah's face *(wajh),* eyes *(ayn)*, two hands *(yadayy)*, ect., I did not hang my argument on these. And while I did cite the Abd Allah report from the Prophet concerning al-Dajjal and his one eye, versus Allah's eyes, I did not cite it as evidence that Allah is a man but as one piece of evidence of the Prophet's own *tafsir* of the *Ayat al-Sifat*. More on this below. No, the reports upon which I relied to make the case that Allah has a human-like form (*sura*, not *jism*) specifically mention Allah's form, *sura*. I mentioned the famous *sahih* hadith in which the Prophet declared: *khalaqa Allah Adam 'ala suratihi*, "Allah created Adam according to His form" (Bukhari, 8.74.246; Muslim, *birr*, 115; Ibn Hanbal, *Musnad*, II:244, 251, ect.). That the possessive pronoun *hi* refers back to Allah was affirmed by the Salaf. I quoted in Philly the great scholar Taqi al-Din Ibn Taymiyyah (d. 1358), who in his ***Naqd al-Ta'sīs***, 3:202 reports:

> "There was no disputation among the Salaf of the first three generations that the pronoun (*hi*/His) refers to Allah, and it is narrated via many isnads from many Companions. The contexts of the hadith reports all indicate this...(B)ut when the Jahmiyya became widespread in the third Islamic century a group began to say that the pronoun refers to something other than Allah...They were denounced by the imams of Islam and other ulema."

That this hadith indicates that Allah has a form after which Adam's was pattered was affirmed by many of the great ulema of the Classical Period, including Imam Ahmad (as we saw) and the famous hadith scholar Abu Muhammad b. Qutayba (d. 889) who explained: "That Allah should have a form is no stranger than His having two hands, fingers and eyes...God possesses an actual form, though it is not like other forms, and He fashioned Adam after it."

My argument was also based on the authenticated reports according to which Allah came to the Prophet in a most beautiful human form. I quoted and discussed there the *sahih* hadith:

Mu'adh b. Hisham < Hisham b. Abi 'Abd Allah < Qatada < Abu Qilaba < Khalid b. al-Lajlaj < Ibn Abbas: The Prophet said: "I saw my Lord in the most beautiful form (*fi ahsan suratin*). He said to me: 'Oh Muhammad! – 'Here I am, Lord, at your order!' He said to me: 'Do you know over what the Sublime Council disputes?' – 'No, Lord, I don't know that.' Then he put his hand between my shoulder blades, to the point that I felt its coolness between my nipples…" (Ibn Hanbal, ***Musnad***[1], 5:243; al-Tirmidhi, ***Jami' al-Sahih***, 9: 106ff, #3288; al-Suyuti, ***Tafsir al-Durr al-manthur***, 7:203.)

Now my argument is based on more than these, but time permitted a discussion of only these in my lecture in Philly. The rest of my arguments are laid out in my book.

Regarding Bro Mubaashir's response to what he presents as my argument, there are three points that I would like to address here. He says,

"As a follower of Imam Waarithud-Deen Mohammed, it is important that I point out that we have been taught that the Qur'an is the number one source of our guidance and is the criteria by which we judge the validity of all knowledge, including the reports (hadeeth) of what Prophet Muhammad said and the debates between scholars. I would also note that students of Imam Mohammed do not accept hadeeth at face value, even Sahih hadeeth, *without first sifting them through the lens of the Qur'an*"

It must be mentioned in this regard that 1.) Bro Mubaashir *did* invoke hadith (*viz.* the Hadith of Jibril) to make a theological point (i.e that Allah cant be seen) and 2.) as I have demonstrated in Part I, it is not the "lens of the Qur'an" through which Bro Mubaashir sifts hadith and views my claims; it is demonstrably the lens of his own ideology through which he read the Qur'an and Sunna and judges my arguments. And while this is perfectly natural and even inevitable – we all to some degree read these sources from our own theological perspective– it is important to call it what it is, his interpretation of the Qur'an, and desist from calling it what it is not, the "clear" position of the Qur'an itself. This is ever more urgent because I have, I believe, demonstrated that his interpretations of the Qur'an and Sunna are not consistent with the Arabic philology.

Bro Mubaashir then advances the following 'rebuttal' of what he has erroneously presented as my argument

> "Allah says in Sura 17:89, 'And We have explained to man, in this Qur'an, every kind of comparison, similitude, parable: yet the greater part of men refuse (to receive it) except with ingratitude!' This, and many verses, tell us that you will find parables, comparisons in the Qur'an and that the purpose of these parables, similitudes, comparisons is to explain things to men and women. If Allah uses parables and comparisons to teach, isn't it reasonable to recognize that His prophet would use parables and comparisons to try and teach the people also? That is common sense, isn't it?
>
> "When the Prophet tells his people that Allah will hold all of the heavens and the earth in His right hand, do you really think he is talking about Allah's human right hand? Do you really believe that Prophet Muhammad is suggesting that Allah's hand is a human hand like Master Fard's or his own and that He will use it to hold the skies and the earth? Isn't it more reasonable and intelligent to reason that he is making a parable to give the people an idea of the vastness and greatness and bigness of Allah, whom they cannot grasp with their vision? We can't see the bigness of Allah, so the prophet

gives us a parable in terms the uneducated Arabs could understand.

"Doesn't that explanation make more sense than trying to figure out how a human being standing on a corner in Detroit or Chicago is going to grow his hand so that it can hold the sky and earth while he is standing on the corner? Maybe he has to levitate into outer space and then grow his hand to hold the earth and sky. Which understanding makes better sense?" [End quote]

In responding to this Response, I must first point out that this last statement is an example of the 'straw-man argument' that I suggested Bro Mubaashir engaged in. Who in the NOI – certainly not me – would suggest that the significance of these verses is a cosmically huge divine hand and, in order to relate these verses to Master Fard Muhammad, assume that while he is standing on some urban corner or levitating in outer-space his hand will enlarge? Come on, Beloved. The Science of the Truth of God (Tawhid) is much more sophisticated and intellectually appealing than that.

But Bro Mubaashir's main point here is that such anthropomorphic references in the Qur'an and Sunna are purely parabolic, having no real existence themselves. He seeks to strengthen this proposition by appealing to his ideas of what is reasonable. Besides the fact that in most cases the use of parabolic or even metaphorical language in general does not seek to deny the real existence of the elements used in the parable or metaphor (i.e. it is not the hand that is non-literal, it is the picture of the hand clutching the heavens and earth that is non-literal or metaphoric), this proposition finds little support in the Qur'an and Sunna itself. This is a point well made by Imam al-Juwayni (d. 1047) (or someone in his name) in his *Risala fi ithbat al-istiwa' wa al-fawqiyya* ("Epistle on the Afiirmation of (God's) Establishment (on) and Aboveness (over the Throne)"):

> "When I studied the Book of Allâh and the Sunnah of His Messenger sallallâhu 'alayhi wa sallam, I found in them texts pointing to the reality of these meanings (i.e. the Sifat). I found that the Messenger sallallâhu 'alayhi wa sallam clarified that which came from His Lord, as well as describing Him with them. And know - without any doubt at all - that he sallallâhu 'alayhi wa sallam used to have present in his noble gatherings the Scholar and the ignorant person, the one with sharp intelligence and the not so sharply-intelligent, the Arab and the non-Arab. However, I did not find anything by which he followed-up such texts with which he used to describe his Lord neither with another text, nor with anything that would cause the meanings to be removed from their (real meaning), or cause ta'wîl to be made of them… And I did not find that he sallallâhu 'alayhi wa sallam used to warn the people from having îmân (faith) in what was apparent in his speech describing his Lord, whether it was concerning al-Fawqiyyah (Allâh being above His creation), or al-Yadayn (the Hands of Allâh), or other than them. And there is nothing recorded from him which proves that these Attributes have another inner meaning, other than what is apparent from their meaning ..."

That nowhere in the Qur'an or Sunna is there the slightest evidence that the Prophet intended the Sifat mentioned in these verses and reports to have a significance other than their apparent one is a point made as well by al-Ghazzali himself, in his *Iljām al-Awām an Ilm il-Kalām* ("Bridling the Common Folk Away From the Science of Theological Speculation"). But al-Juwayni (or Pseudo-Juwayni) makes another important observation above: "I found that the Messenger sallallâhu 'alayhi wa sallam *clarified* that which came from His Lord." This is exactly the point I made in Philly and my reason for citing the Abd Allah report from the Prophet concerning al-Dajjal and his one eye:

> "Narrated by Abd Allah: Al-Dajjal was mentioned in the presence of the Prophet. The Prophet said: 'Allah is not hidden from you; He is not one-eyed,' and pointed with his hand towards his eye, adding, 'While Al-Masih Al-Dajjal is blind in the right eye and his eye looks like a protruding grape'."

The point of this hadith for me was/is the Prophet's physical gesture (i.e. pointing to his eye) to clarify what he means by 'eye'. There are several such reports. See e.g. the hadith reported on the authority of Abu Hurayra and found in Abu Dawud's *Sunan*:

> "[Abu Yunus] said: I heard Abu Hurayra recite the verse 'Surely God commands you to make over trusts to those worthy of them, and that when you judge between people, you judge with justice. Surely God admonishes you with what is excellent. Surely God is ever Hearing, Seeing.' Then he said: 'I saw God's messenger [when he recited these last words] put his finger on his ear, and the next finger on his eye.' Abu Hurayra says: 'I saw God's messenger, when he recited this [verse], he [so] put his two fingers'."

Ibn Majah reports in his ***Sunan***:

> "Ibn Umar reported: I heard Allah's Messenger (s) saying while he was on the pulpit, 'Allah the Compeller grasps His heavens and His earth in His Hand,' and the holy prophet closed his fist and began to close and open it."

These physical gestures made by the Prophet clearly suggest that his intent was for the descriptions to be taken in the physical sense. According to a tradition on the authority of Jubayr b. Mut'im and found in Abu Dawud, Ibn Khuzayma, at-Tabarani and others, God sits on the Throne like a man sitting on a leather saddle and makes it creak.

> "[Jubayr b. Mut'im] narrates: A Bedouin came to find the Messenger of God and said to him: 'O Messenger of God, the men are all in, the women and the children perish, the resources are growing thin, the beasts are dying. Pray then to God in our favor so it rains! We ask of you to intercede for us alongside God, and we ask of God to intercede for us alongside of you.' 'Unfortunate one!' answered the Messenger of God, 'do you know what you're saying?' Then he started to say *subhana llah*, and did not stop repeating it so long as he didn't see his Companions doing as much. Then he said [to the Bedouin]: 'Unfortunate one! One does not ask God to intercede alongside any one of His creatures! God is very much above this! Unfortunate one! Do you know who God is? (God is on His Throne, which is above His heavens, and heavens are above His earth,) like this'—and the Messenger of God put his fingers in the shape of a tent—*and it creaks under Him like the creaking of the saddle under the rider.*"

The Prophet compares Allah sitting on the Throne and making it creak to a man sitting on a saddled horse and making the saddle creak. The anthropomorphism is blatant. The Prophet's physical gesturing hardly allows us to see in this report anything other than a physical description of God's "establishment" on the Throne. This is equally true of the other reports. The Prophet's physical gesturing when mentioning Allah's Sifat is no doubt his own tafsir of these Sifat. This is likely the Prophet's "clarification" which al-Juwayni refers to above.

This issue of the significance of the verses and reports of the Sifat – literal or metaphorical – must be pursued further. To make his point that these are purely (which I assume he meant) parabolic or metaphorical, Bro Mubaashir quotes Sura 17:89.

However, most exegetes who make this same claim start with Sura 3:7:

> "He it is who has sent down to thee the Book: in it are decisive verses (*muhkamāt*); they are the foundation of the book: others are allegorical (*mutashābihāt*). Those in whose hearts is perversity follow the part thereof that is allegorical, seeking discord and searching for its hidden meanings, but no one knows its hidden meanings except God. And those who are firmly grounded in knowledge say: 'We believe in the book; the whole of it is from our Lord'; and none will grasp the message except men of understanding."

The foundation of the Book comprises *muhkamāt*, clear verses whose meaning is sufficiently known and therefore require no further explanation. In contrast to these, there is a smaller portion of the Book comprising *mutashabihat*, uncertain or doubtful passages whose meaning is open to two or more interpretations. The true significance of these is known only to Allah and they thus require further explanation.

The pressing question of course is to which category are the *Ayat al-Sifat*, and by extension the *Akhbar al-Sifat* or hadith references, belong? It is generally assumed today that these are from the *mutashābihāt* or doubtful verses and are thus *majāz*, "metaphorical". This means that the apparent meaning of such a verse is not be countenanced and its hidden meaning is found through *ta'wīl*, metaphorical interpretation (as advocated by Bro Mubaashir). So the Qur'anic references to Allah's hand, for example, do not mean that Allah actually has a hand: the term *yad* (hand) is but a metaphoric reference to Allah's grace. In contrast, among the *muhkamāt* or decisive verses whose apparent meaning is clear and obligatory are the allegedly 'anti-anthropomorphic' verses such as 42:11 ("There is nothing like Him"), declaring Allah's incomparability, and 6:103 ("Vision comprehends Him not"), declaring the inability of human eyes to comprehend God. These latter verses, we are told today, are not subject to *ta'wīl* but are to be understood according to their apparent (*zahir/haqiqa*) meaning.

While today this division of the verses (*muhkamāt* = allegedly anti-anthropomorphic verses/ *mutashābihāt* = anthropomorphic verses) is generally recognized and is even orthodox, in the Classical Period it was the mutakallimun or speculative theologians like the Ashariyya who adhered to this division. On the other hand, the Traditionalist Sunni scholars, that is to say the Sunni scholars (not just the Hanbalis) who privileged the authenticated reports over the so-called "rational arguments" of the mutakallimun, adhered to the exact opposite division: it is the allegedly anti-anthropomorphic verses that are *mutashābihāt* and therefore requiring further explanation, and the anthropomorphic references that are *muhkamāt* and therefore are to be understood according to their apparent meaning. For example, Imam Ahmad specifically identified the main proof-texts of the anti-anthropomorphist theologians – 50:16; 57:4; 6:103; 42:11 – as *mutashābihāt* (*Kitab al-Risalah li-Ahmad*; *Al-Radd 'ala l-Zanadiqa wa l-Jahmiya*). On the other hand, regarding the *sifāt khabariyyah* or Revealed Attributes (i.e. scriptural anthropomorphisms), they are *muhkamāt* and are therefore to be affirmed according to their literal meaning (*'ala zahirihi*; see Ibn al-Jawzi, *Manaqib Imam Ahmad*, 155; Ibn Hanbal, *usul al-Sunna*, in Ibn Abi Ya'la, ***Tabaqat al-Hanabila***, I:246). So too the famous Maliki scholar from al-Andalus, Yusuf Ibn Abd al-Barr (d. 1071), who said in his *al-Tamhid lima fi l-Muwatta min al-ma'ani wa l-asanid* (7:145): "The People of the Sunna are agreed in affirming all the Attributes which are related in the Qur'an and the Sunna, having iman (faith) in them and understanding them *ala l-haqiqa* (according to their apparent and real sense), not *ala l-majaz* (metaphorically)." While there are many such references that I could cite to prove that the Traditionalist scholars understood the Sifat as *muhkamāt* and therefore possess literal significance, I will conclude with the important statement of al-Ashari (d. 935) himself, the one to whom, ironically, the latter Ashariyya and today's orthodox look. He says in his, *al-Ibāna 'an usul al-diyāna*, 89, 93-94, while articulating the position of the People of the Sunna regarding the Sifat against the deniers of their reality:

> "If it is asked, 'Do you believe God has two hands?' the answer is: We (the People of the Sunna) believe it, and His words 'the hand of God was over their hands,' and His words 'before him whom I have created with My two hands,' are a proof of it; and also, it is related, on the authority of the Prophet, that he said, 'God rubbed Adam's back with His hand and produced from it his offspring,' and therefore the existence of the hand is proved...Since God addresses the Arabs only in their language and what He reveals is understood in their speech and comprehended in their converse, and in the language of careful speakers one may not say, 'I have done something with my two hands' meaning 'grace', it is untrue that the meaning of His words 'with My two hands,' means 'grace'...If anybody says, Why do you deny that His saying, '*Do they not see that We have created for them what Our Own Hands have created* (36:71)' and His saying '*Whom I have created with my Own Hands* (38:75)' are *majāz* (metaphorical), the answer is: The ruling concerning the Word of God, the Mighty and Majestic, (regarding these verses) is that they are to be taken in their apparent/literal (*zāhir*) and real (*haqīqa*) meaning. Nothing is to be transferred from its literal meaning to a metaphorical one, except by proof...Likewise, Allah's words 'before him whom I have created with My two hands'. Its literal/apparent (*zāhir*) and real (*haqīqa*) meaning is affirming two hands. It is thus impermissible to alter (these words) from the literal meaning of 'two hands' to that which our opponents

> claim, without proof…Consequently, His saying 'Whom I have created with My Own Hands' must be proof of God's possession of two hands in reality (*haqīqa*), and not 'two graces'."

The point of this particular discussion is therefore this: Bro Mubaashir's suggestion that the *sifāt khabariyyah* are *majāz* and therefore have no literal reality in God is true to today's orthodox position on the matter, but in the Classical Period it was the position of the speculative theologians, in particular the Ashariyya, who were deemed *unorthodox* until late in the Medieval Period (ca. 13-14 century). What's more, the available material for the Prophet himself gives no warrant for this position and in fact contradicts it. If, while discussing the Ayat/hadiths mentioning Allah's hand, I moved my hand to illustrate the point, or I pointed to my eye when discussing Allah's eyes, Bro Mubaashir would likely judge me a gross anthropomorphist who is imposing a crude interpretation on the Ayat and ahadith. But what do we do when it is the Prophet himself who offers such a "crude interpretation"? Do we explain away his interpretation? It would be most inappropriate to do so.

This does not mean that these verses and reports don't use non-literal language to convey a bigger point, as Bro Mubaashir correctly suggests. But as in most uses of metaphor, while the overall point is non-literal (Allah won't *actually* hold the earth and the heavens literally in his hand) the elements deployed in the metaphor do have actual existence: just as the earth and heavens are real, so too is Allah's hand.

In conclusion, I would like to quote the Persian Hujjat al-Islam himself, al-Ghazzali. While it is largely his views of God and his rationalizations for this view of God that inform the orthodox view today, he himself confessed that the Prophet nowhere spoke of this god. I discussed this quote in Philly, but it does not appear that Bro Mubaashir was able to follow my argument (no doubt due to my own failure to clearly articulate my point). In his important treatise, ***Iljām al-awām an ilm il-kalām*** ("Bridling the Common Folk Away From the Science of Theological Speculation") the Persian Proof of Islam quotes the arguments of those who believed in an anthropomorphic deity against the mutakallimun who, like al-Ghazzali, affirmed an omni-located, bodiless god. He says:

> "So if it is said (by the believers in an embodied god): "Why did he (the Prophet) … not say [regarding God]:

- He exists, (but) is not a body (jism),
- nor a substance (jawhar),
- nor an incidental attribute ('arad),
- nor is He inside the universe, nor outside of it, nor attached to it, nor separate from it,
- and He is not in a location (makān),
- nor is He in direction (jihah), rather all the directions are devoid of Him.

> "For this is the truth with a people (i.e. the speculative theologians), and it is possible to express that (belief) in this manner [using these words] just like the speculative theologians have expressed it. And there is no shortcoming in [the Prophet's] (sallallaahu alayhi wasallam's) expression, nor any laxity in his desire to reveal the truth, nor any deficiency in his acquaintance (knowledge)." [End of Quote]

The believers in an embodied Allah take the mutakallimun to task here: given that the Prophet Muhammad was in no way lax in terms of his desire to propagate the full truth as he knew it; though he had no intellectual deficiency that would have limited the truth as far as he possessed it; though he lacked nothing in terms of linguistic and semantic facility that would have precluded his clear articulation of the truth as he knew it; why did he not affirm the bodiless, omni-located god to whom he (al-

Ghazzālī) and the speculative theologians were calling the people? Simply put, the anthropomorphist interlocutors ask: why is there no evidence that the Prophet taught the people to believe in the same god to whom you (mutakallimun and al-Ghazzali) are calling the people? (Note: this is not a rhetorical question from me, as Bro Mubaashir assumes. This is an actual argument advanced and which al-Ghazzali addresses in a most informative fashion). Now, one would expect al-Ghazzali to respond with: "Well, the Prophet DID inform the people of this god, and this is where…" How does he in fact address this objection? He says:

> "We say [in response]: Whoever considered this [i.e. what the Mutakallimun are upon] to be the reality of the truth has explained it thusly: ***That if he (the Messenger) mentioned [the above, i.e. the omni-located and bodiless god], the people would have fled from its acceptance, and they would have hastened to reject (it), and they would have said: 'This is completely impossible', and they would have fallen into rejection (al-ta'tīl)…*** And the Prophet (sallallaahu alayhi wasallam) was sent as a caller unto the creation [inviting them] to the bliss of the Hereafter, as a mercy to all of creation. ***How can he speak with that in which there is the destruction of the majority?*** Rather, he was commanded not to speak except at the level of the people's intellects."[End of Quote]

Why didn't the Prophet, fully capable of affirming the truth of this bodiless god, actually do so? Because, al-Ghazzālī claims, the Prophet was commanded by God to speak "only at the level of the people's intellects." Because the people to whom the Prophet was sent were not intellectually capable of grasping this 'truth' and therefore would have rejected this god as an impossibility and thus rejected Islam, the Prophet withheld the truth of the incorporeal god! It is not necessary here to deconstruct al-Ghazzālī's elitist and condescending presumptions regarding the masses of the Muslim followers of the Prophet (i.e. the Black Sheep!). It is enough to emphasize that al-Ghazzālī here clearly admits that the 'Islam' of which he is said to be the 'Proof' is NOT the Islam that the Holy Prophet articulated, at least the god of his Islam is not the God which the Prophet called the people to! This is a critically important confession that agrees with the observation of (Psuedo-) Imam Juwayni quoted above: nowhere in the sources for the Prophet's teaching is there evidence of this immaterial, formless god.

Peace and, unfortunately, To be continued
Bro Wesley

www.truthofgodinstitute.com

4.] Muhammad Abdur-Rahman - Response to Dr Wesley Muhammad

As Salaamu Alaikum,

Dr. Wesley Muhammad, It seems to me that you have done a great amount of research and I can really appreciate your due-diligence. Nevertheless, you are presenting us with these hadiths that has no relevance of G-d being a man in the Qur'an. When Allah makes mention of His Hand, Tree, Animals, Ants etcetera. These are languages that speak in metaphor, and a metaphor is the concept of understanding one thing in terms of another.

A metaphor is a figure of speech that constructs an analogy between two things or ideas; the analogy is conveyed by the use of a metaphorical word in place of some other word. For example: "Her eyes were glistening jewels". Metaphor is or was also occasionally used to denote rhetorical figures of speech that achieve their effects.

So, Dr. Wesley Allah's "Hand" is the hand that controls, and handles everything"! Let's take a look at this verse in the Qur'an whereas Moses is asking to "see G-d."

Surah 7 Ayat 143:

> When Moses came to the place appointed by us, and his lord addressed him, he said: "o my lord! Show (thyself) to me, that I may look upon thee." Allah said: "by no means canst thou see me (direct); but look upon the mount; if it abides in its place, then shalt thou see Me." when his lord manifested his glory on the mount, he made it as dust. and Moses fell down in a swoon. When he recovered his senses he said: "glory be to thee! To thee I turn in repentance, and I am the first to believe.

The meanings of Ayat 143:

And when Moses came at Allah's appointed time, that is, the time at which Allah had promised to speak to him, and his Lord spoke with him, without any intermediary, with speech which he heard from all directions,Moses said, 'My Lord! Show me, yourself, that I may behold you!'Allah Said, "You shall not see Me, but look upon the mount; if it abides in its place, then shalt thou see Me." The mount never did abide in it's place, so therefore [he] knew at that moment that he was confronted by someone [more] powerful than himself, and BIGGER than mankind, therefore Moses fell out! that is to say, you do not have the power to see me. I don't know about you? but that is telling me and others that G-d cannot be seen and He is beyond our comprehension.

When you find yourself associating something or someone with the Creator of the Heavens and the Earth, then that is definitely

Shirk! Let me give you the definition of Shirk, so that it's not just thrown out their without any knowledge.

Shirk- Associate; Partner; be sharer. Making association or partner with G-d

When Imam Mubaashir stated; "As a follower of Imam Waarithud-Deen Mohammed, it is important that I point out that we have been taught that the Qur'an is the number one source of our guidance and is the criteria by which we judge the validity of all knowledge, including the reports (hadeeth) of what Prophet Muhammad said and the debates between scholars. I would also note that students of Imam Mohammed do not accept hadeeth at face value, even Sahih hadeeth, without first sifting them through the lens of the Qur'an."

That is to say; the Qur'an is our first source, contact, reference before we go to any other book for clear understanding! A hadith is a saying of Muhammad or a report about something he did. Over time, during the first few centuries of Islam, it became obvious that many so-called hadith were in fact spurious sayings that had been fabricated for various motives, at best to encourage believers to act righteously and at worse to corrupt believers' understanding of Islam and to lead them astray. Since Islamic legal scholars were utilizing hadith as an adjunct to the Qur'an in their development of the Islamic legal system, it became critically important to have reliable collections of hadith. While the early collections of hadith often contained hadith that were of questionable origin, gradually collections of authenticated hadith called sahih (lit. true, correct) were compiled. Such collections were made possible by the development of the science of hadith criticism, a science at the basis of which was a critical analysis of the chain of (oral) transmission of the hadith going all the way back to Muhammad.

These debates are indeed healthy, because how else will we send falsehood to its proper place. As the Prophet Muhammad (SAW) taught us as Muslims:

Volume 8, Book 73, Number 135: Narrated Abu Huraira:

Allah's Apostle said, "The strong is not the one who overcomes the people by his strength, but the strong is the one who controls himself while in anger."

So a Muslim should always keep his anger in check. I know it is hard, but when we become angry we lose our senses and this makes us unfit to defend Islam as we are not thinking properly. So what should we do in the face of such attacks against our religion? The answer is extremely logical; we must study our religion so that we will be able to defend it. How can we defend our religion when we do not even know much about it? Thus, if Muslims want to do something about it then they should start learning about this faith (Al-Islam) and therefore we can engage into these healthy debates.

Surah 17 Ayat 81 And say: "Truth has (now) arrived, and Falsehood perished: for Falsehood is (by its nature) bound to perish."

Surah 21 Ayat 18 Nay, We hurl the Truth against falsehood, and it knocks out its brain, and behold, falsehood doth perish! Ah! Woe be to you for the (false) things ye ascribe (to Us).

So all we need is the truth (Al-Qur'an) and we do have the truth. All we must do is reveal the truth against the falsehood and the falsehood shall crumble and fall apart.These points are crucial for a Muslim to understand because if there is no wisdom in defending the religion, then the religion shall never be defended and the false accusations shall continue to be spread against the true religion of Islam.

Muhammad Abdur-Rahman

5.] Imam Salim Mu'min -Response to Muhammad Abdur-Rahman

If there was a possibility of seeing then the particle laa would be used [in Sura 7:143]. The particle Lan is used to deny from the time speaking into the future. Meaning you do not see me now and you will not see me in the future. In other words you wil never see me. If i say laa tarnee then you are saying that you do not see me as we are speaking, but there is a possibility of you seeing me in the future. It makes it just as impossible when spoken as it does now because we are in the future of the spoken word. It was not possible then and it is not possible now. Then we must come to the conclusion that Allah can't be seen physically, mentally, or spiriutally. Only that we come to the conclusion of Allah by inference of His creation, i.e. the mountain. That is the conclusion of Abraham in his search for Allah, and others. They studied the creation and in doing so that did not become subject to the creation like our universities have, but they realised that there has to be a creator behind all of this. That is why you can't read the Qur'an and come away saying this is Allah or that is Allah. If you can read the Qur'an and the second reading becomes open to you, you will agree with the Qur'an that only Allah has the ta'weel. Ta'weel comes from the word meaning first. Allah is the first authority on the writing of the Qur'an and the Creation. And man has not reached the conclusion of the transcending message of the Qur'an. Therefore those who are well grounded in knowledge will declare that it is from Allah. No man wrote this, and no man created this, and Allah does not have to reveal himself in the person of a man to prove His existance. It is on the pagans who see scripture in its physical form and take it as the reality that need a man shown to them as Allah. This is not new for man on earth. And to make him a Black or White G-d is only a mythological scheme to help elevate a people out of the dark condition that they are in. The light is on, we are no longer in "Black Bottom of the Motor City." Meaning we are not ignorant people that are only moved by motor reflex.

6.] Imam Salim Mu'min - Respnse to Dr Wesley Muhammad Response Part II

Allah is not tauheed. Tauheed suggests the coming together of many parts to become one. It is in the second form. Allah is not the coming together of many parts. The tauheed is in the creation and Allah is not creation. The creation, though it appears diverse it has its unity, that is it comes together as one within its many parts. I do not have to elaborate if you know Arabic. All of the verses of the Qur'an has its explicit meaning and its implied meaning. We have the two readings. The second reading becomes transcending, that is the ta'weel is only known by Allah. Many minds have not been unlocked for the second reading, especially the anthropormophist and those of empirical thinking. You need Allah's help to open for you the second readings. Most of the world including the Muslim world have an anthorpormorphic conception. That is why they came up with titles such as Khalifa, Mahdi, and others to say that a man is bigger than all other men that he must have a divine presence, and go as far as to say he is G-d himself. We dont need to go to the anals of Islamic writings to find this kind of thinking, go to any Egypt, major city and you will find the pagans. You can have your reading on the first level but it is the second reading that is much better. Most of the followers of Imam W. Deen Mohammed and Minister Farrakhan are too sensitive to debate whether Fard Muhammad is G-d or not. That's why Dr. Westley has to deflect. He is not ready to scrutinize the teachings of Fard Muhammad and the Honorable Elijah Muhammad in comparison to the Qur'an. I am ready to take verse by verse of the Qur'an from the Arabic text and compare it to the teachings of Fard Muhammad to prove that Fard Muhammad did not write the Qur'an and He is not the G-d of the Qur'an. Let's start with Al-Fatihah. The Qur'an is the best argument for us or against us. So let me know when you are ready to start. Otherwise I will continue to watch and appreciate your research.

7.] Dr Wesley Muhammad - Response Part III, Section I

As-salaam Alaikum Dear Family

In this the final part (itself divided into two parts) of my response to Bro Mubaashir's review of my lecture, I would like to first reiterate my appreciation for this discussion and its participants. It was long overdue and, despite the objections of some, it is productive and of great value, I sincerely believe, for the future of Islam in America. Before addressing Bro Mubaashir's comments, I feel compelled to respond to some comments made by other participants to this discussion, in particular Bro Muhammad Abdur-Rahman and Bro Imam Salim Mu'min. Bro Khalid Abdullah Islam's rants about cognitive disorders I won't dignify with a response.

Bro Imam Salim has said:

"Allah is not tauheed. Tauheed suggests the coming together of many parts to become one. It is in the second form. Allah is not the coming together of many parts. The tauheed is in the creation and Allah is not creation. The creation, though it appears diverse it has its unity, that is it comes together as one within its many parts. I do not have to elaborate if you know Arabic."

Well, Beloved, I do know Arabic. And while elaboration on your statement is not necessary, justification for it is. As I read it I was reminded of the early Sunni principle: *takyīf* in negation is as erroneous as *takyīf* in affirmation. That is to say, it is as errant to say how Allah is NOT without clear textual support as it is so say how He is without such support. Your statement is an articulation of your own theology, which is fine as far as that goes. But no longer can such idiosyncratic theologies be conflated with the Qur'an itself or masquerade as true Islam' and be set up as the criterion by which all other readings of the

Qur'an are judged. That charade is over. For example, why is your understanding of Tawhid and its relation (or not) to Allah to be preferred over, say, that of Imam Ahmad b. Hanbal? In rejecting a claim not too different from yours made by the Jahmiyyah of his day who claimed that he and his Traditionalist Sunni colleagues were polytheists because they affirmed the literal reality of Allah's many anthropomorphic Attributes (Sifāt), Imam Ahmad said in his ***al-Radd ala l-zanadiqah wa l-jahmiyah***:

> "By saying that Allah was ever-existing in all His qualities, are we not truly describing the one God in all His qualities? We gave the following example: Tell us about the palm tree. Is it not made of stump, stem, fibre, foliage, leaves and pitch, and for all its attributes has it not one name? Likewise, Allah, who is to be compared to what is loftiest, is one God in all His qualities…And again, Allah referring to an infidel called al-Walid b. al-Walid b. al-Mughira al-Makhzumi, said: 'Leave me to deal with him who I created, one (*wahid*) (Q 74: 11)' The one so named had eyes, ears, a tongue, lips, hands, feet and many members, and is yet named 'wahid', all his qualities notwithstanding. Likewise, Allah, who is to be compared to what is loftiest, is with all His qualities one God."

The Islam of this paradigmatic Black Sheep included an understanding of Tawhid that could accommodate an anthropomorphic deity with all of His anthropomorphic 'parts'. Forgive me Bro Salim if I am inclined to privilege his understanding of Tawhid over yours. It's not personal, just academic.

Bro Imam Salim further opines:

"All of the verses of the Qur'an have their explicit meaning and implied meaning. We have the two readings. The second reading becomes transcending, that is the ta'weel which is only known by Allah. Many minds have not been unlocked for the second reading, especially the anthropomorphists and those of empirical thinking. You need Allah's help to open for you the second readings."

What is your proof, Beloved, that your's is one of the minds so "unlocked" by Allah so as to know the implied meanings and thus to know that these negate the explicit meanings of the Ayat al-Sifat or verses mentioning Allah's anthropomorphic Attributes? With due respect, there is a lot of pontificating here. So those of us who strive to think empirically are especially those with locked minds? Oh, I thought this was M.A.L.I., the Muslim American LOGIC Institute? Did I make a wrong turn somewhere and stumble into the Muslim American DOGMATIC Institute? Or, less cynically, the "Muslim American Institute of Those Special Minds Unlocked By Allah In Contrast to the Fools Who Lock Their Minds Chasing Empirical Data"? And if the empirical data supports their anthropomorphist theology, this is but proof of the folly of empirical thinking? Wow. Really, Beloved?

Imam Salim says in conclusion, on a more personal note:

"Most of the followers of Imam W. Deen Mohammed and Minister Farrakhan are too sensitive to debate whether Fard Muhammad is G-d or not. That's why Dr. Westley has to deflect. He is not ready to scrutinize the teachings of Fard Muhammad and the Honorable Elijah Muhammad in comparison to the Qur'an. I am ready to take verse by verse of the Qur'an from the Arabic text and compare it to the teachings of Fard Muhammad to prove that Fard Muhammad did not write the Qur'an and He is not the G-d of the Qur'an. Let's start with Al-Fatihah. The Qur'an is the best argument for us or against us. So let me know when you are ready to start. Otherwise i will continue to watch and appreciate your research."

Sensitive? Please present evidence of this charge from any of my responses thus far. From what am I deflecting, Bro Imam Salim? If you have read my responses, you know that I deal directly with the Arabic Qur'an and Sunna. I don't understand your charge against me. On what basis do you judge me as "not ready" to scrutinize the Supreme Wisdom in the light of the Qur'an? Have YOU scrutinized my public works in which I do just that and have you found them demonstrative of my lack of readiness? If so, please share your findings with your brother that I may benefit from your, not erudition (forgive my previous insult!), but divinely unlocked mind. For the record, We in the NOI do not at all claim that Master Fard Muhammad wrote the Qur'an. No sir. Nor do I claim that HE is the God speaking in the Qur'an. It is my claim, however, that the God of the Qur'an is a divine man (shakhs). I thought we were already having the discussion about whether the Arabic Ayat of the Qur'an justifies or condemns this claim. You are free to join this ongoing discussion at anytime. You are right though: the Qur'an is the best argument. What I have been repeatedly pointing out, however, is that what you and Bro Mubaashir and others are juxtaposing to our claims is NOT the Arabic Qur'an itself but your own idiosyncratic reading of the Qur'an. I anxiously await your pointing out to me and us the Arabic Ayat that explicitly denies that Allah Ta'ala is a shakhs (elevated or divine man). If it is in Surat al-Fatiha, as you seem to suggest, I certainly missed it!

Bro Muhammad Abdur-Rahman, thank you for your contribution to this discussion. You made several points I would like to respond to. First, you raise the question to your a-alikes: "So what should we do in the face of such attacks against our religion?" implying that my part in this discussion is tantamount to an attack against YOUR religion. Let us be clear: I am not over here to attack or even discuss YOUR or anyone else's religion: I am here to discuss MY religion, which is Islam; the

Islam that Allah Ta'ala revealed to the Seal of the Prophets Muhammad b. Abd Allah and is codified in the Qur'an. That is NOT YOUR religion. Or rather, it is no more YOUR'S than it is MINE. We have divergent understandings of this religion and that is what we are discussing. But please don't anyone for a second assume you have ownership rights over this Islam that I don't have. You have ownership rights (and responsibilities) only over your particular understanding of the religion, as do I, mine.

Secondly, you state the following:

"You are presenting us with these hadiths that have no relevance to God being a man in the Qur'an. When Allah makes mention of His Hand, Tree, Animals, Ants etcetera. These are languages that speak in metaphor, and a metaphor is the concept of understanding one thing in terms of another."

Where is your proof, Beloved, that the Ayat al-Sifāt are metaphors? You have here, as is often done (e.g. Bro Mubaashir and Bro Imam Salim), made an assumption about Allah's word based on your own theological preferences, but offer no empirical evidence to justify that assumtion. You have the right to make such an assumption, but don't presume that I or we are contradicting the Qur'an because we reject your theological preference and the assumptions about the Qur'an that derive from it. Show in the Arabic Qur'an where Allah identifies the Ayat al-Sifat as mutashābihāt (ambiguous) and therefore as metaphors? Or, show me where the Prophet Muhammad identified these as metaphors that are not to be taken as literal representations of God. I have provided evidence indicating that the Prophet expected us to understand a REAL eye and a REAL hand, etc., when he recited the Ayat al-Sifat. What evidence has anyone here provided that can impeach or impugn the evidence I have provided? I have also provided evidence that it was the Classical Sunni (Traditionalist) position that the Ayat al-Sifat were in fact among the mukhamāt verses and therefore are to be understood according to their apparent meaning, not majāz or metaphorical. You chose not to address that evidence. Instead, as is often done, you chose to 'wax dogmatic' by insisting with no evidence that these verses are metaphors. Your case, Beloved, is totally unpersuasive. The hadith I cite are indeed relevant because, as Imam Ahmad and others have affirmed, "The Sunna clarifies the Qur'an." While the Qur'an is somewhat ambiguous – it neither explicitly affirms or denies that Allah is a man – the Sunna of the Prophet clears up that ambiguity: Allah is a divine man(shakhs) who is incomparable - laysa kamithlihi shay'.

While I do agree with you Bro Muhammad that the "Qur'an is our first source, contact, reference before we go to any other book for clear understanding," the issue here is what do we do when the explicit words of the Qur'an do not provide us with clear understanding? Your claim that "all we need is the truth (Al-Qur'an) and we do have the truth" is to be summarily dismissed. If, when you go to Juma' and, while making salat, do qabd (clasp your left hand with your right), why do you do this? Or, even if you are a Maliki or a Shiite who does sadl (hands held freely by the side while praying), where do you get these practices from? Not the Qur'an. The Book of Allah tells us to pray, but it never tells us exactly HOW to pray. The manner of our obligatory prayers derive almost wholly from the Sunna, either via hadith (e.g. qabd) or amal (the practice of Medinia - sadl). If all you had was the Qur'an, Friday afternoon in the masajid would look profoundly deferent than it does now. In fact, ISLAM would look profoundly different. So let us not act like we can easily dispense with the Sunna – you know well that we cannot.

Finally, you address the important aya in the Qur'an, *Surat al-A'rāf* [7]:143, which reads:

And when Moses came at Our appointed time and his Lord spoke to him, he said: "My Lord, show Yourself to me that I may look upon You." [God] said: "You can't see Me (*lan taranī*); but look at the mountain. If it remains in its place then you will see Me. So when his Lord appeared (*tajallā*) to the mountain He made it crumble and Moses fell dumbstruck on account of the lightning (*sa'iq*[an]). Then when he recovered, he said: Glory to You! I turn to You, and I am the first of the believers!

You presume Bro Muhammad to give us "the meaning of Ayat [7]: 143." How do you know this is the meaning? Are you, like Bro Imam Salim, one whose mind was "unlocked" by Allah and therefore have knowledge of al-Ghayb or the Hidden Things? Or are you basing your tafsir on a critical philological examination of the text? Or, dare I suggest it, neither of these? You explain to us:

"And when Moses came at Allah's appointed time, that is, the time at which Allah had promised to speak to him, and his Lord spoke with him, without any intermediary, with speech which he heard from all directions, Moses said, 'My Lord! Show me, yourself, that I may behold you!'Allah Said, "You shall not see Me, but look upon the mount; if it abides in its place, then shalt thou see Me." The mount never did abide in it's place, so therefore [he] knew at that moment that he was confronted by someone [more] powerful than himself, and BIGGER than mankind, therefore Moses fell out! That is to say, you do not have the power to see me. I don't know about you? but that is telling me and others that G-d cannot be seen and He is beyond our comprehension."

Your claim that this Aya means Allah can't be seen is, as Bro Elijah Shabbazz well pointed out, completely unjustified by the Arabic text. I was most surprised, however, to see Imam Salim, with all of his knowledge of Arabic, co-sign this reading and thus lend the weight of his Arabic learning to a reading that tortures the Arabic philology. But then, unfortunately, Bro Imam does the same thing when he claims:

"If there was a possibility of seeing (God) then the particle laa would be used. The particle Lan is used to deny from the time speaking into the future. Meaning you do not see me now and you will not see me in the future. In other words you will never see me. If I say laa tarnee then you are saying that you do not see me as we are speaking, but there is a possibility of you seeing me in the future. It makes it just as impossible when spoken as it does now because we are in the future of the spoken word. It was not possible then and it is not possible now. Then we must come to the conclusion that Allah can't be seen physically, mentally, or spiritually."

With due respect to Imam Salim, this is another clear example of theology impinging upon philology. First, I am at a lost to understand how one trained in Arabic could claim that the *Lā* of Absolute Negation, which negates categorically and absolutely, is less emphatic than Lan, which is an emphatic particle but of a different nature. Lan is a ta'bīd, which is an emphatic particle that does not express the sense of 'timelessness' as does, for example, words derived from the root 'zl (e.g. azal "eternity"). Thus, Lan has temporal or temporary significance, not eternal. The categorical negation that Imam Salim wants to read into 'Lan tarānī' is actually said thusly: Lā arānī "I am not to be seen," thus with the Lā of Absolute Negation. In order to make "Lan tarānī" a timeless categorical denial of the possibility of God being seen, it would have to be reworded as: lan tajūz an tarānī, "You can never see Me." Thus, Imam Ahmad, who knew Arabic well (he was a pure Black Arab) perceived the matter more accurately than does Imam Salim when he said to the Jahmiyyah:

"And Allah said to Moses: *You shall not see Me* (Q 7:139), but He did not say, 'I shall not be seen'. Who then is more deservedly followed: the Prophet who said, 'You shall surely see your Lord,' or Jahm (ibn Safwan) who said, 'You shall not see your Lord'?" (*Al-Radd 'ala l-Zanadiqa wa l-Jahmiya*, 112-113)

Philology MUST be freed from and privileged above theology!

In fact, *Surat al-A'rāf* [7]:143 is an explicit account of a theophany (a visual appearance of God). The Arabic is clear and unambiguous: *fa-lammā tajallā rabbuhu lil-jabali*, "So the Lord appeared (*tajallā*) to the mountain." The verb *tajalla* is Form V of the root j-l-w, "to appear, become manifest." It also carries the secondary meaning "He manifested His *Jalāl* (luminous Majesty)." The *sa'iqa* or 'lightning' that knocked Moses into a swoon is the destructive radiance emanating from God's *Jalal*, as the Maliki *faqih* (jurist) al-Qayrawani (d. 996) noted: "God…appeared to the mountain and it became leveled at His Majesty (*Jalal*)."Thus, al-Qadi 'Iyad (d. 1149) correctly notes in his classic text, *al-Shifa*, 104: "This verse…means that Moses saw Allah and that is why he fell down in a swoon…His manifestation to the mountain was His appearance to Moses so that, according to the statement (Q 7:143), he actually saw Him." The issue affirmed in this passage is NOT the invisibility of God but mortal man's inability to sustain a vision of His Majesty. As the important Hanafi Qadi Ibn Abi al-'Izz (d. 1390) observed in his *Sharh al-'aqida al-Tahawiya*: "We don't see Him in this life because our eyes are incapable of that, not because He cannot be seen. If someone tries to see the sun, he cannot, not because it cannot be seen but because our eyes are too weak."

Nowhere does the Arabic Qur'an claim that Allah is ontologically invisible. Nowhere does it declare that He is not nor can He be a man. These claims for the Qur'an are theological readings of the text that betrays the philology of the text. Bro Muhammad Abdur-Rahman and Bro Imam Salim are my family and I respect their intellect. I cannot, however, allow them to persist in masquerading their idiosyncratic theological readings of the Qur'an as the clear statements and perspective of the Qur'an itself.

8.] Muhammad Abdur-Rahman Response:

With Allah's name, The Merciful Benefactor The Merciful Redeemer

Dr. Wesley Muhammad you are absolutely right this is definitely not my religion, and that was definitely not the right choice of verbiage there on my part. So I will say for you Dr. Wesley, The Religion (Al- Islam) as stated by Allah in the Qur'an! This religion is universal, and the door has been open for all walks of life. So you do have just as much rights to engage into these practices and principles as anyone else for that matter. Now that I got that out the way, let's continue what is important that is troubling you and your constituents.

You said; I am here to discuss MY religion, which is Islam; the Islam that Allah Ta'ala revealed to the Seal of the Prophets Muhammad b. Abd Allah and is codified in the Qur'an.

First and foremost, the way that your presenting your ideology of G-d being a man is erroneous, and that is not what was revealed to Muhammad the Prophet (SAW). Matter of fact Dr. Wesley, the first commitment that a human being has to do before witnesses, is to bear witness to this faith. I'm curious Dr. Wesley, what did you say? If you forgot here it goes: I bear witness that there is none worthy of worship except Allah, the One, without any partner. And I bear witness that Muhammad is His Servant/Messenger and seal of the Prophets.

Ash-hadu anla ilaha illal-Lahu Wahdahu la Sharika Lahu wa-ash-hadu anna Muhammadan abduhu wa rasuluhu

Allahu la ilaha illa Huwa, Al-Haiyul-Qaiyum La ta'khudhuhu sinatun wa la nawm, lahu ma fis-samawati wa ma fil-'ard Man dhal-ladhi yashfa'u 'indahu illa bi-idhnihi Ya'lamu ma baina aidihim wa ma khalfahum, wa la yuhituna bi shai'im-min 'ilmihi illa bima sha'a Wasi'a kursiyuhus-samawati wal ard, wa la ya'uduhu hifdhuhuma Wa Huwal 'Aliyul-Adheem

[Surah al-Baqarah 2: 255]

"Allah! There is no god but He - the Living, The Self-subsisting, Eternal. No slumber can seize Him Nor Sleep. His are all things In the heavens and on earth. Who is there can intercede In His presence except As he permitteth? He knoweth What (appeareth to His creatures As) Before or After or Behind them. Nor shall they compass Aught of his knowledge Except as He willeth. His throne doth extend Over the heavens And on earth, and He feeleth No fatigue in guarding And preserving them, For He is the Most High. The Supreme (in glory)."

Dr. Wesley since you say you know Arabic please translate this! Especially La Sharika Lahu. Please don't try and dance around this one. Nevertheless, you probably will? Also, translate Ayat (sign) Al Kursi. Let's see where your intelligence takes you my beloved? I don't approach this as a game, nor am I trying to make mockery of anyone! I am simply trying to prick the conscience by speaking directly to the right!

Allah say's in Surah 2 Ayat 256

Let there be no compulsion In religion: Truth stands out Clear from Error: whoever Rejects Evil and believes In Allah hath grasped The most trustworthy Handhold, that never breaks.

When I said; "When Allah makes mention of His Hand, Tree, Animals, Ants etcetera. These are languages that speak in metaphor, and a metaphor is the concept of understanding one thing in terms of another."

This was me speaking in the literal sense, and not specifically addressing Ayat al-Sifāt ? That was you making a kneejerk reaction pertaining to that verse. However, I am not going to play your word games, because I really believe you know what's going on? However you probably don't (wise men/women always told me to never assume anything). Dr. Wesley, I really appreciate these debates and also your profound wisdom towards Al-Islam.

This is Bible, and it reads; It says that there was a man who could not read the book, because it was sealed/locked up! So he took it to one that could read it. Nevertheless, the man that could read it also replied; "I cannot read it, and I am locked out of it! Now the man that was "learned" he could read the words on the surface, but he could not read the words under the surface, which is the hidden (metaphorical, allegorical) meaning. So when G-d Almighty say's to those faithful and sincere believers; No one will be able to touch it! The word for "touch" is Mukhlasin and it comes from the root word Khalasa which means; To be pure, unmixed, alone, exclusive, sincere. So Al-Qur'an has been given to one pure and sincere (heart), and when you "get it" don't go mixing it with that which is impure! So, when you start putting your spin on what is not there, then ENOUGH/STOP because you are mixing your "thoughts or thinking" with that which is CLEAR/ PRECISE and UNMATCHED!

I'm going to use your words that you love saying; I cannot, however, allow YOU to persist in masquerading YOUR idiosyncratic theological readings of the Qur'an as the clear statements and perspective of the Qur'an itself. I love you Dr. Wesley in the path of G-d!

Muhammad Abdur-Rahman

9.] Dr Wesley Muhammad - Response Part III, Section 2

Finally, my Response to Bro Mubaashir regarding *surat al-Ikhlas.* I had hoped that I could also discuss Bro Mubaashir's comments regarding Surat al-Shura [42]11. However, time simply won't permit any more expenditure right now. I have one hundred mid-terms to grade by Monday. I must therefore refer anyone interested to an article I wrote on that very subject which can be found at:

http://drwesleywilliams.com/yahoo_site_admin/assets/docs/JAOS_Art_Body_Unlike.98120904.pdf

Bro Mubaashir says in his review of my comments in Philly:

> "Dr. Wesley addresses one of the challenges of the Qur'an, Suratul Ikhlas, where Allah states that He is One, He is the One on whom everything depends (As-Samad, which is sometimes translated as Eternal), He never had a child, He never was someone's child, and there is nothing equal to the One. *Dr. Wesley claims that the attribute or characteristic As-Samad doesn't mean eternal, but rather solid.* This meaning of As-Samad would lead to the translation that Allah is One, a solid whole. So, according to Dr. Wesley Allah is a solid and for something to be solid it must be delimited, which means that it is limited by boundaries; finite. Hence, Allah is a material thing, not an immaterial thing; He is a limited, finite thing, not an unlimited, infinite thing."

The first part of this quote is fairly accurate, though a tab bit misleading: I did (and do) present 'solid' as an alternative reading of al-Samad, but I did not just 'claim' this. See below. The second part of the statement is an unfortunate mischaracterization of my position as articulated in Philadelphia. While I do affirm that "Allah is a material thing (rather: being), not an immaterial thing," I do not affirm that "He is a limited, finite thing, not an unlimited, infinite thing." On the contrary, I understand that, though the Qur'an clearly presents Allah as a *shay'* which, by definition, is a physically delimited (mahdūd) being, I also understand that this physical delimitation (not limitation) does not imply any metaphysical limitations for Allah. He is unlimited is His divinity, power, wisdom, etc.

Bro Mubaashir then lists various meanings of Samad. This list is problematic in that he jumbles together definitions for the verb *samada* and the adjectival noun, Samad, giving no indication of their distinction. This can be excused though. Inexcusable, however, is what follows:

> "The reason that I have taken the time to list all of the possible meanings of the word Samad is to help us make it clear that you cannot just pick any definition you want to use for a word and say that is what it means, because you saw it in a dictionary... While it is fair to argue or debate the meaning of a word, it is intelligent to choose the word that makes the most sense and is most likely the correct meaning of the word for the sentence you are talking about. So, the task before us is to consider which of these definitions most likely applies to Allah, The Creator of the skies, the earth, and every single thing within; including you and I and Dr. Wesley. To save us all time, let us simply consider Dr. Wesley's *choice* of definition for As-Samad and the definition used by the majority of Muslims in the world. Dr. Wesley argues that because one of the meanings of Samad is a solid, not hollow, this proves that Allah is a solid, physical thing; a delimited being, a finite, solid material being, yes a human being. By *choosing* this meaning of the word Samad, he declares that the Muslim scholars have mistranslated this word as eternal in order to support their own definition of a non-physical, non-material G-d."

This is either pure disingenuousness on Bro Mubaashir's part, or a profoundly imperceptive reading of the case I presented in Philly. Everyone who has watched the lecture knows that I didn't simply "pick any definition you want to use for a word and say that is what it means, because you saw it in a dictionary." I supported my reading and why this is the preferred reading with important evidence from the Classical Arabic/Islamic tradition. Nor did I cherry-pick definitions. To present the reading "al-Samad=solid" as an arbitrary choice on my part and juxtapose it to "the definition used by the majority of the Muslim world" is unfair to the case I made and, further, it betrays a total lack of familiarity with the philological issues involved with this term or its exegetical history. Reading al-Samad in Surat al-Ikhlas as "solid" is not a "Dr. Wesley claim"; it is an early orthodox reading that no doubt goes back to the Prophet himself.

Bro Mubaashir seems to have relied upon Edward Lane's *Arabic-English Lexicon* for his discussion of al-Samad in surat al-Ikhlas. This is a very appropriate place to start, but it would have benefitted him greatly had he turned to the foundational Classical tafsir text for understanding this term, al-Tabari's (d. 923) *Jami' al-bayan 'an ta'wil ay al-Qur'an*. It is foundational because most of the later tafsir work done on this term relies and in many cases simply repeats aspects of al-Tabari's discussion. Had Bro Mubaashir checked this text, he would not (as least not in good faith) presented my reading ("solid") as a personal, arbitrary choice of mine, nor would he have presented the reading "Eternal" as that definition to which "the majority of the Muslim world" subscribes, unless he qualified this with "TODAY'S" Muslim world.

Al-Tabari presents, in quasi-descending (in terms of likelihood) sequential order, 25 exegetical reports about Al-Samad: the first 14 affirming that the term means "solid" or "not hollow," (*laysa bi-ajwaf/lā jawfa lahu*), and only the last two affirming that it means everlasting/eternal! The fact that the first 14 reports listed affirm the meaning "solid" and only the last two affirm "eternal" indicates that al-Tabari saw the former ("solid") as the orthodox reading and the latter ("eternal") as inconsequential. Most importantly, al-Tabari cites two hadiths which trace this reading to the Prophet himself:

> Al-Abbas b. Abi Talib < 'Umar b. al-Rumi < 'Ubayd Allah b. Sa'id < Salih b. Hayyan < Abd Allah b. Burayda < his father: he said: "I do not know about (this word), except that I asked the Prophet (s) who said: 'Al-Samad is the one who has no hollowness."

Al-Hasan al-Basri and Ikrima, two very prominent Successors, reported the same. This is the only explicit exegetical reading of this term cited by al-Tabari which is actually traced back to the Prophet himself. This is no doubt why many famous Companions and Successors affirmed this reading: Abd Allah b. Abbas, who is called the *Tarjuman al-Qur'an* himself ("Interpreter of the Qur'an"); al-Hasan al-Basri, Sa'id b. Jubayr, Mujahid, al-Dahhak, Sa'id b. al-Musayyib, Ikrima, etc.

The lexical support for this reading ("solid") is strong. Fakhr al-Din al-Razi (d. 1210), in his *Mafatih al-Ghayb 'aw al-tafsir al-kabir*, adds to al-Tabari's list two philological traditions; one from Qatada b. Di'amah (d. 735) that equates the root s-m-d with s-m-t, "of even composition and having no hollowness"; the second a lexicographical comment that samad is "the smoothness of a stone that admits of no dust and is impervious." Ibn Manzur (d. 1312), in his indispensible Arabic lexicon, Lisan al-Arab, informs us that the word samad denotes "the head of a mountain raised up in the sky as if it were a column," or "the high place of anything" or "the top of a rock sticking up from the surface of level ground (4:246)." Other formations of the root indicate the same: musammad = "solid (rock)"; samda/sumda = "rock firmly embedded in the earth"; samud = "solid (rock)."

The reading "Eternal", supported only by the last two traditions cited by al-Tabari, is a secondary reading of al-Hasan and Qatada, both of whom give "solid" as the primary meaning of the word. Al-Tabari's discussion therefore indicates that 'solid' was the orthodox reading of this term, and al-Ash'ari informs us that at the same time it was also the popular reading. In his *Maqalat al-Islamiyin* (p. 34) he affirms: "Many people say, "He (God) is solid," interpreting the word of God *samad* to mean solid, i.e., not hollow." That this meaning of al-Samad implied that Allah was a material being (jism) was pointed out by exegetical scholars, such al-Khazin (Tafsir [Cairo, 1930] 7:265) and Ibn Taymiyya (Tafsir surat al-Ikhlas [Cairo, n.d.], 59ff).

Thus, the lexical/philological evidences all indicate 'solid' as the meaning of the root s-m-d. The Classical exegetical and theological literature indicates that this was the orthodox reading during this period, and it makes clear the reason why: the Prophet himself affirmed this meaning. How, then, did we arrive at the situation that we have today where, as Bro Mubaashir correctly points out, the "majority of the Muslim word" reads this term as 'Eternal' and rejects the reading 'solid'? Islamist Franz Rosenthal, writing in ***The Joshua Starr Memorial Volume: Studies in History and Philology*** (1953), presented a philological study of this term and its history in recent interpretation. His words are very important here. Yes, he is a western scholar of Islam, which may cause some readers of this note to object prima facie. But I cite him only as an authority on the modern, Western treatment of this term, for this is quite relevant here. He says:

> "The treatment which the word (al-samad) has received in western scholarship can by no means be considered an exemplary one. As a rule, it is translated by 'eternal', a meaning of as-samad which is indicated by some Arabic sources, but which, though old, has never been credited with much authority...With the publication of A. du Ryer's French translation of the

> Qur'an in 1647, the translation of as-samad through 'eternal' found universal acceptance...the collected evidence makes it sufficiently clear that the fatuous 'eternal' has been the favorite of western translation since the seventeeth century. One of the contributing reasons for its persistence probably was the fact that 'eternal' was a plain and simple word."

Rosenthal is on the money here regarding the lack of authority which the Classical Arabic tradition accorded the reading 'eternal'. The sources confirm this. Important also is his documenting that the popular translation 'eternal' is actually a western convention that is based not on Arabic authority and which gained popularity due to such mundane issues as the simplicity of this translation! The modern Muslim world followed suit, and here my Beloved Bro Mubaashir is presenting it to us as "the correct meaning" which indicates that "Allah is not a limited solid," even though the philology of the term and the Classical orthodox position and the Prophet himself said it indeed meant solid. You see, Dr. Wesley did not "choose" this meaning: the Prophet did and the Classical tradition followed suit. I only presented this fact in Philly and drew my conclusions therefrom.

Bro Mubaashir next takes issue with my invoking, as a possible context in which to understand Q 112:3, the ancient creator-god of Kemet (ancient Egypt) called Min. I suggested in Philly that the fact that Allah is *lam yulad* ("not begotten") does not preclude His being anthropomorphic (possessing a human-like form). The Creator-god in ancient Kemet (Egypt) was an anthropomorphic black god called *Kamu-tef*, "Bull of His Mother" or "He Who is His Own Father." This epithet indicates that this god is *self-created*, i.e. *unbegotten*. This, I suggest, clearly demonstrates that *Surat al-Ikhlas* does not unambiguously or necessarily describe an incorporeal or bodiless deity.

But Bro Mubaashir objects to this exegetical invocation of this ancient Egyptian Black God. He says:

> "But, what about Dr. Wesley's argument that Allah is a self-created human being and that Allah as a man is different from man as a man? Dr. Wesley offers proof of such a being by pointing to a picture of a man from ancient Egypt who is referred to as a G-d who created himself, thus indicating that he needed no father... But, while Dr. Wesley seeks to prove his argument using the ancient Mystery system or other doctrines, Allah tells Muslims to judge all things by the criteria of the Qur'an. What Muslim would leave the proofs of the Qur'an and pick up another doctrine in an attempt to refute or avoid what the Qur'an clearly says? Sura 2:16 says they trade guidance for error, but they realize it not."

This response is problematic on a number of grounds. First, the disagreement between Bro Mubaashir and myself over this issue is NOT whether the Qur'an is the ultimate criterion of truth or not: we are both on that same page. Rather, the disagreement (from my perspective) is over whose understanding of the Qur'an is consistent with its philological and traditio-historical context and thus should be privileged. Bro Mubaashir speaks of my alleged "attempt to refute or avoid what the Qur'an clearly says," as if he has established (rather than just assumed) that Q 112:3 is a muhkam or clear verse and that he correctly understands the implications of its 'clear' meaning. Even if we grant that "He is unbegotten" is a clear statement – no one gave birth to Him - it does not follow that we necessarily understand exactly how this applies to Allah's divinity, nor does that mean that we can extrapolate from this ostensibly "clear" statement and make other non-Qur'anic claims about what Allah is or is not. Bro Mubaashir and others assume they can, but it is exactly these assumptions – not the Qur'an – that I am refuting.

What I have demonstrated with this example drawn from our Sacred Science of Kemet (not "paganism" as Imam Salim calls it) is the spuriousness of the operating assumption in this orthodox reading of this verse that, because Allah is unbegotten, this necessarily proves that He is not anthropomorphic. This assumption is shown to be a logical fallacy when the Qur'an is placed in its traditio-historical context, a context that includes the Sacred Science of Kemet. It is ironic that such an important intellectual from Imam W.D. Mohammed's community, Bro Mubaashir Uqdah, would take such objection to my invoking Kemetic Sacred Science to understand something in the Qur'an. It is ironic because it was this very community that produced the late Baba Rafiq Bilal (d. November 28, 2008) who co-wrote with Thomas Goodwin the groundbreaking book, "Egyptian Sacred Science in Islam: The Sacred Science of Ancient Egypt as revealed in Al-Islam (1987)." The great Professor Dr Wade Nobles, who wrote the forward to the book, says that it is a "thoroughly supported bridge between Islam and the Ancient Kemetic understanding of the most Holy of Holies." Despite my issues with some of the claims made in the work, it is a trailblazer and reflects most positively on the type of erudition that Imam W.D. Mohammed inspired in his followers. It is a travesty, in my opinion, that this work is not more well-known among that community, among the NOI, and among African American Muslims in general.

According to Bilal and Goodwin's research, "a serious study of the ancient religion of Egypt and the religion of al-Islam reveals the two to actually be different expressions of the same truths (p. 147)". The study of these two traditions convinced Bilal and Goodwin that:

> "God Almighty presented essentially the same truths to the pre-historic Egyptians who built the fabulous civilization upon the principles of the Sacred Revelation, as He presented thousands of years later to Prophet Muhammad Ibn Abd Allah in the Holy

> Qur'an. Holy Qur'an is the purification and refinement of this ancient system of knowledge. The truth from God is one truth. In order to convey the body of knowledge which they received, the ancient Egyptians developed the most elaborate educational system in the history of man. Prophet Muhammad, the unlettered Prophet (the Umi Prophet) received and transmitted the same body of knowledge through revelation many thousands of years later…"

Bilal and Goodwin document the nexus between the Qur'anic lexicon and historiography and Kemetic Sacred Science. They document that:

> "Within the pages of the Holy Qur'an, wrapped in the ancient Arabic language are preserved the following aspects of Egyptian history and sacred science (among others): 1: Concept of God, Nature and Knowledge…"

Bilal and Goodwin's discussion of the harmony between ancient Kemetic and Qur'anic notions of God is of particular significance to our dialogue. They write:

> "An examination of the earliest religious writings known to man, indicates that the original concept of monotheism was the Egyptian 'Neter of Neters,' or 'Great Principle,' or 'Great God'. This 'Neter of Neters,' is often described as 'unknowable' and 'unseeable [rather: unseen]'…In the earliest of texts, the archaic Egyptians give tribute to the 'Great God' from which all creation emanated. The principles which 'the Great God' created out of 'Himself' are then named and placed in their proper place in creation. In the Papyrus of Nes-Amsu, British Museum (no. 10,188) a rendering of the creation in the Book of Knowing the Evolutions of Ra and of Overthrowing Apepi illuminates the earliest monotheism. In it, the

> Great God…says: 'I am he who came into being in the form of the god Khepera and I was the Creator of everything which came into being; now when I HAD COME INTO BEING MYSELF, the things which I created and which came forth out of my mouth were very many…Heaven did not exist, and earth had not come into being and creeping things had not come into existence in that place and I raised them from out of Nu from a state of inactivity. I found no place there whereon I could stand. I worked a charm upon my own heart and I laid a foundation in Maat, and I made every form. I was One by Myself…there was no other being who worked with me'."

Bilal and Goodwin follow this up with a quote from the early Egyptologist E Wallace Budge affirming that 'Khepra', the name of a dung-beetle, symboliszed the Great God because, among other things, it represents the idea of self-production! Indeed, the idea of the Creator God, who was understood to be a divine anthropomorphic being, being self-produced was a prominent theme in this Kemetic Sacred Science. An inscription from the Theb. Tomb 157 reads: "O Ra who gave birth to righteousness, sovereign who created all this, who built his (own) limbs, who molded his (own) body, who created himself, who gave birth to himself." Whether you want to admit it or not, this is a perfect analogy to the God of the Qur'an AND the Sunna, who is anthropomorphic, indeed a divine man (shakhs), but who is also unbegotten, i.e. self-originated. This nexus between ancient Egyptian Sacred Science and the Qur'an documented by Bilal and Goodwin, as well as by the late great Cheikh Anta Diop, completely justify my decision to read Surat al-Ikhlas in the context of ancient Egyptian Sacred Science. I thus did not "leave the proofs of the Qur'an and pick up another doctrine in an attempt to refute or avoid what the Qur'an clearly says," as Bro Mubaashir alleges. Rather, I turned to an essential part of the traditio-historical context of the Qur'an itself in order to shed some light on what Qur'an says. And I make no apologies for doing so.

Bro Mubaashir then raises some philosophical objections to my argument. He says,

> "Think about it, what does it really mean to self-create yourself? First of all, if G-d is a man, a human being, where did he exist when he created himself? I mean, he would have to create himself, before he could create the universe and the earth with water and air so he could breathe. Did he float around in the abyss? I guess you could say that when he created himself, he created everything else at the same time. In this way, when he manifested, so did the earth, air, and water, so he had air to breathe and water to drink too. To say "he" created "himself' implies that "he" existed before creating "himself." The act of creation is an action and an action must have an actor or doer. Action cannot exist in a vacuum. Therefore, if "he" created, "himself" as a man, "he" already existed in order to create "himself." So, there is always something prior to that which is created."

While these are indeed relevant philo-theological questions, they are easily answerable. He is correct: if God 'created' Himself, He had to in some way have already existed in order to create Himself. This is consistent with both the Supreme Wisdom of the Hon Elijah Muhammad, who taught that Allah first existed as a 'force' within Triple Darkness, then He created His own Black body out of the matter of the pre-cosmic space; and the Sacred Science of Kemet, according to which the Great God first existed as a formless force and then, through His own Divine Will, created His own body. Where was He before He created the cosmos? The quote above from the Papyrus of Nes-Amsu provides a partial answer when it mentions:

> "Heaven did not exist, and earth had not come into being and creeping things had not come into existence in that place and I raised them from out of Nu (the abyss) from a state of inactivity. I found no place there whereon I could stand. I worked a charm upon my own heart and I laid a foundation in Maat…"

There was 'no place for Him to stand', precisely as Bro Mubaashir suggests, until He "laid a foundation" in Maat (whatever that might actually mean). Ironically, the Sunna answers this very question. According to a hadith on the authority of the Companion Abū Razin, found in Tirmidhi, *Jāmia' al-Sahih*, sura 11:1; Ibn Mājah, *Sunan*, 1, # 182; Ibn Hanbal, *Musnad* 12:17-20;and Tabari, *Tafsir*, 11:7, the Prophet was asked: "Where was our Lord before he created the heavens and the earth?" The Prophet replied: "He was in a cloud, with(out) air above him or below him. Then he created his throne on the water." This is a beautiful example of the convergence of Egyptian Sacred Science and Islam. May Allah be please with Baba Rafiq Bilal.

I await my Brother's responses.

Salaam

Bro Wesley

10.] Imam Salim Mu'min Response

Dr. Westley yes we are family and I am loving you more and more as you write. I will reply to this thread soon. I do have an engagement this weekend to prepare for, but i will respond. In the mean time think on what my Mama told me when i was a lil boy. She said, "Son if you put it in your head no one can take it from you. They may be able to lock your body up in prison but they can't lock up your mind once its free." Well, i guess im a Mama's boy.

11.] Dr Wesley Muhammad Response to Imam Salim Mu'min

Yes Sir Beloved. I sincerely love you as well and pray that we three can be instrumental in uniting the communties. This does not have to be unity on the basis of theological agreement. It can be untity on the basis of brotherhood/sisterhood and a common legacy going back to the Honorable Elijah Muhammad, and on the new basis of mutual respect for and respectful dissagreement with each other's interpretation of the Din. I know you love the Din, I hope you now know that I love the Din; this should be the factor that allows us to transcend our interpretive differences and unite unite the communities. I too must tend to other buisness as well now, so take your time.
Salaam

12.] Kyle J. Ismail -Response

ASA family, I've watched this conversation for weeks and have enjoyed being a part of the audience. I interject at this point mainly to say that I really love the dialogue that is taking place and also adab or decorum of the discussion. I hope that no one thinks less of me for being entertained at the lack of decorum in some instances :)...It seems that some of us believe that consensus can be reached via ridicule or mischaracterizing the views of others. Not only do I believe that this is not the method.....hoping to come to an agreement is also not the goal. The goal instead is deep empthetic and compassionate listening that causes all involved to grow. As a supporter of Imam Mohammed many of us have not involved ourselves in debates and discussion of this nature and quality. His presence was always enough to put an end to any need to debate with great vigor because we trusted him (may Allah have mercy on him). I'm encouraged to speak now also because I feel that such a conversation, if properly valued, can help bring our communities together as believers and as spiritual descendants of the hon. Elijah Muhammad. Truthfully we need it, both in Imam Mohammed's (r.a.) affliation and in the NOI.

This conversation is a reflection of how far we've come and how conversant we've become as students of quran, sunnah, and the classical tradition. Any time we engage in a public discourse on theology the process is more important than any specific goal – the goal to be closer to Allah (swt) and to one another (being that our relationship with Him is both vertical and horizontal). It doesn't take long to conclude (as nascent students of the classical tradition) that this argument is a very legitimate one. Anyone who's read anything of Ibn Taymiyya, ibn Qayyim Jawziyyah, and their leader Ahmed ibn Hanbal they indeed leaned in the direction of very conservative interpretations regarding how the text is to be approached and the arguments of immanence vs. transcendence emerged and re-emerged and I suppose will continue to as a part of what seems to be a historical dialectic in terms of how human beings see God in relation to themselves in society. What I appreciate most about the hon. Elijah Muhammad's conclusions about the nature of God is that he appreciated how inextricably tied together the notion of God to our social and anthropological realities. While Imam Mohammed dealt very deliberately with the notion of Fard being God (he engaged many things with nuance but he made haste in dealing with this concept) having had a tremendous amount of experiential knowledge he wanted to make a specific stand that he felt would connect us with Al-Islam proper. Dr Wesley I'm sure that you are aware that your ideas, and I believe them to be firmly within the boundaries of theological tolerance (to Borrow Ghazali via Dr. J), You may be creating some controversy inside the NOI because many of my friends within this org don't seem ideologically situated where you are. In any case I've gone on a bit longer than what I intended. I'd love for those who have participated in this conversation to blog about how we can come together as the spiritual heirs of Elijah Muhammad and get back on post for our community. – submissions@NewMuslimAmerican.com (on fb - http://www.facebook.com/NewMuslimAmerican). w/peaceSee More

13.] Nazim Abdul-Latif Response

As Salaamu Alaikum my brothers and sisters of this group. I am currently reading the book my our brother Imam Michael Saahir THE HONORABLE ELIJAH MOHAMMED: The Man Behind The Men". In the 8 on pages 131 to 134, Imam Saahir discusses how Imam W.D. Mohammed took on a role of striking a death nell to a racial superiority of supremacy with the CRAID movement. I think this is worthy of our reading. No, I am not at this time answering Qur'an with Qur'anic text per se. However, I am attempting to establish Qur'anic and prophetic inspired actions to solve real world problems.Racism and improper worship of Our Creator on this earth. He, I believe was taking the same type of actions as The Prophet Mohammed SAWS when went to the Ka'aba to destroy the idols.

For several years in the early 80's there was an independent effort undertaken by the Community of Our Beloved Imam, may Allah the Almighty Creator(lets not get it twisted) forgive him his sins and grant him the highest station of Paradise. We were calling ourselves The WCIW or the American Muslim Mission. This effort was targeting White Racism. However ,as Imam Saahir brings out in his book, it was also exposing so-called Black Racism in the cover of a White face. He shows how in the NOI theological doctrine g-d(the g-d of the Black man) is presented as a Caucasian or white appearing image. Fard Muhammad.

The CRAID Committee was, as many may or may not know, the Committee For the Removal of ALL Attempts to Portray Divine. The operative word is ALL for this conversation. I would print the entire section, but want to help him sell his book. So get the book. I didn't leave one form of spiritual oppression,Chistianity as taught today, to go to another form of worshiping White Jesus to White Fard. I accepted Al-Islam in 1975. I have an FOI uniform. But Imam W.D. Mohammed is my Imam that I gave Beyah to. I believe that this community has been in the hand(power and control)of the Creator since it's very beginning.

In his book he gives reference on page 132 to the MESSAGE OF CONCERN. This is still printed in the Muslim Journal today. Get the Muslim Journal to read it.

"Wallace's intellect set free by his parents to question and investigate all things, eventually became a freedom that questioned accepting W.D. Fard, a man as G-d.

He shows in his book a revelation , revelation with a small 'r' of Imam Mohammed at a May 2007 meeting of a select group religious leaders and educators at Wisdom University in Tulsa, Okla. This summit was entitled" Sacred Activism and the Power of Inclusion- A Heartland Summit. At this summit he relayed how as an adolescent he came to the conclusion that man , Fard, was not G-d. Get the Book.

Many Leaders in Christianity agreed with Imam Mohammed's CRAID message according to Imam Saahir in his book. He quotes a Rev. H. Edward Burton Pastor of St. James A.M.E. Church and makes a statement that is printed in his book. His statement is based on their churches understanding of their scripture.It is in the book.

My Dear believers, if we accepted the logic laid down by Dr. Wesley we would be in effect negating all of the progress made in the last 35 years. Associating partners with our Creator(being specific) is the highest form of oppression. We would be putting ourselves back into the womb of darkness after being brought out to a world of mental and spiritual freedom.

Performing intellectual gymnastic about any issue is good and maybe in some cases productive but let's be clear. Shirk is the one sin that can't be forgiven. Out of all of the sins that man can make . This one can't be forgiven unless the mushrik repents. And know that there are many forms of shirk. Well let's practice subtraction and not addition.

As Salaamu Aliakum
Your brother
Nazim

14.] Dr Wesley Muhammad Response

As-salaam Alaikum Family.

Thank you Bro Kyle for your thoughtful comments. I share your sentiment that the process of dialogue is more valuable than any prospective outcome, except that outcome is increased mutual respect and positive steps toward a unified community. This is the goal. For the record, I did not invest the time in this wonderful exchange hoping to "convert" anyone. I respect Bro Imam Salim's right to, as his dear mother admonished, hold on to that which he has in his brilliant head. If this dialogue changed not a single person's theology but helps to generate a new-found mutual respect among we followers of the Imam and followers of the Minister, then the time and effort was more than worth it. The Imam did a great service to Islam in America in general (as everyone in this group already knows), but he also did a great service to the reconstituted NOI (as I heard the Minister himself say). He forced us to reckon with the Qur'an and Sunna in a way and to such a degree that, without his work, I do not think we would have felt compelled to do. This has generated in those of us who have submitted to this compulsion, if you will, a love and appreciation for the Holy Prophet that was generally absent in the past. Allow me to offer a personal testimony. It was the way the Imam and his followers clung to the Qur'an, the Prophet and his Sunna – and the way some of them frequently bludgeoned us in the NOI with these sources - that inspired my immersion into the study of these sources. And it was this immersion that has engendered in me a sincere and profound love for the Qur'an, the Prophet and his Sunna. Having discovered through this study the harmony of the Supreme Wisdom with the Qur'an and Sunna was/is a tremendous blessing from Allah Ta'ala; I sincerely believe that it has forever freed us sons and daughters of the Honorable Elijah Muhammad from the anguish of having to "choose" the one or the other. I deeply love the Honorable Elijah Muhammad and the Supreme Wisdom, and I deeply love the Holy Prophet Muhammad and the Qur'an and Sunna. I am delighted today to know that I can legitimately – not schizophrenically – include myself in both the NOI and the Ahl al-Sunna! I claim the latter as passionately as I claim the former. I believe that this is a basis upon which the followers of the Imam and the followers of the Minister can grow in mutual respect and, ultimately, mutual love, for we both love the Honorable Elijah Muhammad and we both acknowledge the Qur'an as the criterion of truth and the Prophet Muhammad as the Seal of the Prophets; we can both acknowledge the beauty of his character and of his Sunna. It should matter little that we interpret these great sources differently. It seems to me that our mutual acknowledgment of and love for these sources is the adequate basis upon which to build unity and brotherhood/sisterhood. Am I overly optimistic? Dear Brother Nazim Abdul-Latif, I regret that you feel that accepting my "logic" will set this community back 35 years. My "logic" is that we no longer have to choose EITHER the Honorable Elijah Muhammad OR the Holy Prophet Muhammad. My "logic" is that we no longer have to choose EITHER the Supreme Wisdom that had the unparalleled impact on the lives of Black people in America, literally resurrecting us psychologically, intellectually, socially, economically and, yes, spiritually, OR the Qur'an and Sunna that had the unparalleled impact on the lives of Black people in Arabia (Arabs), literally resurrecting them psychologically, intellectually, socially, economically and, yes, spiritually. My "logic" is that we can actually cling to both WITHOUT being social schizophreniacs. This is a logic that will set the community back 35 years? I certainly hope not. Bro Muhammad Abdur-Rahman, I love you too in the path of Allah! I promise you, I am playing no word-games Beloved. I sincerely seek and appreciate honest, non-dogmatic investigation and discussion about OUR religion, Islam, and OUR book of guidance, the Qur'an. I would never waste mine or the people's time with any intellectual games. I believe Islam is THE healing for our desperately sick people. Every minute I spend in this work is inspired by this conviction. You and I simply have different understandings of the muhkamat and the mutashabihat in the Qur'an. But that's ok. Does this have to prevent our embracing each other as Brothers in the Faith? I hope not Beloved.

Salaam
Bro Wesley

15.] Muhammad Abdur-Rahman Response

With the Name of Allah, The Merciful Benefactor, The Merciful Redeemer

This dialogue has generated in me, for you a great amount of respect Dr. Wesley Muhammad. If I ever get the opportunity to meet you in person, I would like to embrace you with a BIG HUGE of love, honor and respect... It takes a lot of courage on your part to advocate what you love so dearly, and trust me it shows! This beautiful way of life (Al-Islam) is definitely a healing process for sick people (Heart/Mind), and you are right, they desperately need it. When I say that I love you, I really mean that! Your love for the Honorable Elijah Muhammad, The Noble Qur'an and Prophet Muhammad (SAW) is enough to acknowledge your wonderful contribution to this way of life. These debate/dialogues came by way of accident for me. Simply because I did not log into the M.A.L.I forum to debate, I logged into the M.A.L.I forum to click "like" that I read from my phone that Imam Salim had posted. Nevertheless, we respond to that by saying; Al-Hamdulillah for allowing this to happen. Now I know you, and now you know me (In a good way, but that is how the bounding begin). Although you and I may differ concerning the Mutashabihatun issues, nevertheless we are still bounded in brotherhood! I have nothing but respect for the Nation of Islam, and Min Anthony Muhammad, Demetric Muhammad here in Memphis, TN knows me very well. They can tell you Dr. Wesley Muhammad, we love each other. Matter of fact, we love each other so much, I have worked with Bro. Demetric Muhammad here concerning our troubled youths, and I have volunteered my position (Associate Imam) to give Jumu'ah Khutbahs at Mosque 55 on Friday's. The good thing about our debating is that we know that we can agree and disagree and still love one another, and that's how it should be my dear beloved.

Allah say's in Surah 16 Ayat 125

Invite (all) to the Way of thy Lord with wisdom And beautiful preaching; And argue with them In ways that are best And most gracious: For thy Lord knoweth best, Who have strayed from His Path, And who receive guidance.

These debates have definitely been with wisdom and beautiful preaching to say the least, and I really appreciated the Enlightenment. Love you again Dr. Wesley in the path of Allah!

Muhammad Abdur-Rahman

16.] Imam Salim Mu'min Response to Dr Wesley Muhammad

Bismillahi,

The negations:

There are two types of negations and perhaps three. One is to negate an act and the other is to negate the existence of something. Perhaps the third is to negate the state of being.

The first type of negation is to negate an act. There are particles of negation that are used with the verb to negate the act. The act may occur in the past, present or future.

To negate an act of the past we may use the particle 'maa.'
To negate and act as we speak and into the future we use the particle 'lam' with the present tense verb putting the verb in the jussive.

To negate an act in the present we use the particle 'laa.' Note: laa is not an absolute in this case.

To negate from the time of speaking into the future we use the particle 'lan' with a present tense verb putting the verb in the subjunctive.

The second type of negation is to negate the existence of something which is used with a noun.

To negate something in terms of its constitution 'maa' is used.

To negate the origin of something 'laa' is used. This is called the absolute 'laa.' It is used with an internal noun [masdar] and negates that that thing ever existed.

To negate something no longer existing but perhaps existed before we may use 'maa or laa.'

The third type of negation is to negate the state of being. This kind of negation is used to negate 'kaana.'

In this type, 'maa' is used with the verb 'kaana.' Also, if you want to strengthen the negation, the lam of juhuud is used with a present tense verb in the subjunctive.
Laisa is used with a noun to negate it state of being.

These are some examples of negations. So, to say the laa used with a verb is the absolute negation is erroneous. Laa used with a noun and putting the noun in the accusative without tanween is the absolute negation of the negation of the origin of that thing.

17.] Dr Wesley Muhammad Response to Imam Salim Mu'min:

ASA Bro Imam Salim. Thank you for this impressive discussion of the Arabic negative particles. The linguist in me loves discussions of Arabic grammar and syntax, and am therefore very appreciative of your post. I am sorry for the delayed response. I am a university professor with a full load this semester. Most of your post, while quite useful for our overall understanding of the Arabic negative particles, is not relevant to our particular discussion, i.e. whether Q 7:143 is a categorical denial of the possibility of Ru'ya (seeing God) or simply a specific and conditional denial directed at Moses. I therefore have nothing to add regarding most of your post. There are however a number of remarks that seem to specifically address my comments, and thus have a bearing on this discussion. First, though, allow me to remind the readers of the context. You argued previously regarding Q 7:143:

> "If there was a possibility of seeing (God) then the particle laa would be used. The particle Lan is used to deny from the time speaking into the future. Meaning you do not see me now and you will not see me in the future. In other words you will never see me. If I say laa tarnee then you are saying that you do not see me as we are speaking, but there is a possibility of you seeing me in the future. It makes it just as impossible when spoken as it does now because we are in the future of the spoken word. It was not possible then and it is not possible now. Then we must come to the

> conclusion that Allah can't be seen physically, mentally, or spiritually."

Your main point Imam Salim seems to be that it is generally impossible to see God, and that this eternal, ontological impossibility is expressed in the Qur'an by God's reply to Moses *lan tarānī*, 'You (Moses) will not see me' (7:143). You suggest that the negative particle *lan* expresses this categorical impossibility of Ru'ya; if the Qur'an wanted to suggest the categorical possibility, but the specific impossibility in Moses's cases, it would have used the negative particle *lā*. To this I responded:

> "With due respect to Imam Salim, this is another clear example of theology impinging upon philology. First, I am at a lost to understand how one trained in Arabic could claim that the *Lā* of Absolute Negation, which negates categorically and absolutely, is less emphatic than Lan, which is an emphatic particle but of a different nature. Lan is a ta'bīd, which is an emphatic particle that does not express the sense of 'timelessness' as does, for example, words derived from the root 'zl (e.g. azal "eternity"). Thus, Lan has temporal or temporary significance, not eternal. The categorical negation that Imam Salim wants to read into 'Lan tarānī' is actually said thusly: Lā arānī "I am not to be seen," thus with the Lā of Absolute Negation. In order to make "Lan tarānī" a timeless categorical denial of the possibility of God being seen, it would have to be reworded as: lan tajūz an tarānī, "You can never see Me"."

To this, you Bro Imam Salim responded with your above discussion of the Arabic negative particles. As stated, most of your discussion is, while very informative, not directly relevant to the main point, so I will pass on commenting (not that I have any comments – it is a good discussion). The parts of your response directly relevant are thus, quoting you:

1.] "To negate an act in the present we use the particle 'laa.' Note: laa is not an absolute in this case."
2.] "To negate from the time of speaking into the future we use the particle 'lan' with a present tense verb putting the verb in the subjunctive."
3.] "To negate the origin of something 'laa' is used. This is called the absolute 'laa.' It is used with an internal noun [masdar] and negates that that thing ever existed."
4.] "(a) So, to say the laa used with a verb is the absolute negation is erroneous. (b) Laa used with a noun and putting the noun in the accusative without tanween is the absolute negation of the negation of the origin of that thing."

I have no problem with Points 1-3. I only point out that Point 3, while grammatically correct and consistent with your earlier statement, contradicts your general point of the 'timelessness' or categorical nature of lan as used in Q 7:143. This negative particle is temporal: it applies from the time of the speaker and into (the speaker's) future, as you correctly point out. While you never use the language 'timeless' with regard to lan, your suggestion that this verse with this negative particle indicates that it is 'impossible' to see God, and that "we must come to the conclusion that Allah can't be seen physically, mentally, or spiritually," suggests this is your intent.

Point 4 requires more detailed comment. 4b is certainly correct, as far as it goes. Two points need to be made regarding 4a: (1) this is correct in one sense, incorrect in another and (2) the relative correctness of this specific point of grammatical taxonomy does nothing to strengthen your main point – the categorical impossibility of Ru'ya according to Q 7:143 – nor does it do anything to weaken mine – the possibility of Ru'ya.

The *lā al-tabri'a* or Lā of Absolute Negation, as a term, does indeed normally apply when the particle negates a masdar or internal noun in the accusative. However, your claim that "to say the laa used with a verb is the absolute negation is erroneous" is overstated.

Fakhr al-Din Razi (d. 1209) who, among other things, was a scholar of Arabic grammar, discusses our passage in his '*Maftatih al-ghayb ya tafsir al-kabir*' (Cairo, 1938, vol. 14:234). He notes that grammatically '*Lan tarānī*' is NOT a categorical (i.e. absolute) denial of Ru'ya. Had Allah intended such, he points out, He would have said Lā arānī or lam urā, both of which mean "I am not to be seen." Lā here functions as *lā al-tabri'a* even though it negates an action, because it has a categorical sense. Al-Razi cites the following example: When a man is asked for a stone in his hand, he might reply 'hadhā lā yu'ākal', 'this is not to be eaten,' thus denying a whole category of action – the eating of stones. However, if he were to prevent someone from eating an apple that was in his hand, he might say *lā tā'kuluh*, 'don't eat this'. In this case the *lā* is not absolute: it negates only a specific action, the eating of a specific apple. The category of eating apples in general is not denied. Thus, al-Razi argues, *Lan tarānī* of Q 7:143 is semantically closer to the non-categorical *lā tā'kuluh*.

That *Lan tarānī* grammatically is not a categorical denial was pointed out by a number of Classical scholars. The Maturidi scholar Abu l-Yusr al-Pazdawi (d. 1100), in his Usul al-din (Cairo, 1963; p. 79), points out regarding this verse that lan is only used to deny something actually capable of existing or happening. The Maliki-Ashari scholar al-Baqillani (d. 1013), in his *Kitab al-tamhid* (Beirut, 1957, p. 266-279) notes also that *Lan tarānī* does not have the force of a categorical denial, which would more correctly be worded: *lan tajūz an tarānī* , 'You can never see Me.' Al-Baqillini uses the following example to make his point: If Moses had asked Allah for a son, God may very well have refused and used the particle lan to do so, but this refusal hardly indicates a categorical denial of all paternity, past or future! No, Allah's reply to Moses' request to see Him, *Lan tarānī*, was temporal (not eternal) and specific to Moses and his circumstances. It does not imply that "Allah can't be seen physically, mentally, or spiritually."

Salaam
Your Brother
Bro Wesley

18.] Imam Salim Mu'Min Resepnse to Dr Wesley Muhammad

Wa Alaikum As-Salaam Dr. Westley, as you can see i too am a lover of Arabic Grammar, especially Qur'anic Arabic. You have brought some interesting points that i must continue the discussion. Because of my schedule i will try to have a response by this weekend. wa Salaam

19.] Mubaashir Uqdah Reply to Dr. Wesley Muhammad's Response Part 1

I would like to reiterate that this engagement with Dr. Wesley has been very interesting, informative, and beneficial. I also would like to acknowledge and compliment him on the arduous, enormous, and thought-provoking scholarship that he has put into his dissertation:

"A Study of Anthropomorphic Theophany and Visio Dei in the Hebrew Bible, the Qur'an, and Early Sunni Islam"

ABOUT MY REPLY

In responding to my analysis of his lecture, Dr. Wesley characterized aspects of my responses as misrepresenting his arguments, passing off my opinions as if they were the truth of the Qur'an, and misrepresenting the Classical Arabic/Islamic Tradition in order to assert my view and today's Muslim world view of a non-Semitic concept of G-d over what he refers to as the Semitic concept of G-d as the true and authentic Islamic idea of G-d. During the course of this reply, which will be multipart, I intend to respond to these characterizations.

I hereby acknowledge and thank Dr. Wesley for caring enough to make clear that he did not intend his use of the word misrepresentation to imply that I was doing so with ill-intentions. I would like him to know that I did not perceive its use in this way, but rather that he believes I have erred and thereby misrepresented what he believes is the correct representation.

While my response will be multipart, I hope not to prolong it and "beat a dead horse," as the metaphor goes. Dr. Wesley presented his lecture to us. I responded to his lecture. He replied to my response. I am now replying to his reply. Hence, we have both taken two turns at making our views as clear as we can at this time. So, I hope to minimize redundancy and at the conclusion of my reply, I'll consider the "formal" part of this debate done for the time being. Of course dialog on other and related topics will continue for all of us.

As I have just become aware of Dr. Wesley when I saw his lecture, I have learned more about his views upon reading his responses during this dialog and by reading through parts of his dissertation. Having what I believe is a better understanding of Dr. Wesley's viewpoint, I feel even more confirmed in my views, although he argues his point of view very well. Therefore, in addition to responding to some of his specific comments, I may reference small parts of his dissertation in making some general observations.

HOPE FOR UNITY BETWEEN COMMUNITIES OF IWDM AND NOI

Dr. Wesley made the following comment, "This past July I was among those fortunate enough to join Brother Minister Farrakhan for dinner at the National House in Chicago, during which he shared with his guests, among other things, his desire to see his followers and the followers of Im?m W?rrithudd?n come together as a unified community descendant from the spiritual loins of the Honorable Elijah Muhammad (hereafter THEM). The Minister acknowledged that our claim that God is a man is the obstacle to this unity." (Response to Mubaashir Part 1)

While the NOI merging with the community of IWDM as one community is an unlikely scenario for several reasons, including the one you've mentioned, I can understand and appreciate the desire to build a bridge that allows our two communities to cooperate in ways that benefit humanity in general and African people in particular. This desire exists among many of us as well and I believe there is room for us to find ways to cooperate.

While the followers of Imam Mohammed differ with many people theologically, the Imam urged us to look for and connect with right-minded people everywhere who respect each other and where we must differ, do so respectfully. Allah tells us in Qur'an 2:62

> "Those who believe (in the Qur'an), and those who follow the Jewish (scriptures), and the Christians and the Sabians,- any who believe in Allah and the Last Day, and work righteousness, shall have their reward with their Lord; on them shall be no fear, nor shall they grieve." (Qur'an 2:62 Yusuf Ali translation)

While at the same time we are told in Sura 4:171:

> "O People of the Book! Commit no excesses in your religion: Nor say of Allah aught but the truth. Christ Jesus the son of Mary was (no more than) an apostle of

> Allah, and His Word, which He bestowed on Mary, and a spirit proceeding from Him: so believe in Allah and His apostles. Say not "trinity": desist: it will be better for you: for Allah is one Allah. Glory be to Him: (far exalted is He) above having a son. To Him belong all things in the heavens and on earth. And enough is Allah as a Disposer of affairs." (Qur'an 4:171 Yusuf Ali translation)

So, in my opinion, there is room to differ and engage each other about our differences, yet the good people amongst us can find common ground to do good deeds.

THE BLACK SHEEP AND THE WHITE SHEEP

Dr. Wesley makes two major points in his opening comments. The first is that the debate is not about the meaning of shirk, but about the nature of Allah. Is He a man or not? This point has been the subject of most of the discussion and will be commented upon later in my reply to Dr. Wesley's evidence on this topic. It is his second point that I would like to address first, which is how most of the Muslim world came to believe in a G-d that we cannot see with our physical eyes rather than as a man, albeit super or divine man who is different from a regular, mortal man.

My reading of Dr. Wesley's words is that Prophet Muhammad and the other original black Arabs conceptualized Allah in one way (the way of what he refers to as the Semitic tradition) and then afterwards the non-blacks, non-Arabs became Muslim and brought their non-Semitic conceptualization of Allah into the Islamic religion, which drowned out by their sheer numbers the black Semitic way of looking at Allah. Eventually, the white way of seeing (understanding) Allah became the dominant concept and the black way was pushed into the background and obscured.

Dr. Wesley says:

"Bro Mubaashir begins his review by echoing the sentiment of Bro Imam Salim Mu'min that "the only way Dr. Wesley's case proves that the followers of the Honorable Elijah Muhammad are not guilty of shirk is if he changes the definition of the word shirk to something other than what it means." This, Beloveds, is deflection. The problem is not at all our respective understandings of shirk: we three all agree that a mushrik is one who associates partners with Allah. The problem is our respective understandings of "Allah" to whom no partners may be legitimately associated. We who adhere to the Islam taught to us by the Honorable Elijah Muhammad understand that Allah is a man - a divine man rather than a mortal man, but a man nonetheless. In my most recent book, "Take Another Look: The Qur'an, the Sunna, and the Islam of the Honorable Elijah Muhammad," I demonstrate that this understanding of Allah is absolutely consistent with the Qur'an and Sunna when these are no longer read through the lens of al-Ghazzali and other non-Arab converts to Islam who rejected the Black Arabs to whom the message first came and their understanding of the religion. These non-Arab converts - particularly the Persians and Byzantines - introduced a new understanding of God and a peculiar way of reading the Qur'an so as to locate this new God therein. I introduced this history in Philly and identified there the great Imam Ahmad ibn Hanbal (d. 855) as the champion of the Islam of the original Black Arabs against those who tried to de-Arabize the religion by (among other things) replacing the Semitic God of the Qur'an with the Greek God of Hellenism." (Response to Mubaashir Part 1)

Dr. Wesley goes on to say:

"In my lecture (and book) I emphasized this Black Arab/White convert dichotomy in understanding Islam because the Prophet pointed it out." He quotes the following hadith as support for this view:

"Zayd b. Aslam related that the Prophet (s) saw a vision and told his companions about it. He said: "I saw a group of black sheep and a group of white sheep then mixed with them [until the white sheep became so numerous that the black sheep could no longer be seen in the herd of sheep.] I interpreted it to mean that [the black sheep are the Arabs. They will accept Islam and become many. As for the white sheep, they are the non-Arabs (i.e. Persians, Turks, Byzantines, ect.)] They will enter Islam and then share with you your wealth and your genealogy [and become so numerous that the Arabs will not be noticed amongst them.]" The Companions became surprised by what he (s) said. Then one said, "The non-Arab Persians will enter our land, O' Messenger of Allah?!" The Prophet (s) then said, "Yes. By He Who Has my soul in His Hand, if the religion was hanging on the distant star, men from the non-Arab Persians would reach it and the luckiest of them would be the people of Faris."

Dr. Wesley continues:

"I have demonstrated that these 'Black sheep' who are the original recipients of the message of Islam are the Black Arabs and they and their Islam are best represented by Ahmad ibn Hanbal. I further demonstrated that the White sheep and their re-interpretation of Islam are best represented by the Persian Hujjat al-Islam al-Ghazzali." (Response to Mubaashir Part 1)

BLACK SHEEP/WHITE SHEEP HADITH

Upon reading this hadith, I see no reason to interpret the black/white reference as a racial reference, nor does it hint that this influx of non-Arabs to Al-Islam would crowd out "true" Islam or the "true" concept of Allah held by the Arabs. To me, according to this report, Prophet Muhammad simply uses the black/white sheep reference as a metaphor for a time when non-Arabs of other ethnicities will enter Islam in crowds and outnumber the Arabs. This is not a bad thing, this is a good thing. Sura 110 tells us that when we see the people coming to the Deen in crowds glorify and celebrate the praises of our Rabb. The hadith says that they will "accept Islam and become many."

If we accept this hadith, it indicates that Prophet Muhammad envisioned many people from all over the world becoming Muslims, but it doesn't prove Dr. Wesley's contention that the prophet predicted a white takeover and corruption of Al-Islam.

I think it also lends support to the notion that prophet Muhammad spoke in metaphors to better communicate to the unlearned Arabs who were fresh out of Jahiliyyah. Surely, Arabia was an agrarian society and the prophet himself was a sheep herder. All of the people he was speaking to would be familiar with the fact that there are more white sheep than black sheep. They would readily understand how a small number of black sheep would be hidden in the midst of a multitude of white sheep. In addition to the black sheep metaphor, the prophet concludes this hadith with another metaphor when he says,

"By He Who Has my soul in His Hand, if the religion was hanging on the distant star, men from the non-Arab Persians would reach it (meaning reach that distant star)."

When considering Dr. Wesley's reading of this hadith compared to the possible alternative reading I have just provided, I am not convinced that the prophet was alluding to a racial problem or a corruption problem from the anticipated influx of the multitudes of different people to our religion.

After all, how could we believe this in the 21st century, when we know that Allah has promised in Sura 9:33 to make Al-Islam the most manifestly practiced way of life in the world? In order for this verse to become true, we must have multitudes from everywhere become a part of us.

IT'S AL-GHAZZALI AND OTHER NON-BLACK ARABS FAULT

The blame for this non-black, non-Semitic view of Allah (i.e. G-d is not a man) is placed on the non-black, non-Arab converts to Islam, whose chief proponent, according to Dr. Wesley, was Al-Ghazzali. He particularly accuses the Persians and Byzantines with replacing the Semitic ideas of G-d of the black Arabs with the Hellenistic ideas of G-d of the Greeks. There are three points that I would like to offer for your consideration.

The first point is that Imam Al-Ghazzli performed his Islamic work several hundred years after the prophet's passing and he came after the establishment of the four major madhabs. While on one hand Dr. Wesley blames Imam Ghazzali and non black Arabs for Muslims not believing in Allah as a man, on the other hand he tells us in chapter 6 of his dissertation that there were different opinions between the Sahaaba and Tabieen about whether prophet Muhammad saw Allah or saw him as a man or young boy.

Dr. Wesley quotes Gibril Fouad Haddad in his study on "The Vision of Allah in the World and the Hereafter:

> "Many sound reports show that the Companions differed sharply whether the Prophet saw Allah or not. Ibn 'Abbas related that he did, while Ibn Mas'ud,

> 'A'isha, Abu Hurayra, and Abu Dharr related reports to the contrary, stating that the verses of Sura AlNajm and other Suras referred [to] Jibril and that the Prophet said that he saw light." (Dr. Wesley Dissertation)

Dr. Wesley continues:

> "As Shaykh Haddad rightly points out here, many hadith reports give the impression of intense controversy among the Sahaba (Companions of the Prophet) over the question of Muhammad's visionary encounter with God. Less sound, however, is Haddad's suggestion that Ibn 'Abbas, the cousin of the Prophet and famed qur'anic exegete, was the lone advocate of the Prophet's Visio Dei (vision), while Ibn Mas'ud, 'A'isha, Abu Hurayra, and Abu Dharr denied it because they read surat al-Najm as an account of angelophanies (actual appearance of an angel to a man) rather than theophanies (actual appearance of G-d to a man). In fact many more persons were involved in this discussion according to the reports, and the numbers are clearly on the side of the advocates." (Dr. Wesley Dissertation)

Leaving aside the issue of who is right or wrong, or whether there were more companions and followers who believed he saw G-d or did not, Dr. Wesley, in this chapter, documents the fact that this dispute existed long before Imam Ghazzali.

Dr. Wesley also makes the following quote from editors of a book, Kitab al-Ru'ya:

> "The fifth problem regarding the Prophet's vision of his Lord Most High in this world. The Salaf and the Khalaf disagree irreconcilably (ikhtilaft mutabayin) over this issue, some affirming, others denying, while

> others suspending judgment (al-mutawaqqif). As for those who affirm that (the Prophet) saw his Lord Most High there is a group of the Sahaba and the Tabi'in and others. 'AbdAllah b. 'Abbas, Interpreter of the Qur'an, and Anas b. Malik, Abu Dharr, and it is reported on the authority of Abu Hurayra, and Ibn Mas'ud...and Ka'b al-Abbar. As for those who are of the opinion that the Prophet did not see his Lord Most High, a group of Sahaba and the Tabi'in also: our Mother 'A'isha and Ibn Mas'ud. And it was disputed regarding him and Abu Hurayra and Abu Dharr." (Dr. Wesley Dissertation)

Let me be clear, Dr. Wesley presents Hadeeth from both sides and gives his reasons for siding with those reports that seem to affirm the prophet saying that he saw Allah and for rejecting those reports that seem to affirm that the prophet saw Jibril. My purpose here is not to explore this issue, at least not at this point, but rather to assert that Dr. Wesley documents a dispute between the Sahaba and Tabieen about whether the prophet saw Allah or not. The implication is that if he saw Allah, Allah had to be in a form and if Allah has a form that form was a man.

For our edification, let me share with you a couple of the Hadeeth from Dr. Wesley's dissertation that illustrate the two opinions. I do not know which hadith Dr. Wesley feels is the strongest, so if I choose one that is not his preference, it is not intentional. I found it interesting reading them and thought MALI members would also find them interesting.

> We are all familiar with the companion Ibn Abbas. Here are Hadeeth that reportedly involve him:
>
> "Ibn Abbas met Ka'b (al-Ahbar) at Arafat and asked him concerning a certain thing. Then he said, 'God is great,' until the mountains returned the echo. Then Ibn Abbas said, "We belong to the Banu Hashim. We

> say, "Verily, Muhammad saw his Lord twice." Ka'b replied, "Verily God Most High divided His vision and His conversation between Muhammad and Musa. He spoke to Musa twice; and Muhammad saw Him twice." (Al-Tirmidhi)
>
> "(Regarding the aya) "The heart lied not concerning that which he saw (53:11)" (Ibn Abbas) said, "(Muhammad) saw his Lord, May He be Exalted and Great, with his heart twice." He indeed saw Him at another descent by the Lote-tree of the Boundary (53:14)" he said: "He saw his Lord." (Regarding the aya) "Till He was the measure of two bows or closer. Then He revealed to His servant what He revealed (53:9-10)." Ibn Abbas said: "Indeed the Prophet saw Him."

While this second hadith says that he saw Him with his heart, Dr. Wesley goes into great detail in his dissertation in an attempt to show that this does not mean he didn't see with his eyes as well. In other words, his heart did not lie concerning what his physical eyes saw.

One more, for good measure:

> [Ibn Abbas said], "The Messenger of God said: "I saw my Lord under the form of a young man (shabb), one beardless (amrad) with curly hair (ja'd) and clothed in a green [or red] garment."

On the opposing side, I'll share with you a Hadith reportedly involving Prophet Muhammad's wife Ayesha.

> "(Masruq said):"I was sitting back in Aisha's house when she said: "O abu Aisha, there are three things,

whoever says any of which, he is lying about Allah in the most hateful manner." I asked: "Which things?" She said: "[First], whoever tells you that Muhammad saw his Lord, he is lying about Allah in the most hateful manner." I was sitting back so I sat up and said: "O Mother of the Faithful! Give me a moment and do not rush me. Did not Allah Almighty say, 'Surely he beheld him on the clear horizon (81:23)?" She replied: "I was the first in the entire community to have asked Allah's Messenger about this, and he said: "It is but Jibril, I did not see him in the actual form in which he was created other than these two times. I saw him alighting from heaven, covering it all. The magnitude of his frame spans what lies between the heaven and the earth." Then she said: "Did you not hear Allah say: "Vision comprehends Him not, but He comprehends all vision. He is the Subtle, the Aware(6:103)?" Did you not hear Allah say: "And it is not (vouchsafed) to any mortal that Allah should speak to him except by revelation or from behind a veilt, or that He sends a messenger to reveal what He will, by His leave. Lo! He is Exalted, Wise (42:51)?" She continued: [Second], whoever claims that Allah's messenger concealed any part of Allah's book, he is lying about Allah in the most hateful manner when Allah is saying:"O Messenger, make known that which has been revealed unto you from your Lord, for if you do it not, you will not have conveyed His Message (5:67)." She continued: [Third], whoever claims that he can tell what shall happen tomorrow, he is lying about Allah in the most hateful manner, since Allah is saying: "Say: None in the heavens and the earth knoweth the Unseen save Allah" [and they know not when they will be raised again] (27:65)

It is reported that Ibn Mas'ud, the 6th convert to Islam, reported:

> "He indeed saw him at another descent, by the Lote-tree of the boundary (53:13-14):" The prophet said: "I saw Jibril by the lote-tree of the boundary with six hundred wings on him shaking off a plume of ornamental flourishes, pearls, and corundum."

I hope you found these Hadeeth interesting and Dr. Wesley points us to more Hadeeth along these lines with some of the companions seeming to contradict themselves.

My point here is that these disputes are not taking place hundreds of years later between the prophet's black Arab companions and foreign white converts flocking to the religion. This debate is between what he calls the black sheep. For me, this indicates that the debate over whether prophet Muhammad literally saw G-d or not is not a debate between the views of original black, Semitic Arabs and "Johnny come-lately" white, non-Semitic, non-Arabs.

Perhaps, it indicates that there was a struggle to keep the concept of G-d free from the idolatrous tendencies of a people just coming out of paganism that continued after the prophet's passing. Look at us today, 1400+ years after the prophet, still struggling to keep our culture and customs from being propagated as the Deen. Intelligent people still worship all kinds of idols or forms of creation. It wouldn't surprise me if this tendency existed in the Muslims of old.

Dr. Wesley blames the non-anthropomorphic concept of G-d on Al-Ghazzali and other non-Arabs being influenced by Greek Hellenism (Greek way of life, including religion and philosophy), and by their sheer numbers (coming to the religion in crowds) foisting this concept upon the black Arabs and drowning out the original anthropomorphic Semitic concept of G-d held by the prophet.

There is no doubt that Imam Al-Ghazzali was a believing Muslim as well as a philosopher and mystic and he was and is very influential in the Muslim world because of his deep and detailed explanations of so many ideas in Islam.
Now, did his philosophical approach to Islam corrupt the Muslim ummah's concept of Allah, as Dr. Wesley proclaims? I do not accept this assertion. While it may be true that Al-Ghazzali's idea of Allah is the same as the majority of today's Muslim world, most Muslims have not studied Al-Ghazzali's writings on the subject. I understand the idea of G-d the way I do, not because of Al-Ghazzali; but, because it makes more sense to me than to believe in anything in creation as a G-d, whether it is a man or divine man, a bird or divine bird, a statue, saint, angel, or divine bird, divine statue, divine saint, or divine angel. It has nothing to do with Al-Ghazzali, it has to do with reason and the experience of history. My reading of the Qur'an does not make me see Allah as a man; it makes me see Him as greater and bigger than anything.

AL-GHAZZALI OR SCIENCE?

Admittedly, I am not a historian and I am no expert on the influence of Greek philosophy on Imam Al-Ghazzali. However, what I do know is that world history shows a progression of human belief and knowledge from its early superstitious and pagan understanding of the planet and world we live in to a more rational, scientific, and educated understanding of ourselves and our world.

Early man worshipped things in creation as Gods; the wind, fire, rain, etc. We believed in powerful spirits, demons, ghosts lurking in the night. We worshipped the sun, the moon, stars, angelic beings, statues; all kinds of things, including powerful men and women, who were our witch doctors, kings, pharaohs, popes and the wizards of Oz.

As man became more knowledgeable of himself and his world, he began discarding those beliefs and began reducing the number of supernatural, "divine" beings in his world. Eventually, a good number of humans realized that even the powerful and great men and women who claimed to be G-d or claimed that G-d ordained them with the right to rule were only mortal men like the rest of us. This is history 101.

It is not surprising that the Arabs just coming out of paganism, polytheism, and idolatry still struggled to overcome the cultural tendencies of their past. Look at how even today we talk about how Muslims mix their culture with Islam and think that their cultural proclivity is the religion. Even in the midst of the most educated society in human history, there are many who hold superstitious, pagan, and polytheistic beliefs. What can we say?

I make this brief summary to say that people of all cultures, ethnicities, and nationalities originated in superstitious beliefs and gradually began growing out of those superstitions with the growth of reason and science. We should not condemn Al-Ghazzali because he picked up the tool of his rational mind to analyze and deduce explanations of religion. He is not responsible for the majority of mankind rejecting the notion of a tree, bird, lion, man, king, pharaoh, emperor, pope, self-proclaimed or mysteriously designated divine man as G-d of the universe. It is not Al-Ghazzali's fault, it is education's fault. Despite the superstitious proclivities of many 21st century people, we have too much documented human experience showing us that nothing in creation is a G-d to be worshipped; not even the most knowledgeable and talented people or most powerful civilizations.

It is interesting that Dr. Wesley would cite the influence of Greek culture and thinking on the non-Arabs who converted to Islam and brought this influence with them to corrupt the true concept of Allah. I say it is interesting, because what he is referring to is

Greek philosophical thinking, not Greek religion. Had the Greeks not started thinking with reason, they would have remained believers in a concept of G-d not too dissimilar from what Dr. Wesley would have us believe is the Semitic concept of G-d.

We are all familiar with the Greek mythologies of the 12 Olympian G-ds residing above the heavens on Mount Olympus, with Zeus as the Chief G-d or Supreme Being. On occasion, as the G-ds observed life on earth from above, Zeus or one of the other G-ds would have reason to manifest themselves as a man or a woman or a cloud, etc. to earthly beings. You would see them sitting on their thrones on Mount Olympus as giant divine human beings chatting about the affairs of their little toys on earth. This is the classic Greek religion and sounds closely related to the perception of G-d Dr. Wesley calls us to accept (minus the other secondary gods).

Greek philosophers such as Socrates, Plato, and Aristotle took a turn away from such superstitious beliefs in G-ds as men and women on top of Mount Olympus; sitting on their thrones. They ushered in an age of reason, which, notwithstanding its own problems and their own "religious" speculations, they helped humans step further away from idolatry. It is the philosophic rational method of inquiry used by philosophers to whom Al-Ghazzali and Ibn Sina are compared. Perhaps, these men helped Muslims use reason and logic to resist the belief in a divine man G-d, just as the Greek philosophers moved people away from the worship of Zeus, Apollo and the other "divine" super human beings.

The Ancient Greeks and Ancient Hindus had concepts of man gods and they were not Semitic people. Many people in Africa, Asia and Europe had Man god concepts and they are not Semitic peoples. The worship of man as god is not a Semitic idea, it is a superstitious idea resulting from a time in human knowledge when we didn't know any better. Humans may have predominantly believed in god this way at some point in human history, just as we predominantly believed in witchcraft and rain gods at one time. But, as human knowledge increases our understanding of the Creator and the scriptures should also increase.

What Dr. Wesley extends to us, however eloquently, is an invitation to return to the worship of creation rather than Creator and an understanding of the scripture that would lead us back into superstition.

I believe human reason, education, and scientific discovery is responsible for our current monotheistic concept of G-d than Greek Philosophy or non-black, non-Arab foreign ideas. I believe it was Al-Qur'an, Prophet Muhammad, and the Muslim Ummah that brought the world out of the dark ages of superstition and creation worship so that we would study creation properly and be catapulted into the scientific age of today where many are free from the worship of created things as G-d.

We do still battle with man's desire to see himself or his image as the Creator though. Abraham had to battle against a man-pharaoh who believed he was the manifestation of god. I had a brother in my Masjid try to convince me that after the Honorable Elijah Muhammad died, the god came into him and therefore, I should follow him rather than Imam Mohammed. Even as a young man, I knew better than this. He told me he had some special powers that he could use with his mind on people. At that point, I quickly got out of his car (smile).

It was the physicalization of religious knowledge and ideas that has put the religious world to sleep. It is reading revelation as purely literal text that has locked us out of religious understanding. It is the attempt to portray physical images as divine; that is, ascribing divinity to things created that has caused people to believe the stories in scripture as literal truths and turn religion into comedy for the thoughtful.

To be continued...

Mubaashir Uqdah

20.] Imam Salim Mu'min Black sheep and white sheep.

In religion black symbolizes the purity of nature and white symbolizes the purity of the intellect. We born black in our original nature, the nature of fitr. As this nature become enlightened, that is white enter...s into the nature, we become whiter and whiter until at a point man no longer depends upon his nature. He then depends upon his intellect. He moves further and further away from his original nature thinking that he can make it on his own, with his own intellect. This is the white sheep entering the black sheep until you see no more black sheep. The rest of the hadith you should be able to get.

Maa kathaba al-fu'aadu maa r'aa [The heart did not lie about what is saw]. The believer senses his Lord in his heart. Surely he saw one of the great signs of His Lord. Have you seen Lat, and Uzza? And Manat the other third? Are the idols that... the people were worshipping Lat, Uzza, or Manat? Is Fard Muhammad Allah? Is the Honorable Elijah Muhammad Allah? Or is this whole movement of the Muslim American experience a great sign of Allah. Meaning this movement belongs to Allah.

21.] Dr Wesley Muhammad - Thoughts on Bro Mubaashir Uqdah's 'Reply To Dr Wesley Muhammad Part I'

ASA Bro Mubaashir. Thank you for your kind words regarding my doctoral dissertation and thank you for the time you have put in to this dialogue with me. For me as well this exchange has been interesting, informative and beneficial. I have not yet had the opportunity to read your Reply Part II, though I skimmed it. I would, though, very much like to express some thoughts regarding Part I of your Reply. There are four main arguments of yours in this Reply that I must comment on:

1.] The Black Sheep/White Sheep reference in the hadith I quoted has no racial reference and no 'corruption of Islam' is hinted at there. Rather, the reference is only to the positive, Qur'an-predicted phenomenon of non-Arabs in general entering Islam, to their benefit and, presumably, to the benefit of the religion itself.

2.] The invisible, incorporeal god that now characterizes orthodox Muslim theology preceded al-Ghazzali by centuries. This fact is proved, you argue, by the debate which I document in my dissertation among the Sahaba regarding the Prophet's Ru'ya or Vision of Allah. The fact that some of the Black Arabs allegedly appeared on the 'negative' side of the debate is, you suggest, proof that the invisible, incorporeal, non-anthropomorphic deity of the Persian al-Ghazzali actually goes back to some of the Black Arabs themselves.

3.] The whole idea of anthropomorphism is 'pre-scientific'. In your version of world history, which allegedly "shows a progression of human belief and knowledge from its early superstitious and pagan understanding of the planet and world we live in to a more rational, scientific, and educated understanding of ourselves and our world," anthropomorphism is such a pagan and superstitious understanding that characterizes the pre-scientific world of the intellectual brutes of yesterday. Our more modern acquisition of education, science and reason forces an abandonment of anthropomorphism. This, you say, is History 101.

4.] You further suggest that it was the Greek philosophers such as Socrates, Plato, and Aristotle who "ushered in an age of reason" and helped lead humanity – the intellectual brutes of Ancient Greece, India, Africa, and Asia – away from their pagan and idolatrous ways. The Qur'an, the Holy Prophet, and the

Muslim Ummah all espoused the same type of god as did the Greek philosophers, and therefore further helped bring the world out of the dark ages of superstitious and pagan anthropomorphism.

Your positions were well laid out and articulated Bro Mubaashir. It is no mystery why you are hailed by many as one of the chief articulators of Imam W.D. Mohammed's interpretation of Islam. If I were not a professional Historian of Religion, I myself would have been totally persuaded by your above presentation. As the case is, however, I am an Historian of Religion and the Honorable Elijah Muhammad said it well: "Of all of our studies, History is most attractive and best qualified to reward our research." A better familiarity with the relevant history would, I suggest, bring clarity to your Points 1 and 2 and force an abandonment of Points 3 and 4.

1. THE BLACK SHEEP AND THE WHITE SHEEP, AGAIN.

You say Bro Mubaashir:

> "My reading of Dr. Wesley's words is that Prophet Muhammad and the other original black Arabs conceptualized Allah in one way (the way of what he refers to as the Semitic tradition) and then afterwards the non-blacks, non-Arabs became Muslim and brought their non-Semitic conceptualization of Allah into the Islamic religion, which drowned out by their sheer numbers the black Semitic way of looking at Allah. Eventually, the white way of seeing (understanding) Allah became the dominant concept and the black way was pushed into the background and obscured."

This is a pretty accurate summation of my position. You then appropriately quote the hadith, which I too will do for the benefit of readers and this discussion:

"Zayd b. Aslam related that the Prophet (s) saw a vision and told his companions about it. He said: "I saw a group of black sheep and a group of white sheep then mixed with them [until the white sheep became so numerous that the black sheep could no longer be seen in the herd of sheep.] I interpreted it to mean that [the black sheep are the Arabs. They will accept Islam and become many. As for the white sheep, they are the non-Arabs (i.e. Persians, Turks, Byzantines, ect.)] They will enter Islam and then share with you your wealth and your genealogy [and become so numerous that the Arabs will not be noticed amongst them.]" The Companions became surprised by what he (s) said. Then one said, "The non-Arab Persians will enter our land, O' Messenger of Allah?!" The Prophet (s) then said, "Yes. By He Who Has my soul in His Hand, if the religion was hanging on the distant star, men from the non-Arab Persians would reach it and the luckiest of them would be the people of Faris."

Bro Mubaashir then offers the following:

"Upon reading this hadith, I see no reason to interpret the black/white reference as a racial reference, nor does it hint that this influx of non-Arabs to Al-Islam would crowd out 'true' Islam or the 'true' concept of Allah held by the Arabs. To me, according to this report, Prophet Muhammad simply uses the black/white sheep reference as a metaphor for a time when non-Arabs of other ethnicities will enter Islam in crowds and outnumber the Arabs. This is not a bad thing, this is a good thing. Sura 110 tells us that when we see the people coming to the Deen in crowds glorify and celebrate the praises of our Rabb. The hadith says that they will 'accept Islam and become many.' If we accept this hadith, it indicates that Prophet

> Muhammad envisioned many people from all over the world becoming Muslims, but it doesn't prove Dr. Wesley's contention that the prophet predicted a white takeover and corruption of Al-Islam."

A number of comments are warranted here. First, it was not my "contention that the prophet predicted (in this hadith) a white takeover and corruption of Al-Islam." The white takeover – yes. The white corruption – no. While historically the white 'corruption' did indeed follow the 'white takeover', I was careful to only claim for this hadith that the Prophet pointed out "the Black Arab/White convert dichotomy." Secondly, the Black Sheep/White Sheep metaphor is undoubtedly a racial reference, Bro Imam Salim's purely speculative theological interpretation notwithstanding. Now, I don't deny Imam Salim or yourself the right to interpret this hadith how you will, nor do I suggest that your interpretations must be wrong and mine must be right. Nor is Bro Mubaashir's suggestion of the relevance of the 7th century agrarian context of the metaphor denied here. I am, however, suggesting that the difference in our methods of interpretation is also germane here. While Imam Salim chooses to interpret this 'black/white sheep' metaphor in accord with certain theological/symbolist presuppositions that he holds, I choose to interpret it in the light of the known history of the Umma, and therefore suggest that Prophet Muhammad was being, well...prophetic.

It is an historical fact that the original Umma was mainly Arab, and that these Arabs were black. It is also the case that whites, particularly Persians, Byzantines, and Turks, entered the religion in large numbers beginning in the 8th-9th century, and these whites, after 'converting' to Arabism (i.e. adopting the language, dress, and religion of the black Arabs), indeed 'squeezed out' the original black Arabs and became the main shapers of Islamic intellectual, theological and political tradition. I document these facts in my books, 'Black Arabia and the African Origin of Islam' and 'God's Black Prophets: Deconstructing the Myth of the

White Muhammad of Arabia and Jesus of Jerusalem.' It is also an historical fact that the Islam of the black Arabs was very different from the Islam of the 'new Arabs', the white converts to Islam and Arabism. Lastly, it is also an historical fact that the incorporeal and invisible god of Bro Mubaashir and the rest of the modern Muslim world was introduced into Islam NOT by the Holy Prophet Muhammad or the Black Arabs of the original Umma, but by white, specifically Persian converts to the religion. I document this in my book, "Take Another Look".

That the 'black sheep' metaphor used of the original Arab Ummah is a reference to the blackness of these original Arabs is confirmed by numerous reports. A good indicator of this is the example of Muhammad b. Abd Allah (d. 762), known also as al-Nafs al-Zakiyya ("The Pure Soul"). He was a pure Qurayshi Arab and pure descendent of the Prophet himself through the latter's daughter Fatimah, wife of Ali b. Abi Talib. He boasted of being "at the very center of the Banu Hashim's lines. My paternity is purest among them, undiluted with non-Arab blood, and no concubines dispute over me." What did this pure Arab descendent of the Prophet look like? Al-Dhahabi describes him as "black-skinned and huge" (*Al-'Ibar*, 4:198) and al-Tabari (*Ta'rikh* 10:203) reports:

> "Muhammad (Al-Nafs al-Zakiyya) was black, exceedingly black, jet black (*adam shadid al-udma adlam*) and huge. He was nicknamed 'Tar Face' (*al-qari*) because of his black complexion (*udmatihi*), such that (the Abbasid caliph) Abu Ja'far used to call him 'Charcoal Face' (*al-muhammam*)."

Muhammad al-Nafs al-Zakiyya, a Qurayshi Arab whose pure lineage on both his father's and his mother's side put him "at the center" of the genealogical lines of the Banu Hashim, the Prophet's kinsfolk, was so black he was called 'Tar face' and 'Charcoal face'. He best represents those 'black sheep' to whom the message of Islam first came and who disappeared from view once non-Arab groups converted in large numbers. Hear also the words of the ninth century poet Abu al-Hasan Ali b. al-Abbas b. Jurayj, also known as Ibn al-Rumi (d. 896). Ibn al-Rumi was not an Arab. His mother was a Persian and his father was Byzantine (some say half-Greek). Yet, in his poetry he presented himself as an advocate of the (now) ill-treated black Arabs, in particular the black family of Prophet Muhammad. Ibn al-Rumi was a Shiite Muslim and thus was an advocate of the rights of *ahl al-bayt*, the Prophet's Hashmite relatives and 'Alid descendents. He fulminated in his poetry against the 'Abbasid abuse of the tombs of the Shiite Imams and their living descendents of his day. Unlike the Umayyads who were pure Black Arabs, the Abbasids were 'whitened' through miscegenation with Persian and Byzantine concubines. They thus developed an anti-black, anti-Arab sentiment. Ibn al-Rumi thus writes to the Abbasid caliph:

> "You insulted (the family of the Prophet Muhammad) because of their blackness (*bi-l-sawad*), while there are still deep black, pure-blooded Arabs (*al-'arab al-amhad akhdar ad'aj*). However, you are white - the Romans (Byzantines) have embellished your faces with their color. The color of the family of Hashim was not a bodily defect (*'aha*)." (Abu al-Faraj al-Isbahani, ***Maqatil al-talibiyyin***, 759)

The Arabs were well-known for their blackness. In fact, Ibn Manzur tells us in his *Lisan al-Arab* that the phrase 'aswad al-jilda', black-skinned, idiomatically meant 'khalis al-'arab,' pure Arab because, he says, "the color of most of the Arabs is black (al-udma)." You thus cannot deny the racial implications of the metaphor 'black sheep' for the Arabs.

There is also no denying that the 'white sheep' reference is a reference to the ethnic whites who converted to Islam. In the hadith itself the Persians are specifically identified. The Persians were/are a proud, racist Indo-Aryan people. Empirius (ca. 200

CE; *Against the Ethicists*, 43) claimed that of all whites the Persians are associated with "the whitest and the most hook-nosed." In Classical Arabic tradition the Persians and Byzantines were recognized and the 'whites' of the empire. Al-Dhahabi points out in his ***Siyar a'lam al-nubala'***,II:168:

> "Red (*al-hamra'*), in the speech of the people of the Hejaz, means white-complexioned, and this is rare among them. Thus the meaning of the hadith 'a red man as if one of the slaves.' The speaker is saying that this is the complexion of the Christian slaves captured from Syria, Rome, and Persia."

Whites, Persians in particular and Turks a little later, gained ascendency in the empire through the misnomered "Abbasid Revolution." It was actually a 'Persian Revolution', as documented by a number of scholars. The consequence of this revolution is that the Arab-Islamic kingdom of the Umayyads was replaced by a largely Non-Arab, Persianized kingdom. Al-Jahiz observed that the Abbaisid empire was Persian ('ajamiyya wa Khurasani) and the Umayyad was Bedouin Arab (Bayan, 3:366) and al-Dhahabi lamented:

> "We rejoiced that [the reins of power] passed to [the Prophet's family, i.e. the Banu Abbas]…nay, it was a tyrannical Khurasanian (Persian) regime which arrived." (Siyar, 4:58)

These Persians introduced into Islam, among other things, a virulent anti-black, anti-Arab racism that shaped the Abbasid caliphate and life in the Abbasid empire in general. That this 'black sheep/white sheep' metaphor alludes to this Black Arab/White Persian demographic of the empire was known by at least some within the empire. See e.g. the case of Khaydar b. Kavus Afshin (d. 841), the Persian general of Caliph al-Mu'tasim. He only superficially converted to Islam and dreamed to see the restoration of his land, his people, and their religion,

Zoroastrianism, which he called the 'white religion'. He mocked 'the black religion' Islam and the Black Arabs, and would kill a black sheep every Wednesday by cutting it in half and would then walk between the two parts. This ritual aptly illustrates the method used by the Persians to topple the Umayyad dynasty: divide and conquer.

The so-called 'Iranian (Persian) Intermezzo' which followed the decline of Arab power in the 9th century was itself followed by the rise of Dawla Turkiyya or the Turkish Empire in the 11th. As Robert Goldston observes in his work, ***The Sword of the Prophet: A History of the Arab World From the Time of Mohammed to the Present Day*** (New York: Dial Press, 1979) 87:

> "although both Abbasid and Fatimid caliphs continued to maintain their titles, between the Mamelukes in Egypt and the Seljuks in the East real power in the Arab world (except North Africa and Spain, where the Seljuks never penetrated) had passed into Turkish hands. There it was to remain until our own day. And what of the original Arabs, those lords of the desert who had formed the vanguard of Islam and presided over its golden age? Almost all had long since become so submerged into the cosmopolitan empire that they were indistinguishable from their neighbors."

This is the exact fulfillment of the Prophet's dream. This demographic shift is part of what I have called the *Aryanization* of Islam: the transformation of Islam's culture, ideology, spirit, and face from Semitic (black Arab) to Indo-Aryan.

The bottom line is this: while you are free to speculate about what theological meaning this hadith and its metaphors might possess, the ethnographic and historical data is perfectly consistent with the *historical* interpretation that I offered.

2.1 ALL AL-GHAZZALI'S FAULT?

No. Nor did I claim that. It is, however, largely (though not exclusively) the fault of non-Arabs, especially his people the Persians/Iranians.

Bro Mubaashir says:

> "The blame for this non-black, non-Semitic view of Allah (i.e. G-d is not a man) is placed on the non-black, non-Arab converts to Islam, whose chief proponent, according to Dr. Wesley, was Al-Ghazzali. He particularly accuses the Persians and Byzantines with replacing the Semitic ideas of G-d of the black Arabs with the Hellenistic ideas of G-d of the Greeks."

This is only partly correct. I do indeed document in my book (not just 'place the blame') that non-Arab converts introduced into Islam the invisible, incorporeal deity of Hellenism which the Honorable Elijah Muhammad called a 'Spook God.' I did not, however, describe al-Ghazzali as the 'chief proponent' of the non-Arab corrupters. In my post I said "the White sheep and their re-interpretation of Islam are best represented by the Persian *Hujjat al-Islam* al-Ghazzali." Al-Ghazzali best represents this revision of Islam, not because he originated it (he did not) but because he provided the lasting arguments for it and is recognized by much of the Islamic world today as orthodox (though this was not the case in his day). These circumstances do not prevail with the actual originators of this doctrine, his Persian predecessors, particularly Jahm b. Safwan.

Bro Mubaashir here replies to what he assumes to be my claim:

> "The first point is that Imam Al-Ghazzli performed his Islamic work several hundred years after the prophet's passing and he came after the establishment of the four major madhabs. While on one hand Dr. Wesley

> blames Imam Ghazzali and non black Arabs for Muslims not believing in Allah as a man, on the other hand he tells us in chapter 6 of his dissertation that there were different opinions between the Sahaaba and Tabieen about whether prophet Muhammad saw Allah or saw him as a man or young boy… Leaving aside the issue of who is right or wrong, or whether there were more companions and followers who believed he saw G-d or did not, Dr. Wesley, in this chapter, documents the fact that this dispute existed long before Imam Ghazzali…My point here is that these disputes are not taking place hundreds of years later between the prophet's black Arab companions and foreign white converts flocking to the religion. This debate is between what he calls the black sheep. For me, this indicates that the debate over whether prophet Muhammad literally saw G-d or not is not a debate between the views of original black, Semitic Arabs and "Johnny come-lately" white, non-Semitic, non-Arabs."

There are two problems with this reply, Bro Mubaashir: (1) I never claimed that al-Ghazzali himself introduced into Islam this bida or innovation. He certainly did not, though his people did. (2) Your use of my dissertation here is inappropriate and evidences what you readily admitted above, viz. that you weren't able to read the whole thing. That is most obvious here, for reasons I will elucidate below.

Al-Ghazzali, who died in 1128, did not originate the corrupting influence of Hellenism in Islam or specifically the Arabic version of the Hellenistic 'spook god'. Ja'd b. Dirham (d. 743) and, especially, his student Jahm b. Safwan (d. 746) did. Both Persians, Ja'd was the first documented mu'attila or denier of the literal reality of Allah's Sifat. This is confirmed by Al-Darimi in his ***Radd al-Jahmiyya***, 7; Ibn al-Imad in his ***Shadharat***, 1:16; Al-Kawthari in his *Mugaddimah Tabyin*, 12; and Ibn Taymiyah in his ***al-Risalah al-Hamawiyyah***, 15. He was executed by order of caliph Hisham b. Abd al-Malik because of this. This Persian convert was, by all accounts, reacting to the popular, Arab understanding of the scriptural Sifat as literal descriptions of Allah. It was Ja'd's student, Jahm, who developed this *ta'til* or denial of the Sifat into a system of thought. He argued that Allah is 'no-thing', *Allah laysa bi shay'*, even though the Qur'an and Sunna explicitly describe Allah as a shay', thing or delimited being (6:19; Bukhari, tawhid, 21). Jahm claimed that He had lā yusaf, no attributes. Jahm's deity was invisible and immaterial, and he claimed that Allah "is not described or known by any attribute or act nor has He any term or limit; He is not grasped by mind...and whatever may occur to your thought as a shay', He is contrary to that". (Does any of this sound familiar?). Abdus Subhan, in his important article "Al-Jahm Bin Safwân and His Philosophy," ***Islamic Culture*** 11 (1937): 221-227 explains:

> "According to al-Jahm, the anthropomorphic expressions of the Qur'an...cannot be literally applied to God, because it would signify that He is a material substance...Hence all anthropomorphic expressions, be they in the Qur'an or in the Sunnah, are to be understood figuratively...he holds that God has neither spoken to Moses nor can He speak nor can He see nor can He be located in a space nor has He a throne for Himself to rest upon...for He is above Time and Space...God, according to al-Jahm, is something strictly unperceivable...he...for the first time in history, introduced *ta'wîl* (i.e. not taking the expressions of the Qur'ân and the Sunnah in their literal and primary sense, but reading a secondary meaning to them instead-of course not in every case)- a departure from hitherto established convention of literal interpretation so loyally followed by his predecessors."

Please note that it was Jahm who introduced the method of taw'il or figurative interpretation of the Sifat into Islam! He innovated this against the general practice of the (largely) Arab Umma at the time which was ithbat or affirmation of the literal reality of the Sifat. No, the Persian al-Ghazzali didn't introduce this god, but his Persian predecessors Ja'd and Jahm did. And as Morris Seal correctly pointed out in is study of Classical Muslim theology: "Jahm's God…was closer to the Greek Absolute than to the God of the Qur'an (Muslim Theology: A Study of Origins with Reference to the Church Fathers, 1964, 58)."There is a simple explanation for this: R. M. Frank, in a thorough analysis of Jahm's doctrine, demonstrated clearly and unambiguously that his doctrine is neoplatonic in structure and that Jahm's was "the first clearly defined attempt to adopt an identifiable Greek philosophical system to an islamic theology ("The Neoplatonism of Gahm Ibn Safwan," Le Museon, 58 [1965], 396). You see Bro Mubaashir, al-Ghazzali did not introduce the Hellenizing theology and its 'spook god', Jahm did, and he offered it as an alternative to the God of the Black Arabs (the black sheep) whom he was apparently disgusted by. Jahm said regarding the Throne verse (20:5) which, at times, was at the center of the anthropomorphism debate later: "Could I scratch that out, I would."

2.2. JAHM'S AND AL-GHAZZALI'S 'SPOOK GOD' AMONG THE BLACK SAHABA?

Bro Mubaashir, I sincerely appreciate your taking the time to read some of my dissertation and I fully understand that for someone with your undoubted schedule it is simply unreasonable to expect the whole 300+ pages to be read. I do, however, wish you could have read more than you actually did, or had more time to digest what you did read; this would have no doubt benefitted your Reply, I believe. As it is, you seem to have completely missed my point.

Bro Mubaashir lifts two quotes from my dissertation which he feels contradict my thesis that (in his words) 'Johnny come-lately, white, non-Semitic Arabs' introduced into Islam this 'spook god'.

He feels these quotes demonstrate that the idea existed already among the Semitic Black Arabs, i.e. the Sahaba. The quotes are as follows:

> "Dr. Wesley quotes Gibril Fouad Haddad in his study on 'The Vision of Allah in the World and the Hereafter: 'Many sound reports show that the Companions differed sharply whether the Prophet saw Allah or not. Ibn 'Abbas related that he did, while Ibn Mas'ud, 'A'isha, Abu Hurayra, and Abu Dharr related reports to the contrary, stating that the verses of Sura AlNajm and other Suras referred [to] Jibril and that the Prophet said that he saw light.' (Dr. Wesley Dissertation)"

> "Dr. Wesley also makes the following quote from editors of a book, Kitab al-Ru'ya: 'The fifth problem regarding the Prophet's vision of his Lord Most High in this world. The Salaf and the Khalaf disagree irreconcilably (ikhtilaft mutabayin) over this issue, some affirming, others denying, while others suspending judgment (al-mutawaqqif). As for those who affirm that (the Prophet) saw his Lord Most High there is a group of the Sahaba and the Tabi'in and others. 'AbdAllah b. 'Abbas, Interpreter of the Qur'an, and Anas b. Malik, Abu Dharr, and it is reported on the authority of Abu Hurayra, and Ibn Mas'ud...and Ka'b al-Abbar. As for those who are of the opinion that the Prophet did not see his Lord Most High, a group of Sahaba and the Tabi'in also: our Mother 'A'isha and Ibn Mas'ud. And it was disputed regarding him and Abu Hurayra and Abu Dharr.' (Dr. Wesley Dissertation)"

Again, Bro Mubaashir believes that these quotes demonstrate that centuries before al-Ghazzali there were at least some Black Arabs who advocated the same type of god that al-Ghazzali later advocated, i.e. those Black Arab Sahaba who allegedly argued against Ru'ya. The 'spook god' is thus an indigenous Black Arab contribution. Bro Mubaashir has profoundly misread my work.

These two quotes actually open the chapter (Chapter 6) that Bro Mubaashir appeals to. In the remainder of the chapter I actually demonstrate that the authors of both quotes are wrong, and that there was NO dispute among the Sahaba as they present it in these quotes. I demonstrate that those Sahaba who allegedly rejected Ru'ya – Ibn Mas'ud, A'isha, Abu Hurayra, Abu Dharr – actually DID NOT reject Ru'ya, with one possible exception: A'isha. With her, however, it is not at all clear that even she categorically rejected Ru'ya. I demonstrate that there is reason to believe that she might have actually affirmed a Ru'ya, just not a ru'ya bi-l-absar or Vison of the Eyes. The bottom line is that I demonstrate that the sources DO NOT present the Sahaba as "disagreeing irreconcilably (ikhtilaft mutabayin)" over whether or not the Prophet saw God: 19+ Companions affirmed that he did – including Ibn Mas'ud, Abu Hurayra, Abu Dharr – while only one companion allegedly explicitly rejected it, A'isha.

I demonstrate that there WAS a dispute among the Sahaba related to Ru'ya, but it was over the following matters:

1.] Is Surat al-Najm a record of the Ru'ya or no?
2.] Was the Prophet's Ru'ya related to the Mi'raj (Ascension to Heaven) or Isra (Nocturnal Journey) or no?
3.] Was the Ru'ya bi 'l-absar, with the eyes of the Prophet's head, or bi 'l-qalb, with the eyes of his heart, i.e. a dream vision?

I demonstrate in that dissertation that the Companions who answered no to 1.] and 2.] DID NOT reject Ru'ya (e.g. the Ru'ya would have occurred in Medina rather than early Mecca as Najm would imply, and that it was independent of the Mi'raj and Isra). I also demonstrate that however one answered 3.], Traditionalist Sunnis affirmed that it was a real vision of Allah.

My dissertation also demonstrates Bro Mubaashir's error in conflating an alleged rejection of Ru'ya with a rejection of an anthropomorphic God and an affirmation of an invisible, incorporeal diety à la al-Ghazzali. Because a Classical figure, Sahaba or otherwise, is on record denying Ru'ya does not mean that individual necessarily rejects anthropomorphism. The text-book case here is the great hadith scholar from Herat, al-Darimi (d. 895) whose ***Radd ala Jahmiyya*** and his ***Radd ala Bishr al-Marisi*** unambiguously show him to be an (some would say extreme) anthropomorphist. Yet, he just as adamantly rejected a ru'ya report of Ibn Abbas and privileged A'isha's rejection. But his reasoning was text-critical, NOT theological. He unapologetically affirmed an anthropomorphic God while just as unapologetically rejecting some very anthropomorphist Ru'ya reports.

Thus, there is no warrant at all for Bro Mubaashir to cite my dissertation as evidence that there were some Black Arabs advocating the invisible, incorporeal god of Jahm and al-Ghazzali. Nothing in chapter six or any other chapter in it suggests that. None of the persons erroneously identified in the two quotes as 'rejecters of Ru'ya' - Ibn Mas'ud, A'isha, Abu Hurayra, Abu Dharr - is on record affirming an invisible, incorporeal God. The lone possible exception and explicit rejecter of Ru'ya, A'isha, was herself rejected by the Black Arabs! Listen to the words of Muhammad b. Ishaqq b. Khuzayma (d. 924), the most prominent Shafi'i in Nishapur at the time and considered the "chief of the hadith scholars (*ra's al-muhaddithin*)":

A'isha did not report from the Prophet (s) that he informed her that he did not see his Lord, May He be Exalted and Great. She simply recited [God's] words, "Visions comprehend Him not" and "It is not for man that Allah speaks to him except (through) revelation." (But) from the contemplation of these two verses and in accordance with attainment of the "Right," it is known that there is not in either of the two verses that which merits charging one who said that Muhammad saw his Lord with lying

against Allah.... the Tribe of Hashim, collectively, contradict A'isha (m) in this matter and they, all of them, used to affirm that the Prophet (s) saw his Lord twice. The agreement of the Tribe of Hashim is...more appropriate than A'isha's isolated statement. Companions who are known did not follow her, nor did any woman from the wives/women of the Prophet, nor any of the female Successors (*Kitab al-tawhid*, 225ff).
Thus, the quintessential Black Arabs, the Banu Hashim (see Muhammad al-Nafs al-Zakiyya) collectively rejected A'isha's unsupported tafsir and collectively affirmed Ru'ya. The lone exception thus proves the rule.

I have not yet read Bro Mubaashir's Part 2. I have skimmed it, and to my amazement found this quote:

> "In Part 1 of my reply to Dr. Wesley, I demonstrate using data from his dissertation that it is evident that Muslims disputed about this topic (i.e. anthropomorphism) long before the so-called non-Arab takeover and domination of Muslim thinking."

I have here demonstrated that Bro Mubaashir did no such thing. He only demonstrated that he didn't read enough of my dissertation to understand what it was saying.

3. ANTHROPOMORPHISM PRE-SCIENTIFIC?

Bro Mubaashir confesses, then opines:

> "Admittedly, I am not a historian and I am no expert on the influence of Greek philosophy on Imam Al-Ghazzali. However, what I do know is that world history shows a progression of human belief and knowledge from its early superstitious and pagan understanding of the planet and world we live in to a more rational, scientific, and educated understanding of ourselves and our world. Early man worshipped

things in creation as Gods; the wind, fire, rain, etc. We believed in powerful spirits, demons, ghosts lurking in the night. We worshipped the sun, the moon, stars, angelic beings, statues; all kinds of things, including powerful men and women, who were our witch doctors, kings, pharaohs, popes and the wizards of Oz. As man became more knowledgeable of himself and his world, he began discarding those beliefs and began reducing the number of supernatural, "divine" beings in his world. Eventually, a good number of humans realized that even the powerful and great men and women who claimed to be G-d or claimed that G-d ordained them with the right to rule were only mortal men like the rest of us. This is history 101."

With due respect to my Beloved Brother, this is History 101 from an admitted non-historian and it thus fails to meet the standards of critical historical writing. This idea that anthropomorphism is 'pre-scientific' and human intellectual advancement à la the Greek philosophers disabused us of such 'superstition' is not History 101 but, in 2011, Wishful-Thinking 101 and is contradicted by the historical data.

Currently in the possession of the New York Academy of Medicine is the important Edwin Smith Papyrus (ESP), which is an ancient Egyptian medical papyrus written during the 18th dynasty (ca 1500 BCE). However, it was shown to be a late copy of an original produced in the Old Kingdom (4400-4200 BCE). It thus reflects medical knowledge as it existed in North Africa (Egypt) 6,000 years ago. And this knowledge clearly was impressive, to say the least. ESP is an extensive anatomical dictionary of the skull, head and throat. Its knowledge of nueroanatomy was detailed and accurate, without the benefit of EEGs, CAT scans, or magnetic resonance imaging. This medical papyrus speaks of 48 cases of bone surgery and of external pathologies. It mentions 'brain', a term unknown in all of the East or West at that period. The author of the papyrus already knew the body's dependence on the brain. Produced by Africans in the Nile Valley probably around 6,000 years ago (following the Long Chronology), ESP's scientific consciousness has won the non-patronizing admiration of modern scientists.

In the Pushkin State Museum of Fine Arts in Moscow there is the Moscow Mathematical Papyrus, dated to the 12th Dynasty (1850 BCE). This papyrus proves the advanced mathematical skill of the Ancient Egyptians. Two thousand years before the Greek mathematician Archimedes (d. ca. 212 BCE), the ancient Egyptians had already discovered the rigorous formulae of the area of the sphere: $S=4\square R^2$. They knew the exact formula for the volume of the cylinder: $V=\square R^2$. In fact, we now know beyond question that the Egyptians actually taught the Greeks geometry. V.V. Struve, in his *Mathematischern Papyrus des Staatlichen Museums der Schönen Künste in Moskau* (1930) observes:

> "*The Papyrus of Moscow,* which gives us, among many others, the proof that a famous discovery by Archimedes (i.e. surface of an ellipse) has to be credited to the Egyptians, confirms in the most striking manner the statements of Greek writers on the mathematical knowledge of the Egyptian scholars. We therefore no longer have any reason to reject the affirmations of the Greek writers according to whom the Egyptians were the masters of the Greeks in geometry…it is again a great discovery attributed to Democritus (i.e. function of the brain) that will have to be pushed back fourteen hundred years before the birth of its presumed inventor. These new facts…force us into a radical review of our persistent value judgment held up to this moment about Egyptian knowledge. A problem like that of the research on the brain's function or that [of the determination] of the surface of the sphere …herby prove that the Egyptian people as well as the Greek people strove to acquire a pure intellectual vision of the universe."

A "pure intellectual vision of the universe" was indeed in the possession of the ancient Egyptians, popular misconceptions notwithstanding. But Ancient Egyptian science not only outshined later Greek and other contemporary sciences, it also baffles modern science and mathematics.

The Great Pyramid of Giza stands 483 ft high and is made of 2.3 million blocks of limestone and granite carved with such extreme proficiency and accuracy that modern science finds it inexplicable. The building techniques were as accurate as the best we have today. The builders clearly knew and used such modern techniques as trepanning (for drilling holes). But this suggests the use of ultrasonic machinery and thus "clearly points to manufacturing methods that involved the use of machinery such as lathes, milling machines, ultrasonic drilling machines, and high-speed saws." System's of measurement had to equal today's. The transcendental number pi (3.14), which is fundamental to advanced mathematics and supposedly discovered in the 3rd cent BCE by Archimedes, was already incorporated into the structure of the Great Pyramid thousands of years earlier: the ratio between its original height (481.3949 ft.) and perimeter (3023.16 ft.) equals the ratio between the radius and circumference of a circle: 2pi. Marshall Payn, in his article "The Case for Advanced Technology in the Great Pyramid," (***Forbidden History***, 270) notes:

> "The Kufu (Cheops) pyramid defies how we depict ancient technology. Over two million limestone blocks rise to the height of a forty-story building. Each baseline exceeds two and a half football fields. Standing on top, an archer cannot clear the base with an arrow. All this comes from what was supposedly an agrarian society, forty-five hundred years ago. And that's not all. The precision and craftsmanship surpass our modern understanding. Occupying an area of thirteen acres, the entire bedrock base has been carved to less than an

> inch out of level. It is oriented within a tiny fraction of a degree from the cardinal points. Outer casing stones and inner granite blocks fit with such precision that a razor blade cannot be inserted between them. Blocks weighing seventy tons (about what a railroad locomotive weighs) have been lifted to the height of a ten-story building and mated to the next block with wondrous precision. How did they do these things? We don't know…Where did the technology come from? We have no answers. Any method of construction suggested, to date, for this pyramid does not satisfy the accepted standards of technology."

The Great Pyramid's northern face is aligned almost perfectly to true north; its southern face almost perfectly aligned to true south; the same with its eastern and western faces. Astonishing also is that the Great Pyramid possesses almost perfect 90° right angles. Very few modern buildings possess corners with perfect 90° right angles. Because it makes no difference structurally and most observers are oblivious, the norm is for corners to be out of true by a whole degree or more. However, in the Great Pyramid the margin of error is almost nill: SE corner 89° 56' 27", NE corner 90° 3' 2", SW corner 90° 0' 33", NW corner 89° 59' 58". But showing an even more astounding level of advanced mathematics is the hard-to-deny suggestion that the Great Pyramid is actually a model and map-projection of the northern hemisphere of the earth on a scale of 1:43, 200. The mathematics supporting this suggestion is persuasive. This means that the ancient builders, probably working anywhere from 11-7, 000 years ago, had an accurate knowledge of the dimensions of the planet.

The alignments to true north, south, east and west; the near-perfect 90° right angles; the incredible symmetry of the four enormous sides; the engineering logistics of raising millions of huge stones hundreds of feet in the air; all of these are 'almost impossible'. Just how supra-modern the Ancient Egyptian culture is was aptly stated by Jean-François Champollian, founder of modern Egyptology: beside the Egyptians of old, he said, "we in Europe are but Lilliputians."

Why did I spend this time talking about the scientific advancement of the ancient Egyptians? First, because it demonstrates clearly that Bro Mubaashir's Darwinian view of human intellectual history is simply out-dated and wrong. Dr. Charles Fince expresses this fact well when he remarks:

> "as history dawns in the Nile Valley at the end of the 5th millennium B.C., medicine is already at a very advanced state and...in fact, it underwent a decline in later ages which was not reversed until the scientific breakthroughs of the 18th and 19th centuries. It is the conceit of modern historiography that human culture has evolved in linear fashion from the simple to the complex, from the primitive to the advanced, from the lower to the higher, reaching its pinnacle in the post-Renaissance civilization of Western Europe. A more clear-sighted perception of history would show us that this flies in the face of the true facts; the progression of human civilization might be more accurately described as a sinusoidal wave, in which the ebb and flow of civilized progress is represented by peaks and valleys. From every pinnacle there is a regression and every succeeding civilization is faced with having to re-discover old truths. The Greek 'miracle' is but the detritus of ancient Egyptian thought and many of the 'marvels' of the modern age are the fruit of recovering older ideas ("Science and Symbol in Egyptian Medicine: Commentaries on the Edwin Smith Papyrus," 349)."

Secondly, this evidence demonstrates the error of Bro Mubaashir's claim that belief in an anthropomorphic God belongs to the 'pre-scientific' stage of human evolution. The scientifically and mathematically advanced culture responsible for this scientific and mathematical Wonder of the Ancient World, the Great Pyramid, was also a culture committed to the true, anthropomorphic Black God! The theological wisdom that complemented the scientific and mathematical knowledge was: "men are mortal gods, and God is an immortal man." Egyptian Sacred Science (not paganism or superstition!) was rooted in the acknowledgment of the same Self-Created Black God that the Most Honorable Elijah Muhammad taught us about here in America. Here me well: that scientific wonder standing in the sands of Egypt was raised by a culture that affirmed and was committed to the self-created Black God! With the knowledge of that same God, the Honorable Elijah Muhammad raised in the 'sands' of America a mighty Black Nation, the sociological enigma of the modern world! As the ancient African believers in this Divine Anthropos took unhewn stone and near-perfectly and precisely joined and raised them, in the process raising the greatest architectural structure of the whole ancient world, the Most Honorable Elijah Muhammad took the an unhewn people – human rubble – and carved us near-perfectly, joining and raising us precisely, in the process achieving the greatest collective human transformation in modern history. The Nation of Islam under the Most Honorable Elijah Muhammad was the Great Pyramid of the modern period.

Herodotus (500 BCE) said: "Of all the nations of the world, the Egyptians are the happiest, healthiest and most religious." How dare we dismiss the Sacred Science of the Egyptians and its God, a Sacred Science that produced the happiest and HEALTHIEST people of the known world, as mere 'superstition and paganism'. The Sacred Science and its Divine Man-God of the ancient Egyptians made them a culturally, intellectually, and civilizationally advanced people as well as a happy and healthy people (vs. the technologically advanced but pathologically depressed and sick modern Western world). The Supreme Wisdom (Islam) of Master Fard Muhammad as taught by the

Most Honorable Elijah Muhammad made the so-called Negro the most disciplined, intelligent, enterprising and wealthy Black community in America. What happened when that community turned its back on the Teachings of the Honorable Elijah Muhammad and embraced the 'spook god' of the modern Muslim world? Prof Sherman Jackson, in his book, 'Islam and the Blackamerican (2005) gives us the lamentable answer to this question, writing:

> "perhaps the most lamentable development (due to the transition from NOI to Sunni Islam) was the seemingly reversed effect that Islam was exerting on the pathologies and dysfunctionalities of the urban ghetto. Beyond the explicitly religious vices, for example illicit sex or alcohol consumption, Islam was fast losing its significance as a fortifier of indigenous constructions of such values as manly pride, fiscal responsibility, or civic consciousness. Whereas under the 'Islam' of the Honorable Elijah Muhammad, education, work, and community-uplift were synonymous with Black Muslim, Sunni Islam was increasingly being invoked as a reason *not* to work (for the infidel), *not* to be educated (in the infidel's institutions), and *not* to be involved in the (infidel) community...In short, on the new, immigrant-influenced understanding of Islam, Sunnism was in many ways becoming a cause rather than a solution to the problem of Blackamerican Muslim dysfunctionality in America."

The Ancient Egyptians' belief in the Man-God lead them to create the greatest, scientifically most advanced, happiest and healthiest civilization of the ancient world; The Black Arab belief in the Man-God of Prophet Muhammad's Sunna enabled them to rise above their degenerate tribalism and other Jahili ways and create the largest empire in recorded history; The so-called Negro's belief in the Man-God of the Honorable Elijah Muhammad enabled him to rise above his peculiarly American

Jahiliyya to become the healthiest, wisest, and most enterprising Black community in America. What did leaving this God for the spook god of the modern Muslim world produce for our people? It destroyed the social, economic, intellectual, and health advancements that was gained under the regime of the Man-God. You call that progress? I will take that functional so-called 'pagan' God over your dysfunctional spook god any and every day. Bro Mubaashir claims: "we have too much documented human experience showing us that nothing in creation is a G-d to be worshipped." While I agree with the letter of your statement as far as it goes, I ask you Bro Mubaashir: what is the documented history showing that God is an invisible, incorporeal 'no-thing'? I missed that in my Hist 101 class. Bro Mubaashir says further:

> "What Dr. Wesley extends to us, however eloquently, is an invitation to return to the worship of creation rather than Creator and an understanding of the scripture that would lead us back into superstition."

No sir. I don't invite us to return to the so-called superstitious worship of creation. I invite us to return to the Sacred Science of our great ancestors and the God of that Sacred Science. That God was/is Self-Created and was the same God of the Prophet Muhammad. The Holy Prophet NOWHERE invited us to the incorporeal and invisible god of Plato and Aristotle, Ja'd and Jahm, and Bro Mubaashir and Imam Salim. Where is the testimony from the Prophet inviting us to this god? Nowhere in the Qur'an and Sunna. But as I have demonstrated, in the Qur'an and, especially, the Sunna there is overwhelming evidence that he called us back to the Divine Man-God of our ancient Religion (which Islam claims only to be the culmination of). Where is the testimony from the Prophet himself that he did not intend for us to take him on his word regarding Allah being a man? Produce that 'documented history', please sir.

Shukran and Salaam

Your Brother in Islam
Bro Wesley

22.] Mubaashir Uqdah - Response to Dr Wesley Muhammad

Thank you, Brother Wesley. It is easy see that you were at the top of your class and are, I am sure, one of the top followers of Minister Louis Farrakhan and advocates for the Honorable Elijah Muhammad's teaching. As Salaamu Alaikum! May Allah reward us for our striving. Mubaashir

23.] Imam Salim Mu'Min - Response to Dr Wesley Muhammad

> "perhaps the most lamentable development (due to the transition from NOI to Sunni Islam) was the seemingly reversed effect that Islam was exerting on the pathologies and dysfunctionalities of the urban ghetto. Beyond the explicitly religious vices, for example illicit sex or alcohol consumption, Islam was fast losing its significance as a fortifier of indigenous constructions of such values as manly pride, fiscal responsibility, or civic consciousness. Whereas under the 'Islam' of the Honorable Elijah Muhammad, education, work, and community-uplift were synonymous with Black Muslim, Sunni Islam was increasingly being invoked as a reason not to work (for the infidel), not to be educated (in the infidel's institutions), and not to be involved in the (infidel) community…In short, on the new, immigrant-influenced understanding of Islam, Sunnism was in many ways becoming a cause rather than a solution to the problem of Blackamerican Muslim dysfunctionality in America."

This is a lie. A big lie. A big lie from a professor in one of the biggest "infidel" universities in America that is too afraid to work with his own people. He too busy sucking up to immigrants to know what goes on in Imam W. Deen Mohammed's community. Immigrant-infuenced? The teachings of Imam W. Deen Mohammed is not Immigrant-influenced, in fact dont bring this shit back here on the page. I don't have a degree from your universities in Islamic studies but i can hold my own with both of you. As we say in the ghetto, go to hell.

How in the hell can you say there is less value on education in Imam's W. Deen Mohammed's community when i wrote a letter to get my X as a means of encouraging education, now i'm debating a professor with a degree from an Ivy League school about Arabic? And i don't have a degree from a University in Arabic Islamic Studies nor have i been to the Middle East. I can on showing progress and i can show where we haven't been doing as well as we should. But one thing for sure, i'm not an ignorant black man from black bottom as Fard Muhammad found us.

24.] Imam Salim Mu'min Response to Dr Wesley Muhammad

Dr. Westley Muhammad, As-Salaam Alaikum,

There is no need to continue to address laa, whether it is nafiya tabree' or nafiya lil-jins, since it is not used in the verse 7:143 and cause no relevance at this time. Thus, surely it would be speculative.

I would not say that Lan is ta'beed nor is Lan ta'keed in general. However, I would say that it is Istiqbaal used specifically or generically. Though it is Istiqbaal, I would not say that it is ta'beed in nature, but depending on the context it may have the sense of being ta'beed. If it was ta'beed in nature then why would Allah say in the Qur'an: 2:95 wa lan yatamannau-hu abadan…

of course unless you were reading the verse in the sense of Qur'an bil-Qur'an allowing 'abadan' to define the particle lan. Or you may say that it is ta'keed in that you want to express the idea of ta'beed twice, once in the nature of the particle and again in the usage of the internal noun. But I doubt this is the case.

I also say that lan is istiqbaal with takraar when time is not specified such as in the Qur'an 2:24 fa-in lam taf'aluu wa lan taf'aluu. In this case there is no time indicator or restrictor, therefore I would say that takraar takes place, which is more perpetual in nature than an emphatic repetition, tautology or eternity.

Within the context of using lan in the context of a specific time or restriction, then the Qur'an uses something in the verse referencing time. Again, we see it in the verse 2:95 with 'abadan' or when Allah says in the Qur'an: "wa lan yanfa'a-kum al-yauma…" thus, al-yauma restricts the takraar by indicating a specific time.

If you want to use a negation with the connotation of "azala" then you could use "maa kaana" or "lam yakun". For Allah says in the Qur'an: 35:44: wa maa kaana Allahu li-yu'jiza-hu min shay'in fee as-samaawaati wa fee al-ardi inna-hu kaana 'aleeman qadeeran. Here maa kaana is used along with the li of juhuud to give emphasis to the negation, thus, Allah was not frustrated, is not frustrated and will not be frustrated.

Again, kaana is used to show sempiternity in the the expression "inna-hu kaana 'aleeman qadeeran" that Allah was, is, and will be Knowing, Powerful. I would rather use the term sempiternal to give the temporal affect seeming that my mind cannot stretch beyond the creation to address that which is eternal.

You may say that lan is only restricted to the condition of Moses, however, I would say that it is temporal as much as the whole creation it temporal. The mountains are temporal, however you will never see G-d in a physical form, but you need a reference to sense Him.

I am having a problem understanding the expression "laa arani" or laa aranee. It appears by your transliteration that "araa" conjugated in the first person present tense verb[I see] is connected with the nun wiqaaya and the attached first person pronoun "yaa" [me]. With the negation laa, it appears as if you are saying, "I do not see me?" Besides show me Qur'anic examples of these expressions, for anything outside of the Qur'an are speculative.

To add words to make a point can be done, but that is not the case here. There are many ways to express a negation. I do not believe that Allah can be seen in any form of created matter so there is no sense in continuing this debate. I am sure that I can research the history of the Black man in Africa and find them worshipping trees, rocks, mountains, etc. as deities.
You can find today in any major city people having pagan beliefs, that is, taking the material world as the only reality, which testifies to the empirical studies in these universities. Peace.

25.] Imam Salim Mu'min Terminates Debate

As-Salaam Alaikum,

I have given Dr. Westley [the opportunity] to make his argument on this page, MALI. In conclusion to this argument, there is no proof that Allah is a man. We don't believe it here so lakum deenu-kum wa liya deeni. For you is your religion and for me is my religion. This conversation is no longer welcomed. Thank you.

www.ingramcontent.com/pod-product-compliance
Lightning Source LLC
Chambersburg PA
CBHW070644160426
43194CB00009B/1571
* 9 7 8 0 9 8 3 3 7 9 7 1 3 *